I Am
My Father's
Son

Winds of Time Novel

B. G. Simpson

Brilliant Books Literary
137 Forest Park Lane Thomasville
North Carolina 27360 USA

To Gene
Father, mentor, teacher, and friend

CONTENTS

In those days men will seek death and will not Find it;
They will desire to die, and death will flee from them.

—Rev 9:6

1

MEMORIES

It had been a long summer with rain coming down in endless sheets of dampened obscurity. Most summer days experienced had that constant downpour, leaving a wet soggy acceptance forever branded in memory. The heavens were enclosed with clouds that surrounded the base of the mountains amidst a peacefully covered landscape. Even with cloud cover, the view was spectacular with its glaciers and massive rivers with mile after mile of unforgiving country of forested land. Yet somehow in the back of his mind, Robert thought if a godlike king had made a specific place to build a new kingdom, it would have been here, the Alaska frontier, an isolated land with frosty peaked mountains and icy wintry winds. It would have been the last place Robert wanted to hang his hat, with its extreme cold weather and darkness that would show its ugly head during the ferocious winters. He was almost sixty now and still had the strength of an ox. He wanted his life to turn out better than it did. Of course, somehow, he knew this hard life wasn't something chosen of his own free will, but one of destiny. It was more like a dream that, slowly through the years, had led him toward Alaska's borders, a place or road that he went down without much thought put to this predicament. Alaska had become a part of what was left of his long life, a life he had learned to accept with the addition of trudging through the snow or soggy forest each day, depending on the season. His days had cut a trail of some of the most unforgiving country he had ever experienced. Robert had built his own log cabin home about half a mile up off of the main riverbank that had frequently been visited by bears or wolf packs looking for food. The cabin had an able-bodied comfortable feel to it-built four feet above the ground on a six-step landing, placed perfectly on the back part of an open field with two mounting walls of thickly timbering trees built-up on two sides, about a hundred and fifty feet apart.

He raised a pup that was half wolf and half Alaskan husky with beautiful blue-gray eyes. The pup quickly bonded with the old man. He called him Skittles. He had found the pup at the edge of a riverbank two years back when he fell into the challenging waters. The pup was almost taken by the river. But before the river could pull him under, Robert had fished The trivial pup out of the torrential water with a fishnet he had made from old materials found on the riverbank's sandy shore, from a life vest and a long wooden stick laying among floating debris. That day, he stopped fishing and decided to take the pup back to the cabin and get him warmed up after his near-death experience. He lit a fire in the potbelly stove from wood he had stacked neatly against the wall. The furry pup was attracted to a bag of Skittles candy that fell out of Robert's coat pocket and broke open on the cabin's floor. Being that all pups are curious, he licked up a hand full before Robert could stop him. That's when he thought up the obscure name.

Many a day of Robert's past had been spent filled with regrets about his life that he could never fix, leaving a trail of emptiness in its wake-too many hours of silent loneliness to think about all the things that went wrong in his life. Yet life would go on as he had contented with his past and was learning to deal with it.

He had been married once, but he had ever not learned from the years past that every decision he had ever made had unrealized consequences as its final deductions. He had been a father to a beautiful boy who was back in Southern California, who had started etching out a life of his own. Robert Littleton had done the best he could with his son, yet through the years, they had changed and went their separate ways. Not that there wasn't love between a father and a son, it was more complicated than just showing up every day at each other's door. He had moved pretty far from norm, and James now had his own life to contend with. Life got complicated with distance. There wasn't a day that went by that Robert didn't think about James. How they, at one point, were so much alike in certain areas; but with time, even their similarities began to gap. Melody, his wife from the past, became bored with him after fifteen years and decided one day to up and leave. Robert and James were left behind with the house payments and relentless bills that seemed to pile up. Back then, James was seventeen, and Dad was working six days a week trying to keep things together. James had what most people called a silver tongue. He would convince certain friends to camp out at the house for several months to help with a little cash so Robert and James would have enough money to buy food for the Month. He put every last penny he had into the house hoping Melody would change her mind and come back home, but it never Happened. After about three years of struggling, he decided to finally let the house go. They had lived in a community of San Diego, which was part of a town called Imperial Beach. He was Surprised one day when he came home and half the furniture Was missing, not even a note was left behind. He spent hours In remorseful bitterness left in the miseries of sleep deprivation Before taking that long drive every night back to Julian. He worked the graveyard shift for a local supermarket chain that offered him a full-time position. They stocked the shelves at night with groceries, after the store was closed.

Earlier, in Robert's life, he had spent his free time learning Martial arts. He had trained with his good close friend for four Years in a Kempo Karate studio built from the ground up. How He ended up in the Alaska frontier-he didn't quite have that figured out yet. The only thing that seemed to come to mind was visiting Alaska once when he was a young boy.

He thought Alaska to be one of the most beautiful landscapes anyone could ever envision. And he also thought if everything else had dropped off the end of the planet, Alaska would be a place he would head for, and that's probably why he was here.

Within a year, he had built a cabin about twelve hundred square feet in dimensions, cozy and warm with a dormered skylight to brighten the main room from above. The outside had a beautiful woodsy porch with a view of the whole valley half a mile up the side of a slanted hill overlooking a thickly forested landscape. It was breathtaking. From time to time, Robert and Skittles would go off and set traps for a wolf or two, not to rid the community of all wolves, but try to keep them from overpopulating. He was in the middle of building a barn and corral so he could eventually own a horse to help him on some of the trips he would make into town, usually once a month for supplies, pulling a sleigh behind him. The town of Skagway was a good twenty miles down the trail closely following the river. Robert had left for Alaska after he had lost his last job with thirty Thousand dollars left to his name and a small retirement account That he had wired each month to a local bank in Skagway. He decided this great adventure would give him a new insight, a new beginning, a fresh start. From the other direction, his cabin was only thirty miles from the Canadian border; with its inclement season, he'd cross its boundary without being aware. Up through jagged mountains, it wasn't uncommon to drift back and forth over the borders, laid between delineated imaginary lines drawn by bought rights.

James was scheduled to come out and visit for the whole summer. He was able to kill two birds with one stone; one, visiting his father, and two, finishing up his studies on his father's property. James had conducted quite the scholastic achievements, shortly to get his doctorate in marine biology. He was ready to study hundreds of species found in the Alaskan waters just off the coast. James worked it out to stay with his father through a local government agency hooked up with fish and game. James thought to use this valuable time to get closer to his father, since they hadn't seen each other for over five years. This was the perfect setup for father and son to get reacquainted.

Memories had been tossed to the wind of better days left behind, as Robert reminisced about his past. With time, things had become different. Slowly, through inured years from earlier brought extreme change, and with change, there seemed to be a price to pay for the mesmeric atmosphere now facing him. Modifications didn't always make sense from a day-to-day basis, to be a normal routine, if there even was such a process in this forgotten land.

Robert had finished the roof on the barn before the rain started again. By midday, the rain began to come down like slanted sheets off a waterfall. Skittles stayed back under the protection of the porch and whined while wagging his tail.

He whipped his head in Skittle's direction. "You're supposed to be tough." Robert shook his head as he leaned down to pet the wolf-dog. He figured he had spoiled him with too many times in front of the open fire under warmer conditions of a spoiling master.

He was scheduled that next day to make a run up to the mine on that Sunday of June 2 to open up a new vein he started a month before. Skagway had a history of being an old gold rush-mining town at the end of the nineteenth century, when Alaska was first starting to populate. Robert was hoping to find His little spot of paradise from gold, left behind in a small corner Overlooked by old miners and now forgotten from bygone years, in the twilight of a new millennium. Maybe something had gone amuck, and just before a great discovery, the mine had sealed itself off from being revealed as the find of this new century, now, waiting for a pair of patient hands for discovering at that perfect moment. A time revealed like Kodak moment, as if purpose had her own plan for those willing with grateful hearts and worthy hands. At least, that was what he had hoped for.

That night, Robert sat down and wrote a note and left a map for James to follow, just in case he got hurt or buried alive and ended up missing. He pointed out in the note that he'd left early Saturday morning and wouldn't be back until Sunday to meet James for early morning breakfast.

He had built two beds and put them in the loft up above the cabin main floor so James would have a place to sleep on first arrival. There was no electricity, no phones, no internet, and no people up where he lived, just the big blue sky, the rugged frontier, and dangerous bears and wolf packs. Once, when Robert was fishing, a large brown bear had come up behind him and surprised him. His heart began to pound, sensing the intensity of being faced by this mammoth beast. He was frozen for a brief moment before his instincts began to kick in. Deciding quickly, he gave up his catch of twelve fish instead of a body part he'd greatly miss. Even though living in the Alaska frontier was quite beautiful, it stayed raw in its truest form. In the not too distant future, he started carrying a high-powered bow with metal tipped arrows. A few months back, he had to shoot a grizzly bear that had been wounded from a bear trap by a poacher. He even had to kill two poachers that has threatened to shoot and kill him two years back.

While still early in the morning, Robert left the cabin for the mine after appending the note and map to his front door and then started the climb up those rugged mountains jetting toward the sky. He looked back, for a moment, at the infinitesimal cottage lost in the background of timbered land, from a thousand feet below. A heavenly setting displayed equanimity in the events that were to come. His cabin, from a distance, wasn't much to look at, but it was his home. He felt pride that day while looking back at what he had built with his own two hands. He was a rebel now in this distant land. Without rhythm or reason despite the seasoned, strong in the inside, headed for the right trail, for all the wrong reasons, yet he was pulled to move forward toward a certain destiny without knowing why? He was making memories, but something didn't feel quite right that morning when Robert had slid out his bed. He was pushed by an incessant reality not yet known. He was at a loss about the feelings that he didn't quite understand. His stomach churned into a twisting knot and a sense of fraught warned him to turn back, yet he kept moving forward, always fighting the emotions of peaked danger, to make a better way for a good life. He felt a continuing and constant push to keep up his stride. He glared up at this concentric mountain jetting above. Skittles kept closely knitted to his side, a warm heart of adoration, always together seeking adventure. He was his best friend, a beating heart of camaraderie. He was carrying a pack on his back, and so was Skittles who seemed pleased to lend his assistance in this rough country they both considered home. He had ten-inch buck knife looped through his belt and a heavy pack strapped to his back. He was heavily breathing in the mountain air, which caused him to feel alive. This was living, this was his life, and this was the direction he had to go, a destiny only for the strong of heart, not for the weary wanderer of a forgotten soul. Looking up, Robert noticed it was starting to rain, and then it was coming down as if a wall of unrelenting sheets was moving toward them while mounting a thunderous sound like a stampede of horses. A pedantic wall of water pushed toward them without warning. The ground became alive with the movement of water and earth. The changing of circumstance didn't alter his plans of moving forward. He had bought Skittles a doggy umbrella that hooked to his collar. It looked kind of funny, which caused him to smile because pink was the only color the trading post had left. It didn't appear to bother the wolf-dog, considering he and every other dog out there in the wild blue yonder were color blind. The umbrella kept most of the rain out of Skittles eyes. The wolf- dog led the way trudging up the mountain as Robert quickly followed behind.

That morning, the air was crisp with a slight wind from the west as this beating storm pressed against them like a treadmill leading nowhere. The mountain was alive with brisk and banishing surfeiting streams that moved at all angles, flowing against them like gushing waterfalls. The wind bestirred through the upper branches of the trees, making the forest look like moving tendrils drifting side to side. The rain gave life to the ground as the water doffed the muddy earth down each mountain pass. Every cranny of dirt and fallen foliage of drifting debris rushed toward them. Even the mastered eagles of the sky had enough sense to stay out of the torrential downpour. It was at best, maybe several hours trip from the cabin with normal impediments of circumstance, but this day was different from other days treading up this mountain pass. A rough pair of mountain and a man's world turned inside out drained their energy. There was no room for error, for errors could mean the end of life, and as life flowed down in raging waters from above. Robert took notice of the elucidation of their situation and pushed harder, pushing past the adversity of pain, pushing past the last man standing. He was taking three steps forward and one back before making headway, and the constant beat of the wind and the water eroding the ground all around seemed to pull every last breath of air from the sky. It was the act of iterations to meet and end. They had slowed themselves from their forward trudge to keep from falling down. Robert had made two ski poles from light pinewood to keep sure and steady. By the time he reached the mouth of the mine, four hours had passed, and he and Skittles sat to take a break just past the mouth of the opening. Robert lit a fire to warm his hands and face to take the chill off. The two weary wanderers were already showing signs of fatigue, and their journey had just begun. The tough part ahead was making the drops, and then coming back up. Robert broke out a couple of slices of beef jerky and assured the wolf- dog that the meat came from a cow and not his fellow wolvers that roamed the forest. Skittles gave him a crying whimper and a couple of sniffs before taking the sinewy rendition of what used to be, considering that it might be edible. He then wolfs down the jerky as reward for trudging up the mountain.

The aged mine left a surreal feeling floating in the air. It had that usual damp musty smell to it like old gothic buildings that had been smothered by years of neglect, too long in the closed quarters of the mountain without human care or upkeep. The water caused damp air to ferment, weighing heavy on the lungs. Robert had reinforced the mine's opening in several areas with a number of milled logs he had cut and logged close to the entrance. He didn't want the mountain coming down on his head as he was trying to live the American dream, by finding the mother lode. At times he had worked his way into the deep bellows of the earth, past the barriers of where normal people existed, past the point of no return, dark, secluded, unbecoming. This was a harsh trail to take in the belly of the mine, like it would devour those who pressed deep within her secrets. It wasn't considered safe by any means, yet Robert again had a portended feeling in his gut. Something wasn't right about him surreptitiously going out on a limb to find this plain mystery of hidden gold, like a madman driven by the constant rage of an inward voice that was gently cajoling to keep him moving. Keeping him pressed for the prize at the end of the last tunnel would pull him to a better way of life. He wasn't even sure his true purpose of being here held any significant meaning at all, but here he was again making his fifteenth trip into the shadowy darkness. Robert stood up and pulled in a deep breath of air. He looked past the entrance toward the darkness that lay before him. He felt odd and at the same time exhausted like the years of overworking was finally catching up to him. Robert held his breath in the silence of the dimly lit fire, trying to hear this mountain calling to him, as if shadows of breath had held secrets not revealed until the proper moment of revelation. His hands had mirrored a bit of trepidation as he tried to relax and get his composure back. He wet his head and face to try and draw focus of what was to come. In his past adventures, beneath the tunnels, he had been almost a mile deep at one point and had put together the old generator that once lay dormant. It was something built before his time, as if the ghost of memories past lay haunted through shadowing walls of excavations long gone. This was an old rusty rendition of a steam generator reconstructed later to use gasoline by someone not known. Robert made the aged classic better by changing the generator to his own personal needs of safety. Furthermore, he filled the generator with fuel just before trekking down several drops that he and Skittles were somewhat leery of. The generator pumped air into the lower levels so they would be able to stay longer than what was considered normal, and the lower portions of the mine weren't possible to mine without air. After the first two-hundred-and-fifty-foot drop, the air was almost nonexistent. From that point, they wouldn't last more than an hour. Thinking back, from his son's point of view, James had been accused of having one of those analytical minds for mechanics that Robert never understood. He had a way about him, being able to figure out complicated technicalities like some men take to writing, and others find strength in mathematics or music, or climbing mountains or having an eloquent tongue being able to manipulate the multitudes. James had figured his father lacking in the communications area of his life made up for it in genius. It doesn't figure, Robert thought. *I guess this is my calling.*

Momentarily, both Robert and Skittles had warmed up to a point to shake off the jitters before making that first drop. Robert's heart rate had calmed to a decent level to where he Felt a little more stable than when first entering the mine. They were ready to go. He was the first to stand, and Skittles caught on quickly by the forward movement of his master. He put out the fire before readying themselves for the journey in the dark. He had belts and ropes with several flood lamps to light the passageway beneath them. He put a hard hat on, a thin pair of work gloves, and waterproof pants and coat. He also stuffed two archeology picks into the duffle bag back at the cabin. The generator seemed to be working great, as he felt the chill leave him as they left the vestiges of the rain behind. He felt the air pull past him on a downward path. He eluded a sense of trepidation with an overwhelming sensation verboten of regulations. This caused his shoulders to tense and brisk tickle of air ran down his spine. *As long as they had air, they'd be okay,* he thought, after blowing out a huff of air. He was all strapped in like a professional locked and loaded and ready in a mountain man's sort of way. He had strapped a harness around Skittles midsection so he could lower the wolf-dog down at the same time that he descended, like a counterweight with the wolf-dog and duffle bag on one side and he on the other. Small spurts of moisture began to seep through cracks and crevices, from overhead, and insular trickles of water ran toward the center of the mine. This had Robert a little concerned when reaching the lower extremities, yet knowing also there was an even deeper tunnel that would take most of the runoff caused him to feel somewhat claustrophobic. Robert slowly stepped off the edge as Skittles whined his concerning stares. The abyss that lay before them waited in the silence of the dark. The descent left a cold eerie feeling of apprehensiveness in Robert's bones, a cautioning that caused him to go slower than normal, and the pounding of his heart made him aware that this was the most weight he'd ever taken down. And getting everything back up was another matter that he would have to face once returning. He turned the LED light toward the wolf-dog to make sure he wasn't spinning heedlessly out of control.

"You're okay, boy? We'll be fine. No need to cry." Robert said as he reached over and pets the wolf-dog on the head to reassure him that their journey was one of a true course.

Robert moved the ascenders, first left then right while trying to keep the wolf-dog angled so he was about waist level for counterbalancing. He could hear water pouring into the lower end of the tunnel. This caused him a bit more concern. What was waiting for them at the bottom? And where was the water going to congregate or run off? They slowly dropped farther and farther into the black. The air pulled past them as if flowing toward an exit, yet Robert knew of no other exit except where they had come from. Two hundred feet later, sweat was dripping from Robert's face, and his heart was beating a rhythm he'd never thought possible. Looking past his feet, he could tell the bottom was close. He reached mentally below as if his life depended upon an errorless journey. His heart's pounding caused his hands to shake, as the last forty feet triggered an enervating feeling that engulfed his every sense, every nerve in his body stood on end. Robert ignored his intuition of giving up this insane idea as many men before him had gone and pushed harder. He unclipped Skittles as he leaned against the wall once on solid ground, then bent forward trying to catch his breath. Robert unclipped his own belt as he turned the lights on, facing a side rail next to the tracks. The antiquated bulbs hung on wired string were looped in Circles placed twenty feet apart down the mysterious lit tunnel as if an elusive presence was stringing him along. An eerie sound of trepidation echoed down the tunnel walls, like forgotten memories haunting him, pulling him toward an abyss he knew not of. Where was that sound coming from? And why did the sound cause him to want to turn back? This caused Robert to slow his breathing to listen. The walls and tunnels felt alive with life like a haunted ship moving with the waves of the ocean. As if old memories were here to make him know who he was, why he was here, and where he had come from? It was speaking to him like he was food for thought for this graveyard of the forgotten, as a ship moves at the constant churning of water, the ground moved in shudders beneath wood beams from bow to stern, as the weight of memories pushed him forward forever churning, never giving in, or never stopping their impediments of loss. The tunnel in front, extended down at an angle of another long tunnel. He felt this maze had picked him to be the smartest rat as this endless maze had entrapped him. Robert looked both ways right then left. Without light going down these opposite tunnels, nothing could be seen. The blackness filled in like inclement holes removed of incremental hearts beating with life, compared to grave collectors collecting bones from men who once walked these trails deprived. The dust of their bones lay as memories wasted beneath the bellows of emptiness. Robert turned on his LED light and flipped it around in Circles to check to make sure nothing was propelling toward him in the dark, or some hidden secret was about to be exposed. He pulled in air and let it out in a huff. Everything seemed to be all right, was his reasoning, but why did he feel like someone else was down here watching his every move, as if he was on someone's eternal clock. He marked the tunnel wall with a bright orange chalk line with An arrow pointing up so he could find his way back home. They walked a good four hundred yards before they came to the next level. Skittles wagged his tail, looked toward his master, and then barked. Even the wolf-dog seemed a little bit off, like time had stopped at the top, and they were inverted somehow in someone else's world where time didn't exist.

Robert pulled out a map and flipped it around several times following a highlighted line of yellow toward an exposed trail that he had carefully mapped out. His eyes focused, something looked different, but what was it? With his index finger, he located the next drop. Robert picked up his duffle bag and continued to follow the line of several exchanges from different tunnels, first going down to the left then right, then left again before coming to another long drop into another cavern that was deeper than the first. At this level, he remembered the air being kind of fetid; and with water working its way to the bottom, he became a bit more concerned. Robert stopped and stared at Skittles as if finding strength from camaraderie.

"Are you ready, boy?" Skittles barked twice while wagging his tail, communicating back as dogs do from time to time through their way of knowing, that sixth sense. Robert smiled with a touch of uneasiness, picked up the large duffle bag again, and signaled for Skittles to follow along. With the path dimly lit through these haunted corridors, he moved on. He slowly made his way down left as pictured on the map. Five minutes later he turned right while holding the map in his hand trying to get his bearings. He looked a bit confused at first, but then he'd remembered at this level before, he felt the same feeling come over him. It was the mountain. It was causing this confusion like it knew no one had any business being this deep, and the mountain would stop one's progress of moving forward.

Ten minutes later, he turned left again facing another long tunnel going at a steeper incline; and then five minutes later, he hit the last turn before Robert saw the other drop twenty feet ahead. A whirling of air left a fetid smell toward this apocalyptic hole that lay in front. Robert reached up and covered his mouth, and then tied a handkerchief around his mouth and pulled it up, to relieve some of the smell. This almost caused him to pull back from this hole in the ground. His imagination reflected vivid long tendrils not seen with the eye, but he could feel it drawing him toward this unabated hole as if hell was here, ready to swallow him up. Robert grabbed the wolf-dog and staggered backward. A sense of lethargy shot through him as the vertigo of falling returned, yet he continued to stagger forward to this future unwanted grave, pushed by an incessant urge to reach his end. He had remembered this being the easy part, while coming back up would be the hard part, and he was already spent. Moving headlong, he hooked three different eyehooks with a Overseen pressure gun and shot the eyehooks into solid rock Above the hole, threading two more ropes through the eyehooks, And connecting Skittles' harness to the other end of the rope. He Clicked both belts in snug and tight and freed up any slack while Giving a hard tug to make sure it would hold. Once finished, he slowly dropped off the edge with Skittles closely knitted to his side.

He then turned his head to his closest companion, "You okay, boy? We're almost there. This is the last drop," whispered as if trying to instill confidence. The wolf-dog whined a hushed out bark as he wagged his tail, not sure if his master was talking for his own self-assurance or for his. Before long, they're both propelling slowly a foot at a time into the dark. Thirty-five feet later, Robert felt a draft from tunnels that cross their path at nine o'clock and three o'clock prospectively. Skittles turned his body around and faced Robert while whining from being spun about from the draft of air. This was one area where the air was blown in from above. The air hit Robert's face, cooling his sweat beaten brow. As he sucked in fresh air, he turned to look at Skittles to make sure he was okay.

Two hundred and fifty feet later, Robert and Skittles reach the bottom of the last drop. Robert bent over, holding his knees while trying to catch his breath as he tried to fight off a dizzy spell. Skittles sat and waited for his fearless leader to get his composure back. Once focused, Robert reached over and turned on another set of lights that lit up another long tunnel diffusing the light below as he reflected a disconsolate expression in his eyes. Why was he even doing this? He didn't have anything to prove to anyone; there wasn't a consolation prize at the end of this journey. He could die trying to retrieve this gold. But something unremittingly pulled him toward the bottom of this place. Something set the tone deep within him as if giving reason to a better way of life, a better place to start anew, but what? He unhooked Skittles and released his own belt while taking another look at the map. This tunnel was the lowest level that Robert had ever been to. And this septum showed the tunnels were in tomblike form for the disregarded and the dying, a place where memories have been laid waste from the world above, someone else had paid a dreadful price at the cost of life for this gold. The air felt heavy on his lugs, damp and restricting. An unsettling feeling went down Robert's spine. Something didn't feel right, but that feeling had never stopped him before. For what was this aggregate reasoning of ideas that didn't really make sense in his head? Why did this darkened place of earth make him feel not at home, a place interred of the damned and dismembered, as if the reasonings for dying were deferred.

After they were both unhooked and the map read, he picked up the duffle bag again and headed down to the left after marking off the hole above with another orange chalk line placed above. Fifteen minutes later, they're at the end of this last long tunnel. He noticed right away that something was different about what he saw from a month ago. Off to the left, he could see that some rocks had been knocked loose from the left side of the wall. It gave it an impression of synchronicity, which stumped Robert because this place never had company before, except for him and the wolf- dog. Who else would know to come down here? He set down the duffle bag, unzipped it, and pulled out the pick and started working on the hole that seemed to have partially started from someone else's perspective. It was obvious that movement from another's hand had taken place here, but whom? The mountain appeared to have an agenda of its own, not including those who walked in the corridors of recent excavations. The Alaskan mountains were famous for such tremors from unsettling ground with constant movement; nothing stayed the same for very long. This place was more than dangerous, yet Robert felt propelled to keep focused on this monotonous dream that kept playing in his head. It was his past that pushed him to focus on an agenda, an agenda he didn't quite understand.

He continued to work on the left side of the wall as sweat beaded on his forehead. The corrugated light caused Robert's face to cast a sallow reflection. He was tired yet kept on pushing, still persisting, ever plotting. After diligent picking he broke through to the other side. Robert turned the LED light into what seemed to be another room. He flipped the light up and down and noticed something strange about this place uncovered. He noticed right away that the floor of the next room dipped down about eight feet lower than where he was presently. Robert turned back around and grabbed the other pick.

He then crawled backward into the opening of the hole and lowered himself down into this other room, off to the left in the deepest part of the mine he'd ever been. This other room gave him a jolt of adrenaline, which he didn't know he had left. He noticed that at one time, this place had been full of water shown by the different water lines that had pervaded through the soils at several levels; but now, where had the water gone? To the right side of the room, he could feel air coming through a small opening in the wall just in front. Skittles was still at three o'clock position above him. He looked up at Skittles and gave a bleak smile of hesitation.

"Stay there, boy…I'll be back in a minute."

Robert began to work on the hole that was in front of him, which appeared to be where water had at one time come through this small opening. After working for twenty minutes on this one section, he opened a gap about two feet wide. He could see water glistening off the top of a large water basin that was a foot lower than where he had made this bigger hole. He viewed this to be an underwater lake of some type that stretched out to the other side of another large opening, about seventy feet across to where the cave ended. As soon as Robert turned the LED light toward the ceiling, hundreds of bats flew out of the hole toward him and then up to where Skittles was barking nonstop. Robert dove for the floor while covering his head, as the bats passed over his and Skittles head. Skittles jumped out of the way to avoid the fly by. Robert got up and brushed himself off and then looked up at the other hole. Skittles came back into view.

"Are you, okay boy?" the wolf-dog barked with a wag of his tail as Robert drew focus again on the hole in front. He pulled a glow stick out of the duffle bag, stripped down to his boxer shorts, snapped and shook the glow stick while it turned a bright fluorescent green and dove into the water with the glow stick in his mouth, and a sense of urgency pushing him forward.

Because of the static temperature of the cave, the water felt cool but not cold. Robert noticed when he opened his eyes underwater that the whole wall before him was sparkling a shiny gold color, illuminated by light from glow stick. Something was left behind, not seen by gold diggers from the past. Robert's eyes widened while a rumble of unsettling earth closed-up the hole behind him.

2

THE RESCUE

He was a tall young man with dark features like his mother. James was six feet two inches with a size 13 shoe. Boys with big feet sometimes give an awkward impression of youth, and dad never missed a beat of father-and-son bonding. James was a boy that Robert adored to the bone; a gift given as a token of love.

When Robert was going through the divorce with James's mother, he kept his mind clear of negative thinking. He didn't want his still impressionable son, blaming his mother for the marriage not working out. According to Robert, he felt that being human sometimes, we lose our way in life and make mistakes that can't be fixed. James had presently figured Dad was right and continued to love his mother, still standing strong with support even though he knew his mother was making mistakes. When Robert was emotionally unhinged at times, he would try and hide it from James. What Robert didn't understand though, was James was going through the same hurts, feeling the loss of a mother who was trying to live another life. James never roamed too far from Dad's side. He'd spent many a day planning his schedule around his father's schedule, he remembered the camping trips to the mountains with family and spending time down in Mexico with grandpa and grandma with all of mom's cousins and sisters. *Mother,* James's thought, *was from*

Mexican heritage, with an endless supply of relatives. James would crack jokes about how Mexicans would find humor in little opportunities about how they saw life. White people, he would say, didn't think their jokes were so funny because they didn't understand the hidden meanings of the language or culture. Dad would smile when James would say jokes about both sides and get away with it because he was half Mexican and half Caucasian.

James had an older half-brother named Tito, who was Melody's son from another relationship. Tito was somewhat spoiled being the first grandson but seemed to change over the years and became quite the man that made his parents proud. James was different than Tito, but even still today, he calls his big Brother to find out how things are and to ask about his daughter. Neither boy seemed to be drawn to an athletic life though. They liked to play baseball or toss the basketball around in the hoop, but not on a competitive level. Tito was into reading books, which surprised his mom. Yet Tito had a more analytical side to him that impressed Robert as much as it did his mother. Now James was more the crowd pleaser and with a pretty boy face. James's father had to always force the young ladies out the door and wondered why more fathers hadn't come knocking at the house at ten o'clock at night. What touched Robert the most was how James had this incredible soft side to him that intrigued his father. He was a peacemaker when it came to his friends and family, and Robert saw it as a blessing wrapped in a neat little package of concern, love, and personal consideration.

James had a way with people and mastered the art of persuasion. Robert thought this was probably why he attained so many girlfriends. One weekend, when James had turned eighteen, he asked his dad if could have a small get together with a few close friends.

Three days later, one hundred and fifty kids showed up on a Friday night with two bands that played until one o'clock in the morning. Robert's neighbors were not happy about having a block party with cars blocking the whole street at both ends. One of the neighbors walked two blocks to get home and decided to stop and bang on the front door. James offered the angry neighbor a beer, which was not supposed to be there, and then the cops showed up. James had made all the other boys at the party hand all the beer over the fence to a backyard neighbor before the cops started looking for evidence of liquor. The neighbor's son called James and gave him a heads-up before the cops made their rounds. James was even smart enough to make all the drinkers spray a peppermint breath sweetener in everyone's mouth; somehow, James pulled it off. He even started talking football with one of the police officers and recognized his last name and said he was a good friend with his son. James promised to shut everything down and personally would go to each neighbor in the morning and send his apologies. The cops finally left, and then James quickly shut down the block party within a few minutes. Dad was working the graveyard shift and didn't hear about it until the next day, when his neighbor came over and gave him an evil eye stare. After that, the parties of the future had to be at someone else's house.

When the boys were little, the family would take trips once a year to places like Hawaii or Mexico and four times to Florida. Both boys seemed to remember vivid details about all the trips that Robert had forgotten about because of the years that had passed without much notice. Sometimes the best parts of life in a marriage are forgotten when things begin to fall apart. The negative always seems to take the lead role when offering Memories that were worth their weight in gold-like the gold that James's father was after. James only tried to remember the good times, and even today, he would find something funny to say about his times spent with the whole family, without remembering the bad. Robert would smile and laugh about all the little things that James expressed with great emotion. His son didn't usually want to do certain chores and leave his dad out of the project. Even working on the cars, he would go in the house and look for Robert so they could at least spend a few minutes together talking about the future or some distant dream that Robert saw as far-fetched but never discouraged is son to reach for what he thought might be possible. Yes, those vivid dreams were like the frosting on a melting, moistened butter cake that his mother would make in the winter. He remembered her sitting the cake up in the window to cool. This made him reach up and wipe a tear away that had found its way across his check. What happened to all those good times? What touched Roberts heart was that James would always be affectionate toward his dad even around his friends. Most of James's buddies thought he had to be some type of super dad to draw James's affection. Even in the public eye of his peers. But somehow, Robert knew that it had nothing to do with his abilities as a father. It was James adherent personality shining through. Robert, throughout James childhood, allowed his son to make mistakes without finding any reason to criticize the end result. This meant more to James than constructive criticism or beating him over the head with the end result. When James and Tito were younger, Robert took on the responsibility to coach a young adult basketball team during the summer two years running. Both teams that he had coached won their division both years. Robert was offered job to coach bigger named teams on the A level in San Diego County, but he turned it down knowing this would take more time away from the family and saw it as too great a sacrifice. James would try to emanate his father's likeness, like the way he talks, how he walks, the way he expresses himself with his face, or how he laughs. He would cause everyone to laugh. He was big teaser, his dad would say. When James began to see his mom and dad falling apart, he tried to be the peacemaker at the tender age of ten years old. He would shed tears with Mom then dad and tried to bring their emotions together. Robert knew what James was trying to do and sensed the breakup would affect James more than it did himself in the long run. Even though he still loved Melody with all that was in him, he knew eventually he would recover from the divorce, way before his son would. During that hard three-year period, James caught dad once in the closet sitting on the floor and smelling the perfume on mom's clothes, trying to capture those last few memories of her. James sat on the closest floor with his dad.

His dad embraced him like a child looking for comfort. Robert knew that James had developed an insurmountable love toward his son that became supportive in the nick of time, showed in his father's moments of weakness. Who would care otherwise?

Even today, James was the one who called Dad first when he'd feel down or needed someone to talk to. James became the perfect example of how any father would want their son to be like. Grandma would criticize Robert for not being harder on James when he was in his teens, yet Robert saw something past all the BS that grandma missed because of her absence. He saw a tender side of James that overlooked all mistakes and wild parties or being led to do the wrong action sometimes. Once when

Dad took James to work at the age of thirteen, James thought it would be okay to walk up to the CEO of the company like he was family and introduced himself while explaining who his dad was and to look out for him because he was the type of man, who would set the world on fire.

Robert was somewhat embarrassed but sensed his young son looked past all the insecurities that his father had and only saw his potential without seeing anything else.

James was really good at being friends with almost anyone but struggled like Dad did with being intimate. His only true intimacy was with the passion he had shown toward his father. Robert knew if he was at a point in his life that he had to choose between what his father wanted him to do and his own dreams. He would have followed his father's, yet somehow James knew that Robert would never allow that.

After going through a maturity stage in his life, James decided to hit the books and go to college at the tender age of twenty. The only requirement that Robert asked of his son was to take the same passion he had toward his family and use it in his education, with the same drive, the same imbued personality as with his father. That's exactly what James did. He studied his butt off over the next four years to get his bachelor's degree and then decided to keep going. Five years later, James had developed an incredible passion toward his field of study in marine biology and the hidden secrets beneath the ocean's waves. That trip to Alaska had become forthcoming. He was bit nervous. Yet spending the summer with his father was his final redemption to finish up his schooling with his aging father close at hand. This made sense to him. Robert hadn't seen his son for over five years because James did exactly what dad wanted, and that was to put his passions into school. He was almost done. Father and son missed each other, and the guilt of not being around Dad left James feeling somewhat isolated. He was missing a father's love.

The now much schooled twenty-nine-year-old got on a plane and headed for some place lost in an era before all time had started ticking the hours of a world known clock, in a quaint little town from the back woods of Skagway, Alaska. He thought, *why would Dad separate himself so far from the real world?* What James didn't understand yet, was his father needed this time and Wide open space to learn to love again a journey that caused his Heart to pump blood through his system. And to be in the wild made him appreciated the little inconveniences that caused him to feel there was reason to go on this journey placed in his path. It gave him purpose. He just needed a good dose of reality pointing him in the right direction. With his heart in this forbidden territory, without the usual basics or necessities that others couldn't do without, like the Internet, iPads, iPhones, video games, none of that would help people live normal lives because the numbness would never stop. Most people had become like mindless zombies or lifeless automatons, he was done with that way of living, punching a clock and dealing with an uncaring boss. In James's father's mind, he believed was all BS. He figured if this raw land was good enough for people back in the eighteen hundreds, it was good enough for him in the here and now.

When the plane landed in Juneau, Alaska, James had to take another small plane to Skagway. Then he rented a four-wheel drive vehicle to climb the side of this giant mountain that weaved its way around some of the most beautiful timbered land that James had ever seen. He had seen his father's personality drifting in among the trees in their secret beauties of a life missing from the real world left behind in an endless sea of overpopulated cities. James began to see what his father had seen, something beyond sight of the normal human eye. What he would ever see when clouded with so much monotony left in the stranded byways of millions of people, who loved with an unnatural way of thinking. The people of the world now were living in a cookie- cutter world blinded by barriers, too many wasted moments on nonessential things like, Facebook, YouTube, texting constantly, worrying about who's doing what to whom, instead of worrying about their own little world of confidentialities. This new old-fashioned way of living was a way Robert began to feel a connection with his world, when he'd become disconnected from the other. It caused James's eyes to water when he sensed his father's rugged personality pervading in the tops of the trees, soaked up in the soil, felt in the open air, realized in this comforting environment of yesteryear. It was all ubiquitous of a purpose meant for everyone, but was it? He caught on that the surreal world left behind was caustic to their cause. Thinking other people's minds were empty, without resolution, just strung along in their unfulfilling destinies looking through eyes of unfulfilled purposes. This land was all a part of some past that penetrated his soul and heightened his sense of a better way living, and now it just hit him. James knew then, why his father had chosen such an area. He thought if a godlike king would find the most peaceful place on earth to do his bidding, he would have chosen Skagway, even though the name was misleading. Sometimes sensing the best lessons in life are not the words taught by some great scholar but just the simple sights of God's natural beauty. It displayed a better picture of how calming and healing earth could be. It used to remind Robert how James's personality was when he was younger, clean, fresh, and beautiful as a young boy should be, finding the positive side to almost anything connected with. Once, when James was seventeen years old, he brought a homeless man home without letting Dad know. James fixed him a hot meal and let him sleep on his own bed while he took to the floor. This was James's accommodating personality that his father saw that no one else did. He was a natural at showing a better side of life that had been missing from so many others.

It was a message he wanted to share with every living human being that was on the face of the earth, in other languages, on national TV, shared with the pope or local neighbor or whoever thought it worthy to examine his son's ability to love. Robert knew the love of a son was something special beyond what anyone else could understand. Even today, Robert looks back at Melody and smiles, thinking of the great gift that she helped produce in young James. He has turned out to be such an inspiration.

Thinking forward, James drove to the cabin on long twisting roads into this mammoth back country. He stopped to view a map he'd bought at the Skagway airport. Most of the roads at this level was all dirt with hardly any access to the thickly timbered land. James finally made it to the end of the road that pointed him to the left on an even smaller dirt road that twisted and wound farther into the darkness of a distant land. James felt to be in another world. He saw what looked like the pictures his father had sent him four weeks back. In the distance, he could see the porch had that old rustic look to it, like in the pictures, and off to the back side of the property lay a half unfinished barn and coral. James got out of the jeep and took his bags and equipment to the front porch and glanced up at the door. Right away, he saw the note and map tacked up against the door. James pulled it off and opened the note attached to the map. The note explained how his father had gone up to the mine to work until Sunday, but being it was already Monday, James sensed something was wrong and began to make haste. James quickly unloaded all his gear inside his father's log cabin. He set off to plan and grab what he needed for a trip up the mountain by throwing everything he could think of into the large duffle bag. He had found in a pantry behind him leading to the stairs to the basement. And a weapon of choice, an old SKS with rope for traveling down tunnels, two boxes of shells in the pantry with other supplies that involved climbing gear and survival snacks like dry foods, beef jerky, nuts, water, matches, and anything else he could get firsthand. James stopped for a second to realize that if his father were hurt, he would need a first aid kit and a way to get him down the mountain. Not knowing how far his father had gone inside the mine. He'd have to reconsider the terrain's conditions and the fact that the mine was at least one hundred years old. He had no idea how unstable the area was or how determinate in strength he would be before finding the old man in some dark hole. James looked through every nook and cranny before sitting out the door. James filled five water bottles, found a small bottle of whisky for sterilizing a wound, and heavy boots and gloves. Then he saw the LED flashlight sitting on the kitchen table. He checked it for worthiness just before heading out the front door. James looked at the map before leaving the porch and gazed up at the sky. He thought now would be the best time to leave before losing anymore daylight. The rain would start up again in the late afternoon. He considered the possibility that his father might have been hurt, or stuck somewhere, lost in one of the tunnels. This made him worry more, and a sense of urgency pushed him to get going. He wondered if dad was maybe trapped without sufficient air, with only a few hours before trauma would begin to set in. James put his head down and jumped off the porch and headed in the direction laid out by the map. He looked down at his compass. And then he noticed the clouds were beginning to roll in. James got to the of the mine in about two hours. He began to take in every detail about the entrance, the contours of the land, the sinkholes around the entrance, and any loose gravel or rocks above the facial. He saw the new wood beams right away. They were mostly six by six inch wide and eight feet long. They appeared to be placed at the right junctures of weaknesses. James knew his father was trying to take every precaution, yet going in alone was not too smart. This was going beyond the boundaries of safety. James stopped just long enough to break out his flashlight and then took a swig of whisky to calm his nerves. Normally, he wasn't one to drink, but sensing he needed to be focused, he thought the shot of whisky would calm his nerves. Two minutes later, James began to feel the whisky does just that. Before moving forward, he refilled the tank to the generator, and checked all the gauges to make sure it was running properly. He began to think like a student. He would plan each moment so not to lose his cool, or slip down into one of the many holes dropping in darkness. Within a few minutes, James made it to the first drop. He noticed right away the ropes dangling into the forefront. The air from behind him seemed to pull past him toward this apparently bottomless pit. He looked down and felt the darkness give him a sense of vertigo. The blood ran to his legs as he'd backed up and slipped on a rock. After shaking his head and taking a deep breath, James clicked on the LED light that Robert left on the kitchen table. It hadn't really made a difference, even though it was brighter than a normal flashlight. He put his gloves and hard hat on and strapped the rope dangling over his head around his waist. An unsettling chill went through him as he looked back at the hole again. The light wouldn't penetrate by what he thought. The darkness below appeared to be too far to even fathom. James was afraid of heights, so he took another shot of whisky before considering making that drop below. This was into another world were sounds of a different making led him to believe he wasn't alone. He felt watched, from every corner covered in shadows of a pervading world of eerie darkness. A world of bats and rats and critters that slithered in the night. He reached for the ropes and closed his eyes while letting out a long huff of air. James flexed his shoulders and viewed his situation. *Practice makes perfect*, was his thought as he pulled down on the ropes that lead to another world below. James connected two ascenders to the top of the rope before connecting it to his belt. After having the ascenders attached to the rope and looped through the metal eye loops, he steadied himself. He then pressed forward with all his weight and took the first plunge that couldn't wait. He tossed his duffle back over his shoulder, while the hair stood up on end on the back of James neck. His heart was pounding like a locomotive. He tried to reassure himself that everything would be fine. He took a deep breath and slowly let it out. He tried to get his composure back, but without being able to see below, he felt a touch of panic. Whatever was underneath him would have to be experienced by thoroughly trusting in the rope, along with his ability to stay composed. With his limited ability to master this craft, he began to think back at some of his father's stories about climbing. James remembered that ascenders were the key of holding his body weight. It was rough going at first, and James almost panicked when he felt the air pull past him, like a rollercoaster flying by. Using the light, he let out a sigh of relief when a smaller tunnel came into a view to his right, as air flowed out in a steady stream. It was just the generator doing its job, an efficient running machine giving him fresh air to breathe. Fifteen minutes later, James was at the bottom of the first drop. He was breathless. He sat for a moment to get his strength back and took several chugs of water before continuing down a winding path that lay ahead. The darkness below was different from the darkness above. The environment was stranger, more elusive than before. He broke out the map while resting. A little unsure of his direction, he wanted to make sure before trekking forward without knowing what direction, he was headed. He saw on the map where the tunnel forked left and then right and then shortly it hooked left again. James saw the string of lights overhead. He guessed his father had turned them on before moving on down the line. He noticed the tracks dead ahead with a push cart with steel wheels, showing age with dust and packed on mud with its rusted conditions. Above his head, he saw the orange chalk markings that his father had left behind and took a mental note of its exact location. He sketched in the chalk mark on the map as a red flag to take notice when coming back. James got up quickly and hurried farther down the tracks not looking back at what was behind him. He was on a good pace of getting were he needed to be. Twenty minutes later, James was at the next long drop that went down even farther than the first drop. Again, James saw the ropes attached to the ceiling above and began to pull on the ropes as before then reconnected them to his belt. His heart was still pounding, even though his confidence had faded a bit. He dropped below without giving it a second thought. He had to get to his dad before something bad would happen to him. He was more than worried. This second drop was even tighter than the first. The tunnel made him feel like he was dropping into a world of scarier conditions than before. And unsettling chill crossed his mind, as the smell of aged dampened dirt filled his lungs. Something had died down here that laid wasted in some distant corner giving off this pungent smell. What if he couldn't get back up the same way that he came? James shook his head to clear the thought and then continued on this elusive dream of dropping into blackness. Within thirty minutes, he'd reached the bottom of the second drop. James had traveled forty-five feet farther than the first drop, which he couldn't even fathom; but after looking at the distant meter he had on his belt, he knew it wasn't a dream. It was real, and this trip in the dark was an insane idea coming from an old man without a sense of self-preservation intact. He was crazy, living in a pipe dream of lost causes and broken dreams, trying to retrieve the mother lode. The air at this level had a metallic heaviness to it. James sat for five minutes to get his bearings and to take another look at the map. Considering he was making pretty good time, he started moving slowly forward until he saw the tunnel end. At the left side of this tunnel, James could hear a dog barking faintly on the other side of this cave in. James put down his gear, grabbed the smaller shovel out of his duffle bag and started digging. Hearing Skittles barking nonstop on the other side of this cave in gave James the impression that the wall in front couldn't be more than a few feet thick. An hour after restless digging, James was able to make a hole big enough to see Skittles coming up to the entrance and sticking his nose out for James to touch. A chill went through James's gut. His father had to be here somewhere- but where? Skittles was more than happy to see that James met his introductions. Just a little more digging and he'd be able to push through. The rocks and dirt and whatever else lay on the other side started to give way. James kept digging for an added ten minutes before he had a hole big enough for him to slip through. A pleasurable smile broke out his face. He could tell the room behind this wall of dirt was at lower level. He finally pushed through. After getting to the other side, he left most of the dirt to support the ceiling. Then he began to look for his father.

Skittles barked at James while digging dirt from around him. This was his way of helping. The wall to the right of the hole was at a three o'clock position. Finally, James was able to crawl forward with the pick in his hand as he sidled on his stomach and dropped below with head and arms first. Water leaked out from the other side in a trickle of trails. James noticed the water right away when his right hand splashed in a silky mud puddle. Skittles wanted him to make an opening where the water had left the puddle. He was barking and scratching in the twelve o'clock position of the room. James reached up to pat skittles on the head and then pulled out water for the wolf-dog to drink. Some of the water dripped off the wolf-dog's mouth. Not much was lost to the ground. Skittles appeared to be happy to get relief from the last two days of being stuck in this hole and showed a little nervous tension. Ten minutes later, James had made a three by three foot hole where the water was leaking. He looked through the hole flicking his flashlight in a round circular motion in a complete Circle. From about seventy feet to his left, a large flat rock laid up on the side of the water basin, and James recognized the form laying strung across this rock with his legs dangling over the edge. His father's chest moved up and down. He knew he was breathing. James's heart fluttered when he realized his father was alive. And at the same time, he felt a hardened lump rise up in his throat. James pushed the emotion down and swallowed hard.

He was more concerned about his father's condition and getting him to safer environment, than his own. James stripped down to his boxer shorts as his father had done earlier. With flashlight in hand, he slid into the water basin and swam to the other side. A cold chill went through him, but after a few seconds, he begun to relax. James noticed right away that his father had several cuts and bruises on his legs, chest, and face but didn't see any visual breaks or limbs contorted in any unusual way. Thinking maybe his father had avoided rocks from falling on him. James cupped water into his hand and splashed it on his father's face. Robert sat up and blinked with a huff of air.

"What...what took you so long?" Robert snapped out, tired and testy, as usual.

James had peculiar look about him. "Well, first of all, I didn't know how to get down here, and why are you even here anyway?"

A grimacing smile flanged on his face. He slowly opened his right hand. James looked down at what was clutched in his father's closed fist.

"Is that what I think it is?" James asked.

"It's been here all this time...no one ever found it in all these years." Robert pointed toward the bottom of the water basin. "It's under there. I mean...tons of it, more than we can carry out of here for the next two weeks." Robert grinned from ear to ear while holding this enormous nugget in his outstretched hand. Then James caught the gesture of his father risking his life and expelled a petulant frown.

"You could have died down her if I didn't show up! I almost didn't come... the flight was cancelled at first, but then I found something else at the last minute. The airlines changed their minds when the weather turned and let us go. You're just lucky I showed up when I did...don't ever do something stupid like that again, Dad! Nothing is worth losing your life."

Robert continued to show his pasty white grin while judging his son's physical condition.

"You look older...I mean you put on a few pounds," Robert said."

"That girlfriend of yours feeds you good?"

"She doesn't cook, Dad. I told you before. I do the cooking."

"So, what does she do, besides make babies?"

"She takes care of the babies, Dad. We have two in diapers, like I told you in the letter."

"Are you all ever going to settle down somewhere, or just a have a litter and part ways?"

James's face turned hard. "You make us sound like were animals. Don't go there. I know you don't deal with people very well anymore, but you need to let go of the past and get on with your life."

"I'm doing 'just fine, James. I don't need your sentiment about life's little abrupt letdowns. Conditions seem to always work out..."

Robert stopped mid-sentence and asked, "Do you have anything to eat?"

James's eyes moved from his father's glare toward the small room he'd left behind. "Yeah, back in my pack. First let's get you to the other side before you turn into frozen lamb chop," James barked out.

"I've already done that. Just help me to the other side of the water basin."

Robert and James both slipped into the water while Skittles continued to bark from the other side.

Five minutes later, James climbed through the hole he had made earlier and pulled his father through the opening. He reached over into his dad's duffle bag and pulled out a towel for his father to dry off and dried off himself. Robert looked over at his son with a somber expression.

"I want to come back and dig out as much gold as we can in the next couple of days. I mean, after I get my strength back."

James developed an incongruous expression. "Dad, I didn't come here to spend it treasure hunting in a mine that's ready to collapse. I came here to spend time with you. If that's not what you want me to do, I'll set up shop somewhere else."

Robert raised an eyebrow. "No...no, it's okay. I was looking forward to seeing you too. It's just...well, you need to calm down that's all." Robert was at loss for words. "We can talk about this later." He didn't want to cause a problem this early with his son, and he sensed a sore spot developing between them. He got up after getting dressed and headed back toward the tunnel above them. He stayed quiet about the adventure of mining gold for the next few hours, as if it was a bad idea, and headed up the first tunnel following his son. Both men made it out of the next hole and pulled Skittles through as well. They stood in the tunnel for a minute, getting a good look at each other. Breathing hard while leaning forward, this wasn't easy by a long shot. This was kicking their proverbial butts. Robert sat down on one of the rocks and took a drink of water and offered some to the wolf- dog. He pulled a sandwich from his pack while sharing part of it with his dog. They both chugged more water before finishing the sandwich. Robert dotted the top of his head with a handkerchief before getting back on his feet.

Back in the day, well in 1898 to be exact, Skagway was quite the mining town with a residence that reached over twenty thousand people. Most of it was run by criminals with large amounts of drinking establishments, and hundreds of prostitutes. James had remembered looking up its past to get a feel for its history. Maybe this would be a peaceful place to hang your hat, but from the past, it was called Hell-Town because many men lost their lives here, and no real organization ever got established. Too many criminals ran all the projects going in and out of the mines, and the trails were dangerous with small ledges that became icy and slippery during the winter. Many animals lost their lives tumbling down into the steep gorges, falling to their deaths, and then later trampled underfoot from the masses that walked the Klondike trails. Skagway became a ghost town within a few years because too many had lost their lives from the upheaval of the gold rush craze with the extreme weather and the lack of organization, many were left behind in unmarked graves. Some were killed by the elements, some by the wolf packs, and still others from wandering off too far from camp and losing their way.

James, Robert, and Skittles finally made their way through the top of the mine-now seven o'clock at night, yet still summer most everything up on the mountains were still lit up. They were glad to get out into the fresh air. James could hear a wolf howling in the background while Skittle's ears perked up. The walk back to the cabin was all downhill, and the rain had stopped about four hours earlier as shown by the ground. Robert sat for a second to catch his breath, and James turned to see his dad perched on large granite rock. He saw the pale look in his eyes, and his hands were shaky. James had never seen his father this way.

Robert looked up. "Give me a minute to get real air back into my lungs. It's been two days." Robert coughed and sputtered several times before getting back up on his feet. He wiped the sweat from his face. James had a look of puzzlement as he evaluated the countryside and the mountains that jetted above. Then he looked back at his father. This was a world he'd never imagined.

Not thinking clearly, James asked. "Why does it rain so often?" He'd tried to make small talk with his father, even though something lay deeper under words not said. Robert didn't comment right away. He was still trying to catch his breath. James could see he was overwhelmed from his bout with the Mountain, like some mysterious ghost had followed him and left A pressing expression of adherence glazed in his eyes.

"What do you do for fun around here?" Robert's eyes shot back in his direction. "What, like dancing girls, and hoopla?" James shook his head as a return answer. "I guess I set myself up for that one."

Robert let out a chuckle. "Look, there's not a lot to do around here unless you want to drive into town and go to a bar, but you don't drink. I'm sure you're not the type to chase after bar girls. That's usually what most men do in Skagway, besides hunt."

James flipped his eyes around. "I'm not thinking of cheating on Amanda if that's what you're insinuating. I have kids and responsibility. I wasn't asking for personal reasons. Amanda and the kids came with me. I was asking with them in mind. They're staying in the hotel in town."

Robert's curiosity perked. "Why would you bring your family up to this godforsaken country, James?" James raised an eyebrow.

"She didn't want me to go, Dad…I had no choice in the matter."

James heard a wolf howling even closer than before. Several moving shadowy silhouettes cast across the ground reflecting from the quickly fading sun. Skittles turned rigid while the hair stood up on the back of his neck. the wolf-dog growled in the direction of the timbering trees. James turned to look back at his father.

"Are we going to be, okay?"

Robert smiled and took the rifle off his shoulder. "I brought along some added protection. The kind that's illegal in the states now."

James reached into his duffle bag to find the other gun that he had taken from his father's log cabin.

"Is that my gun you stole out of the house?" James looked over at Robert with a sense of missed elucidation.

"I didn't steal it. I brought it along in case we ran into trouble, like possibly now."

More howls in the background. Skittles raised his head with ululations, which echoed back to the forest.

"We've got to go," Robert said. "We've been here too long. This is their territory. The wolves are getting edgy."

"Why didn't you say something earlier about being in their territory?" James had a look of fear in his eyes. He expelled hesitation about his father. Robert passed his expression off without confutation.

"Just make sure you have that thing loaded." Robert pointed out with a hand gesture to take the safety off. "That's the safety," he spoke. More howls were closer. Skittles took off toward the trees.

Robert yelled in his direction, "Skittles, get back here!" He whistled in short bursts to draw his attention, but it was too late. He could see Skittles running at the edge of the forest. Every muscle in his body was erect with his teeth and tail set In a fighting stance. The leader of the wolf pack burst forth and lunged toward the wolf-dog. Skittles was ready for the Alpha. He flew over the top of Skittles who ducked as the Alpha flew by. Skittles seized this opportunity and grabbed the Alpha's back leg and bit down hard. There was a crunch and a taste of blood as the Alpha howled in pain. They fell together in a twisting tumultuous procession of snarls, heated adrenaline, and rage of dominance-twisting and turning as they rolled down the incline. Skittles leaped at an angle and grabbed the soft flesh of the Alpha's throat. Matted splotches of blood began spilling out over the ground. Skittles continued to rip at the other wolf's throat, and undulating beat of life quickened his demise, as the heat of life flowed from the Alpha's throat. The other wolf gave his last breath and dropped to the ground. Skittles stood on the dead Alpha's chest as he howled to warn others of his victory. The rest of the pack took off through the forest, in the fading light as the sun began to set with deluged reds and yellows in the sky. The wolf pack regrouped beneath the covering of forest blocking them from sight.

James walked up to Skittles and rubbed the top of his head. "Good boy!" he said, as he glanced past the visual of timbering trees. A clear sight of focus showed through on the wolf-dog's face. An adversarial presence caused him to focus. The wolf-dog had blood on his mouth, and on the front of his chest. James sensed the wolf-dog, even though he'd won the fight, knew further battling had just begun.

"Good boy, Skittles. Way to go," Robert assured his best friend. Both men looked at each other with fading confidence as they considered the specter. They would soon be surrounded if they stayed here.

"They'll be back. We have to get to the cabin before they come," Robert explained. The two made tracks as the wolf-dog followed after, down the winding mountain, staying away from the edge of the forest. The land rose up around them like a presentiment that made no sense.

That's the fastest James had ever seen his dad run since he couldn't remember.

Robert turned his head to briefly to say, "Hurry, let's get a move on. We only have a few minutes to get the lead on them."

James felt, at that moment, something strange was about to be directed int their path, if not in the next few hours, soon after. The land was full of secrets yet to be told of mysteries not thought of that stretched for mile after mile of this beautiful land, as if purpose was embedded in the mountains, in the valleys, in the wind that brushed the tops of the trees. A definitive recital was about to take place without their acknowledgement. James could feel the air penetrating his lungs like dreams from centuries gone by. He felt the calm in the air, even though chaos could be rounding the next corner at any moment. It filled his mind and heart like thunder fills the sky without much warning. Something destructive was on its way. And the big blue sky and those below would be the witness of a battle yet to come. He could feel boldness and beauty mixed in a whirling twirling sense of memories coming to mind, something not of this earth-a coming retribution, the settling of difference, for position and power from a world gone awry.

James's heart was ready to pound out of his chest. He felt a lump of flab in front of him. *Too many chili-dogs and hamburgers,* was his thought. Here his dad was fifty-nine years old and beating him down the mountain. He figured too many days inside the classroom without any exercise had made him soft. Skittles, knowing and sensing danger, kept running back and forth in front of them to protect them in a fighting stance like the wolf-dog knew what was to come. Robert could see that the wolf pack was slowly surrounding them. He could see the cabin in the distance about half-mile away. The sun was about fifteen minutes from setting and then darkness would take them, as if the demising of day would release encumbered secrets not seen in the darkness of night.

James brought his revolver out from under his jacket while yelling, "Dad, it's too late we have to make a stand."

Then Robert whipped around and called for Skittles. The wolf-dog ran back to meet him.

"How many are there?"

Robert turned to count them on both sides. "Maybe around eight, maybe twelve, possibly a few more than that?"

"What should we do?"

"They must have another Alpha. This isn't usually how they behave after you kill one of their own."

James looked at his father. "Dad, maybe that wasn't the Alpha that Skittles killed, maybe he was an outcast. I read about that once from a journal when I was in college. Sometimes they'll send an outcast to prove his worthiness to be let back into the pack. The pack…will do that sometime."

Robert stared at his son, surprised to hear he knew so much about the subject. "Get set, and don't lose sight of them while I break out the rifle. Maybe I can pick off a few before they make their run at us." Robert saw his face drain of all color. James shook his head as he got down close to the ground. James looked over at his father.

"Why are they coming back?"

"Because we killed one of their own."

Robert adjusted his sights on the rifle, loaded the barrel with three bullets. He quickly lied on the ground to draw focus. After several seconds, James heard a shot crack an echo off the mountain. He flinched while wrinkling his face.

"I got one!" Robert yelled. *Crack!* Another shot fired. "I got another." Again, Robert could see the pack taking off toward the forest in the opposite direction. He looked back through the sites to make sure of the two kills. Two of the wolves were definitely lying quiet still.

Robert got up quickly and grabbed his pack. "Come on, James, we only have seconds to get to the cabin before its dark. They'll be back when its dark."

James was a little confused about what Robert was talking about, but it seemed better to cut and run and live another day, than to stay and contemplate his remark. Robert took the lead as his son followed after. Skittles past them on the run and shot down the hill. James couldn't believe how fast his dad was moving. He looked like a gazelle capering from one spot to the next, without a moment's notice of being chased. James had trouble trying to keep up. Out of breath, he made it to the front porch while Robert held the door to the cabin open. He closed and bolted the door with a crossbar, knowing from experience that a wandering bear could push open poorly locked doors easier than predicted.

James stared at his father as if eternal memories flashed past him of his youth. He had this bewildered expression written in his eyes, as if compilations of the day were racing through his mind, as a fluency of fluttering photos drifted quickly by in his head. The voracious creatures were gone for now, but the effects of what happened that day remained in memory.

He suddenly looked up at his father. "How do you live like this?"

Robert noticed the petulant look in his son face as if the arduous task ahead would be appropriated. He was a father with an inexorable stature expressed in his aura. Robert looked up from the fireplace flames. Without saying a word at first, he got up and walked to the kitchen. He turned, slightly considering his son's frame of mind while pouring another cup of hot coffee, a hot kettle with warm memories gracing his face. He'd seen that look before, even though unsettling, he knew James would learn that his dear old dad had been changed by the land that surrounded them. The land would change all men within time. For the right to love in such a hardened place was not based on strength alone, but having a connection with every living, breathing thing that roamed this land. And now, James had to face the fact that it was already starting to change him. The land made men face their ultimate fears that tore at their hearts when living with immeasurable circumstances. Faced with challenges in everyday life caused them to take notice of this great wilderness. It was alive. It expelled its own air like it was a living, breathing animal roaming the country side looking for victims. It was a teacher and student all in one. It was a place where the thousand sets of eyes roamed the land without a word said or understood, but somehow knowledge and wisdom were its greatest teacher that lived in the bogs and stormy nights. It lived on clear days of sunshine and deep blue skies. It wandered through the trees and whispered on top of the roughly forged rivers and scaled the mountains or deep valleys, it was the presence of entities to come, realized enigmas already experienced, and terminus happenings not yet conceived.

Robert finally looked up and answered, "This new life I have, has given me purpose…better than sulking about what I use to have." He then huffed out a sigh of acknowledgement as if his own personal credence gave him reason to go on. Then he looked up from his reproachful stare.

"That little run down the hill kept you on your toes-didn't it?" Robert chuckled forcefully like he found humor in the fact that they were running for their lives.

"Hey, it's not funny like you would think," James belted out. "They could have killed us."

Robert still has a diminutive smile written in his eyes. "You think I came up here just to sit and slowly die?" he glared at his son, after taking a long sip of coffee. "How do you think people had to live back when this country was nothing but empty prairies, during a time when there were only cowboys and Indians, and by the way, the Indians shot back? The animals we can contend with, they don't have weapons to use against us except their teeth and claws."

James glared at his father like he had lost his mind.

Robert gave further explanation. "You think everything to learn is in those books you were reading back in college? That's only a part of your education, son. Real life out in this forgotten land will teach you more about life than you could never ever read in those books from college." Robert used his hands to point past the door. "That, out there, is real survival. That's what has changed me, that fear you feel when you're being chased just to live. That's the real living. Feeling yourself pumped with your own blood running through your veins the adrenalin. The fear is what changes you. It makes you think."

James showed a disconcerting stare as he wrinkled his brow. "Dad, why all this change, what was so terrible about your life?"

Robert began to get a distant stare in his eyes. "It wasn't so much of my life being terrible, James. It was people not giving a crap anymore about others..."

James knew that his dad had included his mother into the mix of thing. "James, I didn't have anything left for myself except you and the little ones you have. I just needed a reason to live again...the gold, this land, and all the things that make this place special."

James caught the gesture of his father sensing he had found a reason to go on that didn't include his past. His father was starting over without all the other hang-ups that faced other people.

"James, you have a family that loves you, and a good future with two children. I have this new life." Robert's bottom lip showed a touch of emotion before he changed the subject. "How'd you like those drops down inside the mine?"

James shook his head and blinked several times. "It was the scariest thing I've ever done. My heart was pounding so hard, yet after looking back, it seemed to make me feel stronger, like I was worth something that normality in everyday life I would never feel, unless confronted head on by something that seemed so real. It gave me reason to be here. It caused me to feel alive." James glared at his father; who continued to sip on his warm cup of hot comfort while taking in his words.

"Mom would see you different now." His eyes flickered with a touch of emotion. "She's on her own, you know. She got her own place. I told her you were in Alaska now, she was curious so…" James didn't finish.

Robert understood the overtones of James's words yet said nothing in return. He went to the stove to stir his mystery meat stew with a large spoon. The smell drifted through the cabin causing both men's mouth to water.

James flared his nostrils to breathe it in. "You made this from deer meat?"

he nodded in anticipation as he shoved a spoon full in front of James. "Wait till you taste it. It's one of my specialties."

James blew on the spoon while his mouth watered. He took the spoonful and slowly slurped it down.

"You know the cabin will sleep eight. The beds on top are king-size. I made the frames myself. Maybe if you have free time you can help me finish the barn before it gets too cold. I could pay you in gold?"

James shook his head. "Dad, you don't have to pay me for Helping you. I can lend a hand a couple days a week, but I'm not Going back into the mine. You're on your own if you go back."

Robert dropped the giddy grin. "James, I only want enough to help the family and pay off your school loans. Maybe set aside some for the grandkids. It's the least I can do. I owe you, James. For all that you've done for me over the years."

James raised an eyebrow. "Dad, you don't owe me anything. You're my dad. Why would you even suggest such a thing? I'm Not taking any gold from you. You're crazy for bringing it up."

Robert said no more about the gold that he found in the cave, but he knew he had to do something about it before others discovered what was left behind. From time to time, people from all over the world wander inside the mines to see for themselves. Robert didn't want the chance of someone finding him out. He was going back in the morning with fresh supplies and Skittles at his side.

James fell asleep almost right away. Traveling over ten hours on three different planes, plus his adventures in the mine that day, had left him exhausted from going eighteen hours strong. He was spent. When he woke in the morning, his father appeared to be gone by first glance, but he hadn't really looked below. When James turned to sit at the table to eat breakfast of scrambled eggs and fresh bacon. He noticed the large gold nugget sitting on the top of the table.

3

THE VISITOR

It was cold when Robert rolled out of bed about five in the morning. He had thought about that gold all night long. He would find drifters from time to time making their way across the property. He couldn't help but think that there was a chance that others would show an interest in the mine, especially when a find could change anyone's life to extreme. He also knew that no one was supposed to be near its borders. It was locked up for the longest time. It was abandoned by the local authorities. But Robert decided to make that trip back the next day, still confused about his true purpose of bringing back the gold. He had felt something else was pushing him to go back into bellows of the mine but what? Robert shook his head and walked back into the cabin, which caught James off guard who sullenly raised his eyes with the door quickly opening. At the same time, he remembered James wanted nothing to do with the gold. He saw it in his eyes. He didn't want to jeopardize his son's career, and he'd forgotten about his wife and children he had left in town.

The wolfdog nudged his hand as if saying good morning, Robert went to the door and let the wolfdog out to do his business. He was already dressed, made coffee, and had taken out the duffle bag, and began to load all the gear from the day before. When finished, he stepped out on the porch to take a quick look up at the sky. It displayed a perfect day to make this trip back into the mine. Nothing seemed to be out of place. Only the peaceful quietness in a vast wilderness as an occasional bird was heard chirping among the trees. Yet Robert knew this day would have the perfect weather to take that challenging journey back into the tunnels, but he also sensed that he needed his son's help. He wondered if he could convince James to do the one thing he said he wouldn't do. After pacing back and forth for several minutes, he decided he would ask the one question that had been pressed upon his mind. He wandered back into the cabin with a placate stare in his eyes. Yet Robert's heart felt ready to explode.

Without a word, he stood over James as if he was a suspended mime waiting for recompense. He waited for some remedial answer that might squeak out of James to give notice of their' current situation. James contemplated the gesture of his father's overshadowing demeanor. He was hanging over the top of him like a piñata ready to drop from the top of the ceiling. It caused James to flinch like an eerie pendulum was overshadowing him.

"What…? Quit. I've seen that look before. You can't get it out of your head, can you?" James said.

Robert moved the corners of his mouth to spread his agitation a bit more, for his son knew his indomitable personality was pushing through. "I need your help today. I'll make it up to you."

James rubbed his eyes while trying to process what his father was trying to do. "No! I'm not going back into the mine. It's too dangerous. Besides, I have to go and get Amanda and the kids. they're expecting me."

Robert remained stationary for quite some time, still holding a blank stare while staying quiet. James couldn't believe his persistence. Then Robert spoke after a minute had gone by. "James, only this once. I promise. I'll never ask you again. Besides, if you say no, I'm still going."

James got an unsettling cringe plastered in his eyes. "And who's the adult here, Dad?"

Robert narrowed his eyes. "I know it seems a reversal of character, but it's something I've always wanted to do. And there's something…I'm not…quite sure…but I know I've got to do this…"

"What about Amanda and the kids?" James asked.

"Call the hotel and leave a message. Tell her the car broke down, and you had to wait until Wednesday to get it towed."

James stared unblinking. "But that's telling her a lie, Dad."

Robert showed a smarmy grin. "It's only a taradiddle of a lie-not a real lie, but yes, a deception."

There was a pause in James's expression. Robert continued his abetted request. "Come on. This would mean a lot to me."

James got up from his chair and stared at his father, trying to find some logic in his insane psychotic, delusional way of thinking. Finally, his eyes widened as he pointed his finger in his father's face. "Only this one time. Besides, I'm going to be in trouble already with Amanda. She'll be livid when she finds out where we went."

A smile broke out on Robert's face. Then he finished packing, and James went to get his gear. He had an impermanent scowl written across his face as he turned his eyes toward his father. Robert ignored the gesture of a heated face and went to get his gear. After several minutes, he made haste toward the porch like a sixteen-year-old kid getting his first car. He stood and waited patiently as if doubling up with his sidekick ready to do a dirty deed. He blew out a puff of air as it turned misty and decided checking his list from earlier would be a good thing to do.

He looked up at the sky once more, making sure that the weather was holding.

"I'll pack a lunch to take with us." Robert said, as he ran back inside to get a few things of necessities. He flashed his eyes towards James standing across the room. "We'll bring a thermos of coffee and extra water, and oh…there's some doggy treats in the cupboard for Skittles." He pointed to the pantry behind him. "He likes the beef kind."

After twenty minutes of rushing, both men scrambled to make sure they had packed everything they needed. Robert threw more glow sticks and batteries inside the duffle bag. Then it dawned on him that most of the gold was underwater. He turned his view toward the basement and headed down stairs. At the bottom, inside an old cedar chest, he found two small canisters of oxygen. He came back up the stairs and stuffed them into the duffle bag also along with two pair of snorkel masks he saw hanging on the wall. Just after, both men were headed out the door and on their way, before the sun was coming up over the horizon on a perfect day. Robert knew they were both easily packing sixty pounds apiece. After yesterday's altercation with the wolf pack, neither one wanted to take any chances; so, they loaded up both handguns, and Robert had the rifle strapped to his back.

Half a mile up the mountain, they noticed the dead wolf was gone, and only leftover footprints as seen from evidence. Robert looked behind him before continuing his walk up the mountain trail, wondering if he was doing the right thing. He closed his eyes and sucked in the cool air. The valley floor was covered in dew from the night before. An eagle could be seen flying atop the trees. He was circling, looking for his morning meal most likely. He glanced at his son who walked in silence in front of him. The forest seemed alive that morning with wild life wandering its soft ground of twigs, pine needles, and moistened earth. The wolf pack was nowhere in sight, but human scents would drift among the trees, and they would make the connection.

Robert acknowledged that the mountain would shake in protest when the gold was extracted from its bellows. He caught up to James and stopped him cautiously. "Hold up for a second," he whispered. Robert saw a bear coming down the mountain, while Skittles began to growl. "He's only interested in the river. I don't think he wants to deal with us." Robert shot off a round into the air; it echoed off the top of the mountains. The brown bear stood and sniffed at the air. He made the connection and saw the two men and wolf-dog coming his direction. The brown bear trailed off onto another path while the men stood still and waited.

Once again, the two men and the wolf-dog continued their' journey in the chilled air, leaving the silence of a new day left behind, reflecting the end of a long night's cold rendition of finalization. James viewed this vast arena of nature, sensing her beauty and her pain as they both took part of this journey ahead of them.

A hushed pulse of life lay out among the timbering trees, as the breath of the living reached out like branches through muted movements of creatures below. This ambitious land collated memories to be devoid of future blunders of the human kind. It was awe inspiring from James's perspective. Squirrels and deer and birds could be seen gracing the forest floor, going about their day in usual fashion as life hurried along without the plans of the wild being considered. A glacier in the distance raised its mighty form of blue ice in the background, of mountains and valleys staged by man and beast, both etching out trails of fleeting footsteps into a world of rage and beauty going passed the point of recovery. History was being made, and time had been set. James was sensing what his father had talked about the land, what it could edify, and its remembrance of ageless teachings. James sensed the creator in the midst of them, a reverent adulation of unseen history. He had limited his days among his peers for the last nine years of his life without acknowledging the constant changing of the natural world. Robert stopped for a second, and James looked across his shoulder in a parallel gaze. His eyes met with his sons. "It's beautiful, isn't it?"

James raised his view toward the mountains. "It's breathtaking. Kind of hard to notice the beauty though when you're being chased by a half-crazed wolf pack."

Robert smiled at the implications. "They eat their dead you know, out of respect?"

James stared at his dad's insinuation. "Well, then don't be dying on me up here in these mountains. I wouldn't want you to be their next meal." Both men looked at each other and smiled.

"Don't worry," Robert said, "I don't plan on leaving this world just yet. Besides, there's living to be lived yet."

James put his hand on his father's shoulder. "By the way, it cost me a bundle to come up here."

Robert looked over his shoulder toward his son. "Well, then maybe we'll both get lucky and retrieve plenty of gold."

James shook his head. "I'm more worried about what we get out of the mountain, Dad. I'm more worried about what will happen to us if we get in the mine, and we get trapped."

"Why do you think we'll get trapped?"

"You know, this is not meant to be. Finding one's self a mile below the surface, this is not normal by any means. The mountain knows we're here."

Robert considered his son's statement. "This place is a part of my journey. You're here to be a witness." James raised an eyebrow but remained quiet about his hesitation.

Suddenly, the entrance of the mine stuck out like a bull's-eye facing them. Once inside, nothing looked any different than how they had left it from the day before. The mine had a clammy, musty smell that weighed heavy in the nostrils like spongy dust turned liquified. Both men broke out their flashlights. Skittles muttered a whiny growl as they headed toward darker shadows. Even the wolf-dog didn't like what he felt. This suffocating place beneath the earthy mountains had left a hidden message not yet revealed as this unannounced journey brought them forward to future mysteries. By his lack of showmanship, the wolf-dog seemed to be better off not thinking but used his intuitive instinct to push ahead.

Once they're in the central part of the entrance, they were set for worsening conditions, where trusses are tied to wood beam ceilings, and old gothic generator's aged in years of dampened repudiations set the standard of what used to be. Robert filled the fuel holding tank and lit up the generator. James stared at his father for a brief moment. His expressions showed a reflection of the younger Robert from days gone by, expressed in his own character. Robert wondered if this boy turned into man was ready to face what was ahead. He wondered if James would be able to deal with the sudden drops again.

James pulled his father from memories to say, "How long will the generator run on a full tank?"

"Maybe eight hours," he said. "The tunnels pocket the air into each little area. We might have air for a good two days before it's totally gone."

"I see." James returned. "Did you bring that transponder from work that the institution gave you?"

Robert turned to shine a light on his son's face. "No, I left it in the loft on the nightstand."

James lowered his head and rolled his eyes out of the view of Robert's stare. They both dropped off from conversation and headed for the first drop, without passing judgement one way or the other. Robert had almost memorized every turn and bend, every corridor unrevealed from light above. His map was tucked away in his jacket pocket. He was thinking about everything he had brought with him. He mulled it over in his head, a visual picture of each item. Twenty minutes later, both men and the wolf-dog made it to the first drop. The rope was still where they had left it from the day before. Robert reached into his duffle bag and pulled out two more ascenders and a set of walkie-talkies and handed one to James and a second set of ascenders. James looked up.

"You want me to go first?" Robert smiled and pet Skittles on the head.

"If you don't mind, I'm a lot slower going down than you, so it seems more logical for you to go first." James handed his father the ascenders.

"Then you'll need these if I'm going first." James said, noticing the other two ascenders still connected to the rope hanging above.

"Oh, I forgot I left them."

James clipped himself in to the existing rope, wrapped it up and under his legs, then clicked the ascenders into the right position, before giving a tug on the rope. He looked one last time before dropping off the edge.

"See you in a few minutes." Robert reached and touched him on the shoulder.

"Take your time. There's no hurry." Then James disappeared. Skittles let out a dismal whimper as James heard the sounds of nervous tension in the wolf-dog's character.

Robert yelled down the hole. "Don't forget to call me when you reach the bottom!"

A few seconds later, James yelled back. "I gotcha."

Robert broke out the thermos of coffee and made a break of it. He figured he had a few minutes before James reached the bottom. He put a small plastic camping bowl on the ground and poured water into it for Skittles. "Drink up, boy. Don't know when we'll get another chance." The well-informed muted mutt wagged his tail and gave his best friend nudge of affection. The wolf-dog's eyes had a reflective glimmer in them from the dim light reflecting off the walls. Skittles licked up most of the water while some dripped off his chin. Robert took a gulp of hot coffee then inventoried the duffle bag. After being satisfied with his list, he searched for something to hold the gold in. Back behind the side of the generator, he found a sturdy wooden box with a top cut on three sides. He evaluated its strength by pushing in on the sides at all angles to make sure it was sturdy. The box was about two and half feet squared. It appeared to hold some type of cable system from an earlier time. Robert figured a hundred years earlier that some type of cable pulley system was used to bring two or three workers up or down at a time. He assumed that later on, the pulley system was removed to keep people from going farther into the tunnels at lower levels. To the side, there were leftover scraps of metal and wood hanging around the general area of the generator. Robert didn't really see anything worth salvaging.

The walkie-talkie let out a static sound, and then James's voice came on over the speaker.

"Dad, I'm at the bottom."

Robert reached over and grabbed his walkie-talkie and then pushed the call button. "James, I'm bringing a wooden box down with me. I'll be down in about twenty minutes." Then Robert stopped for a second and looked at the duffle bag with handles, knowing that he had hauled too much gear. There was too much weight to haul in both directions. Then he noticed the duffle bag was strong with thick handles. This gave him an idea. Hooking the handles to the rope seemed a better way to go than using an old wooden box that might break from brittle wear and tear or tumble down on someone's head. Robert remembered the rail tracks at the lower end might come in handy. The box car on the tracks would save them some hauling. Robert could picture pulling gold up in the duffle bag was the best route to take. A smile broke out on his face. He called James' back. "Listen up. I have an idea."

A few seconds went by before James came over the speaker. "Yeah, what's going' on Dad?"

A few more seconds clicked by before Robert answered. "Hey…the duffle bags…they can haul the gold. I mean if we're able to secure the gold from the water basin, we'll have to leave some gear behind, but… it could work."

James shook his head, thinking about going under the water. "Dad, this isn't going to be easy. Its underwater."

Robert dropped the smile. "Look, we'll figure it out when we get to that part."

"Ten four. See you in a few." James clipped the walkie-talkie to his belt and glanced toward the ropes. The slack in the ropes loosened when James unties his weight signaling his father it was time to move on.

Robert hooked his belt into the rope looping it up under his legs like he did before. With the duffle bag attached to his back and Skittles at his side, he edged into darkness. For some reason, his load felt a lot heavier than the day before. Within a few minutes, his heart was pounding in is ears from the burden. With Skittles at his side, it was almost too much weight to bear. The burden caused his hands to sweat inside his gloves as a histrionic sensation ran through his mind. His shoulders was tightening, and he was almost out of breath. The wolf-dog looked over and wagged his tail nervously. Robert's condition was paling. He stopped for several minutes to get his breath back. He knew they would have to pull the gold up separate before coming back up, knowing it would be twice as hard ascending. He became nervous of what lay ahead. Robert had beads of sweat on his forehead, and his hands were a bit shaky. His heartbeat hammered in his ears as the sweat ran off his face. A sudden emotional wave went through him, as he tried to clear negative thinking. Taking a deep breath, he stopped and looked down. The darkness caused an eerie feeling to cross his mind. He felt like he was beginning to lose control. Skittles spun in a circle, moved his paw in the direction of his master while licking his face. Robert held a hesitant smile and understood the wolf-dog was sensing his pain. This was his way of comforting him. Robert's age was starting to show as the years of wear and tear caused a vitiated expression to reflect in his eyes. Before they reached the bottom, Skittles started to growl. Something was different than before. Something might be down here besides them.

It was five minutes later before Robert reached the bottom. James was worried when he saw his father ten feet to his right. He looked completely exhausted. James saw how pale he looked and understood the all too clear message by the glint in his father's eyes.

"Dad, I don't think this is a good idea."

Robert sat on a rock that was up against the tunnel's wall trying to regain his composure. He waved a hand at James in his general direction. "I'll be okay. Just need a minute to catch my breath." He stared at his son while breathing hard. "It was too much weight," Robert said. He put his head between his legs and felt his heart rise up in his throat. Something wasn't right, but he kept that to himself.

James shook his head as he gazed down the next tunnel to come. An eerie darkness brought a cold chill to the air. "You're a crazy old man. You know it."

Robert acknowledged by a shake of his head. He hadn't comprehend that Skittles was still attached to the other rope.

James walked over an unhooked the wolf-dog. Skittles fur Stood on end as he took off down the next tunnel. "What is that crazy dog barking at? Wait a minute. We've still got another drop ahead."

Robert whipped his head around to view his son who moved suddenly with a surge of panic. They both wondered if the wolf-dog had made some type of discovery. Their imaginations began to run wild.

"Someone else is here?" James said. They could hear the wolf-dog barking in the distance. Robert pulled out his handgun from his duffle bag and slipped it behind his back and tucked it into his pants. Maybe some other animal was down here, or other miners had found them out? When the two men reached the other drop, they noticed Skittles standing over the hole. Something of a physical presence has upset him to the point his fur was ruffled. Robert reached down and grabbed his collar to get control.

4

THALIANA

The wolf-dog leaned forward, scraping up dirt with his claws and barking at the hole that lay below him. James held a worried expression as he tried to figure out what had Skittles nervous. After about ten minutes, James made it to the second drop, seeing Skittles off in the distance. He looked back quickly to see his dad trudging behind, winded and spent, showing an achromatic manner in his expression. James's LED light showed ghostly shadows cast against the wall, as if a miserable sign of change had croggled in the dark, following after them as unnerving predators slowly revealing a bleak ending of life.

Robert yelled in the direction of the wolf-dog, "Skittles, come here boy!"

James shot a glance back and saw a sallow glaze of sweat permeating his father's face. "There's someone down there, or your dog is going crazy."

Robert glared uneasily. "Most likely, someone is down here, like you said, but I wouldn't bet on it being anyone important."

"Whatever, your dog is nuts. If you don't mind. I'll take Skittles down with me on this second drop." James sensed his father's inclement condition and extra weight would be too much. he wanted for his father to nod before getting hooked up with the over anxious mongrel who needed to calm down. Then he stepped off the edge with Skittles attached to his side. Two shadowy bodies slipped off the edge into a different world. He couldn't see in front of him and boggled his flashlight. With the movement of Skittles spinning about and lack of focus, he dropped the flashlight into the darkness below.

"What the…" James had started to yell, as he heard the doddering whimpers of the hound. Skittles was mesmerized by what he sensed below. James tried to keep his wits about him as he felt cooler than usual as air shot past him, his heartbeat was an unsteady rhythm as anxiety laced his every thought. Sweat began to form on his face as the darkness beneath gave an uncanny feeling that rose in the air. James reached into his jacket pocket and pulled out a glow stick. He snapped it alive as the green phosphorescent light left an unnerving glare set in his eyes. James felt a sense of trepidation run down his spine. He put the glow stick in his mouth so he could see both firsthand. With whimpers and whines, the wolf-dog appeared a bit skittish. This caused James to feel concerned about their efforts of dropping into the unknown. He reached over and put his hand gently through Skittles fur. "You're okay, boy. We're almost there."

James hadn't thought about if he was putting them into a difficult situation by taking the overexcited wolf-dog with him, without considering he might be out of control once loosed. He tried to change his focus back on the ropes, as he felt around with this limited light of comprehension. The possibility of danger that lay below never entered his mind. His mind had not been focused on his safety, and not on the changes of his environment. James had lost his perspective at how the bottom laid below. An esoteric understanding was remitted by the lack of knowledge at hand. The bottom felt too far away to be understood as a visual of distance. he lacked experience in climbing, but sensed underneath the surface of his fragile coherence, he was being assessed by some unknown source. The direction from top to bottom was irrelevant to his thinking, for his mind was overcome like a pilot flying blind, unaware of direction. The air pulled past him from below as his hands began to shake. Fifteen minutes later, James and Skittles reached the bottom of the second drop. Once finding his flashlight, he looked at his surroundings top to bottom. James noticed the glow of light down the tunnel to the right. Still a bit uneasy, James unleashed Skittles into the unknown shadows of flickering light. Skittles took off down the last tunnel with a spurt of energy.

Robert, at the top, sensing something out of the ordinary, started to descend without waiting.

Anxiety laced the air as James tried to follow after echoing barks off the tunnel walls. Incomplete shadows and flickering of light gave way to a damp pungent smell of old musty air. A disheartening stare reflected in James eyes.

From behind, Robert began to slowly catch up.

James came around the last corner to find the wolf-dog just up ahead, calm now, wagging his tail at something James couldn't quite make out. He could see the wolf-dog facing something in the corner, something out of ordinary, something a bit strange.

Robert came around the last corner and saw an ineluctable change in his son's face. The lights were still flickering causing the shadows to dance upon the wall.

"What's wrong with your crazy dog?" James asked while looking back.

Robert shook his head. "I don't know; why don't you ask him?"

James shined his LED flashlight toward the corner of wagging tail and whimpers. he could see Skittles facing something darkened by the bend of corner's shadows. Suddenly, a young Indian girl stood up. She was leaning in braced up against the wall, innocent looking, small in stature, unique in a way that neither man could quite understand. She appeared to have a purpose for being here. Skittles slowly slid to her side and licked her hands as if making friends of this small statured so quickly. Skittles looked back at the two men and barked. At first, the young girl seemed timid, yet within minutes, she began to warm up to the acceptance of the friendly hound. She smiled when Robert turned to view her. She was around five feet four, a hundred and ten pounds, with along black hair reaching to the lower end of her back. She had almond shape eyes with high cheekbones with soft stunning skin tones. and embedded features not seen for some time. She was singing a song that caught Skittles' attention, a delicate lullaby that had a calming effect. Both men looked at each other. Who was she? And why was she here? It didn't appear to make any sense to either one of them. And Skittles had his own way of seeing the world, which both men would never understand.

Robert saw something in the Indigenous girl's manner, which touched him. On closer inspection, he noticed she had tattoos on her arms that bore symbols of a culture he'd never seen before. She appeared to be from a time not thought possible. An ancestry of a time forgotten and not seen or heard of for recorded centuries, a past unrevealed as of yet. Her voice was that of an angel as the men were mesmerized by her aura. She had a voice like nothing Robert had ever heard before in this world but somehow inwardly pointed out that she was fit for a position of leadership. She gave the impression that there was more to her than what was seen by the eye or understood by the ordinary man. The Indigenous girl reflected peace as seen of these two men. Even in the dilemma of being cornered, she appeared to be held to a higher calling. She was wearing animal skins that fit tightly to her body with Indigenous person jewelry, moccasins on her small feet with headband, and a feather rose in the back part of the band inlayed with beautiful colors of green and red. She finished her song and leaned down to pet the wolf-dog. Her voice was calmly alluring. James sat down to get drink of water. He acted like he was seeing something for the very first time-unique, beautiful, and drawing. Robert did a double take when he saw James sit down.

"What…is it, break time? We've got company."

"I was thinking to get a breath of air. Is that all right with you?" James asked. "Dad, come on, an Indian girl?" As if he didn't acknowledge her there, for the simplest of reasoning they were buried a mile beneath the earth; and seeing strange things in these unrealistic circumstances, hallucinations could have been typical. "What next, Geronimo and his warrior princess?"

Robert turned and looked at her, still a bit leery of her presence. "I don't know, let's ask her?"

Robert made eye contact with the young Indigenous girl and pointed to himself.

James shook his head. "No, Dad, don't embarrass me with the cave dweller gestures of me Tarzan, you Jane. Come on… be realistic."

Robert dropped the smile. "Okay, almighty smart one, how would you communicate with her?"

"I don't know, Dad, but not with hand gestures. She might think you were born in a cave."

"Well thanks for your moral support, junior. I'm glad you have my back on this one."

"Dad! Don't be so emotional about it. Just treat her like a normal human being, not like a brainless cyclops."

"What's that supposed to mean?"

"It means don't seem so brainless about your introductions."

"Yes, boy of my youth, I've got it."

The Indigenous girl breaks the ice. "My name is Thaliana. I'm from a world not known to you."

Both men turned in astonishment as they looked at each other. Robert's eyes sparkled with a sense of his heart in the eyes of the youthful Indigenous girl. There was something unique about her that he couldn't put his finger on. He felt as if he was being turned inside out, leaving no secrets unrevealed. she has a spirit reflecting an ancient quintessence, which was embedded into her character of a delightful form. She portrayed a gentle smile when she revealed an intangible charisma, an aura of not being of this place, deep in the earth, separated from the light above. James's heart was touched by her guileless effects. His eyes sparkled with the soft glow of light.

"You know, as men, we have to be committed to do the right thing. I feel like you have a place of great importance. What can we do to help you find your way back home? Robert felt a lump in his throat as he took her hand. He had no idea what would come out of his own mouth, considering her like a daughter in the gentle protection of a father's guiding hand. A bit confused, she looked down and smiled. Robert misunderstood her reason of being here, as he quickly looked back at James to win his approval, he said, "We're here to help... I mean, if you need our help." A single tear pooled in Robert's eye, as if his past memories haunted his present situation had been worn by the effort of time. He was moved by the young Indigenous girl's incarnation. It was like they were caught in a fantasy transmitted through her presence, through her warmth, as a quiet resilience was instilled through the darkness, as light shown back on this place secretly held. A soft glow of light sprung forth from her personal presence. Her stare stayed affixed on this old man holding her hand. She felt the comfort of experience reflected in his eyes.

"I don't yet know my exact resolve, but I sense my purpose in being here is to show you great warriors your purpose."

Robert and James looked at each other wondering what she was talking about. This young Indigenous girl knew something that they were blind to.

Robert then spoke from his mounting curiosity, "So why are you here?"

Thaliana showed a regal acknowledgement. "I've been sent as a Guardian from the Seventh Realm of Heaven. You were about to make a grave mistake. I'm here to give you counsel so you keep to your present journey."

Robert and James both looked surprised. "What do you mean, young lady, what's the real reason for you being here?" The Guardian would give an account of the most bizarre story either man had ever heard.

Shew signaled with her hands. "Please sit," she insisted." This will take a while to explain." Robert took out the thermos of coffee and sandwiches to make a lunch of it and offered water to their host. Thaliana took the drink, finding satisfaction in the cool water tipped from an animal skin. She looked at them hesitantly before starting. "I've been appointed to watch over you, Robert Littleton, since you were born. You are a part of those chosen of a king of realms." She turned to look at James for a brief moment to include him.

Robert has an expression of bewilderment. Still confused, he kept silent.

From where she was standing, they looked like two schoolchildren who had lost their way, by obeying orders from their teacher. She seemed to be there to scold them or exude some type of purpose from a lesson learned. She wasn't sure how they would take a peculiar story of what she was about to share, but she seemed to not want to frighten them. She stared at Robert for a brief moment, maybe looking past all the rough spots of character through his eyes, not quite sure if he would be the right person, or maybe she had been misinformed and needed to seek another. He appeared a bit older with the lines cresting at the bottom of hidden eyes. Maybe she was in the wrong tunnel or took a wrong turn?

She looked back at both men caught in a trance from dazed like wonder. Then she began the astonishing account of thousands of years ago.

"Well. I'm not sure where to begin, so I'll tell you about this place first and then maybe the rest. You'll see how it all fits together into its congenial arrangement, or as it was meant to be." Thaliana seemed a little nervous at first, since this was her first time being a Guardian, and wasn't quite sure if she would be accepted after such a bizarre beginning.

"This place is special, like you have thought all along," as if reading Robert's mind. "It's a place of beauty that's been saved for people such as you. At least, that's what I've been told. It's also, a place I knew as a little girl in my youth, many years ago before your time, I once lived here. A king of realms has a special purpose for all things. Maybe not as you would think in a human type of way. He knows your heart. That's why I'm here, to give insight of your purpose."

Thaliana stepped forward and then placed her hands on Robert's shoulder as if checking that he was really there in front of her. He thought it a little peculiar, yet Robert sensed that there was something right about Thaliana's reasoning, even if he didn't understand its meaning yet.

"I died here many years ago… a young girl of nineteen. Even though my years here were but few, I served my purpose of what I had to learn. My father, of this earth, was a great chief of the Tlingit nation from a long time ago, a people from about a thousand years before your time. my people of then lived and survived on the beaches of the southwestern areas of the Alaska Panhandles, close to the foothills of these great mountains. Most of my people were tucked between the tidewater and the rugged timberland that you have experienced. That's where we survived and lived for hundreds of years, then the Norsemen from the north came. They were mass murderers, rapist of our women, and would burn our old people at the stake. My king obliterated those people off the face of the earth. You cannot find much of them left in history. These Norsemen, as they were called, had made their choices of treating others with total disregard. They were a crude and heartless people, but somehow, they served a purpose in being here, as you have been appointed to serve a purpose of being here now. My father, back then, was a leader of numerous Indian warriors that roamed this great land for many centuries. He was a man of honor and strength, a warrior chief who loved his people as a father should love his own, who would have died for its cause, which he did at his final end. He believed that each warrior should stay true to his people and his journey, at all costs, no matter what of your circumstance."

Robert sensed she was talking about present day circumstances.

Thaliana looked up, as using the mountain as an example of what she was referring to. "This place is sacred. That's why you were drawn to it as a boy, and now again as a man. You are meant to be here. This is a place where your heart has found peace. A place set apart from all other places you've been, a place for truth and pureness to be imposed that only a good heart can hold. I'm also, here because you have given up on your destiny, but I was hoping to lead you toward the right path."

Robert was so fascinated by Thaliana's strange words that he almost totally forgot why they had come down here in the first place, thinking maybe his true resolve was now being exposed.

"This gold you seek is not meant for men of the earth anymore. Maybe at one time it was but now it stays behind as an association to the history of all mankind. **It's symbolic of what's really important in life, nothing to do with precious metals or the glitter of life. It's about doing the right thing when the cost can mean your life.** Its only purpose now is to teach men to turn from going the wrong direction. As they are aimlessly walk-through life, causing destruction, without an eternal plan in view, yet instead they can change from their malicious ways that leads to their death, and find life again through a changed heart." She looked at both men to keep their attention.

"I had three sisters and three brothers of my youth that I left behind. Two sisters and one brother are now within the Seventh Realm. **They share in the joys we have of that place and have learned the eternal ways of happiness are not what a man seeks from learning but are accompaniment of what's in a man's heart to lead him in doing a king's work. It's what's on the inside of a man's soul that led him to take the right path in life.** The others of my youth had lost their way and had taken a different journey that I have no knowledge of. My love still goes with them even as I miss them today in memory." Thaliana stopped for a brief moment to remember the siblings of her youth.

"I have a different journey now. My position of Guardian includes pointing the way for those like you. It's your destiny Robert Littleton to change your direction. I saw your name brought up before the council. My king knows of your life being a difficult journey, yet one worthy of its purpose. I was hoping you would be open to my story so you could be encouraged as you once had been in your youth. Your time is soon. You're almost home." Robert felt a lump rising in his throat. He lifted his hand to wipe at his eyes. Thaliana acknowledged his building emotion. **"My king knows of your sorrows. he understands your pain. He feels your struggles."**

Robert pushed down the emotion as he looked back at the Indian princess. "Your words are strange to hear." Thaliana looked at him with concern. James remained silent but taken back by the aura of this young Indian girl.

"I carry a message that needs a quick acknowledgement for time is running out. All you have to do in accepting the message is to believe what I have to say has merit, and for you to make the right decision. Your life, though difficult, has been a worthy road to take. **Your son understands this journey as the right path. This land has led your heart to find a life here. What lies ahead for both of you is something I can't explain now, but in time, you will know of your true purpose.**

"As a son takes a special place in a father's heart, he becomes unique among men because he loves without having boundaries. His spirit is like one that travels the world for centuries that has learned about a father's love as he prepares his heart for what's to come. A son holds more value than that gold you seek beneath this mountain. This place, where the glaciers rise and fall in the blue that completes this valley or as the dirt and rock under your feet, serves purpose. There is reason in all things. My king's will and testament of things to come will be exposed before the next full moon. **He left this land as an example of his presence hewn in among trees, the mountains, the continuation of every living and breathing thing is reflected in the ground, in the water, in the air, in the stars and planets above. All shows resolve.**

"I've but only a few weeks to acknowledge a plan for you and your son, to make the best of what's left. The wolf packs in this great wildernesses give representation of how life can be quickly stolen away, or as the eagle that soars above represent those of a watchful eye. Everything formed by a master's creative hands becomes a part of his creative plans." Robert and James were perplexed by her words as they sat listening in wonder.

"I too was once drawn to this place as a little girl. My memories remain fresh from my youth as if it was yesterday that I roamed through this timbered land." She stared at Robert like she could see through all the painful memories of his past. Thaliana touched his face with gentle hands as if he had an inordinate part in her life. Her eyes glimmered in the vague light of the tunnels glow. Her heart was focused on a mission she'd been prepped for. Robert sat flummoxed by the gentle words said.

"You know, this place had once been a land thought of for kings. I lived in caves and tunnels such as these in my youth. My experiences of this place were why I was chosen to be your Guardian, as all journeys have an inordinate plan of their conditions."

"But why after all these years?" Roberts asked.

Thaliana revealed a hesitant smile as she waited a few seconds to get her words. "I don't know the exact purpose of my king just yet. I'm only shown bits and pieces of his true plan at a moment's notice. My job of Guardian over you is to keep you from straying from your determinate destiny."

"Actually, I do understand, to a point," Robert said, "what you're talking about. But I've never had the courage to continue toward such a path. It was a path that led to too much sorrow, too many obstacles along the way that stole my courage."

Thaliana's eyes sparkled from the corrugated light cast by the bulbs flickering above them. She took Robert's hand and led him to the next room, without saying a word. Both men followed her to a lower level that the two had been exposed to the day before. Thaliana's face glowed from the shadowy light that gave elucidation to their pathway. Skittles barked twice then followed after. Water was still dripping off the water basin opposite of the room. A radiating golden color of light lit up the opposite room reflected off the top of the water. A nervous wag of his tail, and a whimpering whine, Skittles looked up past the lower end of the room. The water basin lay at an angle impeding a clearer understanding of what laid below. Robert and James saw something that they could not explain by words, but their bodies and minds could sense an aura not of this world. Nothing they'd ever seen by human eyes made sense of reasoning. Something more magnificent than anything they could ever imagined formed as clouds of golden brilliant light that almost blinded them. The susurration of energy shot forward as if set afire. Both men became fearful as they dove for the ground. They felt insignificant in the presence of something overwhelming that hovered over the top of the water, as if an amorphous being floated gently in a certain space of coherence. It didn't appear to be a part of any physical matter. A separation was felt between the aura of this supreme being and the walls of water, as if matter itself had no barring of its presence; yet at the same time, everything around this aura felt saturated by what existed as an incessant presence that wasn't held to the laws of time or physical conditions. The area became a dwelling place, an apotheosis holding the contents of a unique entity as if the physical things around it showed efficacy by its presence. A voice exuded from a circumscribed void without resolute matter that brightened as they came closer to the mouth of its opening. Equanimity and power revealed as an indomitable force to be reckoned. Something of power and glory became blinding, not only to human eyes, but to understanding as well.

"I am the father of all, and you have purpose. Let your Guardian led you."

When this presence spoke, the mountains shook as if this space had been altered. Time and space were nonexistent in the realm of this void. Thaliana lowered her gaze in reverence. Even Skittles lay on the ground and covered his head. Robert's heart was pounding, and his body shivered from the fear that engulfed him. Sweat broke out on his face and arms. **James felt a similar experience, as both men knew at that moment, their reason for being at this place, at this time in their lives, would make a significant turning point in their direction**. Momentarily, the presence of this indomitable enigma slowly dissipated among the rocks and walls and slipped through the water like never there. Robert glanced at Thaliana in a subdued humbleness. He had a refined awareness churning in the pit of his stomach, as if punched by a rude awakening.

"I didn't know he thought of me as important. My world never seemed so alive to have a divine presence visit me and my son in such a way."

Thaliana's eyes were filled with worry, even though she knew Robert was being open-minded about what he saw and felt. "You have no idea of his appointed journey for your life. I'm really not supposed to tell you, but you became one of his favorites from the very beginning. He has things invested in you that are not understood by any other. You have no idea of your true resolve, but someday soon you will. I'm commissioned to share of what I've seen and experienced from my days of training. I wish that you would remain open-minded for it's not that easy to understand. For this place I'm from is not of this world but a world not quite understood for it is of a future not comprehended by those of earth. Your future is beyond anything you could ever dream of. A place of solute existence with all the best of everything ever created. Dreams can't express the opulence of this place not held to barriers of time. A place that baffles the ordinary mind, brings healing to a broken and sick heart, dries up the tearful eye, and mends those of broken relationships. It's a place that goes beyond what those of earth could conceive. The gold you seek here is nothing as the gold you will see there. It's transparent or transcending to the eye. There is a place that has already been chosen for you to live, a place that can only be envisioned by knowing the heart, a place to rest, and a place to grow. You see, my king loves to show off in a way. He goes overboard on everything. Gabriel said he likes big numbers, and every time he fashions something, he tries to outdo his last production. Gabriel said you're a lot like him in many ways. That's why my king has taken a liking to you. The way he explained it, was that you would always do the same. I mean, you put your heart into everything, as if to give it your best. Gabriel said that our king feels your pain and knows your heart like he would his own. He also said that he spent several earth days trying not to interfere with his original plans for you, but as all things can change course, so did his plans. This is why I'm here today, to help you find your way back to where only a good heart can function."

Robert's eyes sparked with incomprehension. He was baffled by words of operant understanding. He wasn't sure what to think of this Indian girl who seemed to be of a higher representation.

"So being my Guardian, you reap the benefits of this king who reigns in this Heaven of Seventh Realm?"

"Yes, but this place is called the Seventh Realm of Heaven, not Heaven of the Seventh Realm. There is really only one heaven, but it's much bigger than you can imagine. Make sure you get that right. Sometimes it becomes a little bit confusing to most. One more thing of great importance that I haven't mentioned yet, there'll be others that will come."

Robert raised an eyebrow with a setting wrinkle in his face. "What do you mean there'll be others?"

Thaliana's eyes had a chagrin flint of acknowledgement. "I thought that maybe you knew, that's why I was here?"

"Knew what?"

"That I was here to protect you."

"Protect me, protect me from what?"

"I'm not of this earth anymore. I have been given powers that give me presentiment of what's to come. Nothing of what you would understand as seen by your mortal eyes."

Robert was bit confused. "I don't understand what you mean?"

Thaliana walked up to Robert and reached over to touch his face. "The Dark Angels are coming. They're to wage war against my king. They'll track you and your son, now that I've come. It won't be long before they're here. "Thaliana turned and looked at James for a brief moment, and then back to Robert.

"I'm a warrior princess from the Seventh Realm of Heaven. Being a Guardian I hold title along with position. They'll know I'm here to give you counsel."

Robert and James both looked at each other. "What? You Mean here in this place?"

5

THE FALLEN

Thaliana stood staring toward the dark of the tunnel, sensing danger was already here. She bowed her head and folded her arms across her chest in military fashion, like making ready for something not usually seen in a technique of any military known of man. Spontaneously, wings jetted from behind her back as a swish of air caught both men off guard. Feathery, flamboyant, fraught caused both men to duck and cover. Thaliana's legs, shoulders, and chest became covered with golden-plated body armor. Her wings were a fathom abreast. Her nails grew talons as sharp golden claws. They gave off a sparkle of light. Her face, neck, and head were also shielded with the golden armor. Her face shield had spikes above in a circular notion all around. The air became heavy all of a sudden, and the mountain trembled as if encumbering circumstances were about to unfold. Thaliana pulled a golden bow like the Greek god Artemis from the back of her wings, which had no arrows, yet it held a glow that was not of this earth. She took a fighting stance in this tunnel beneath this earthy ground as she touched the haft of her yielding sword. Two Dark Angels rushed toward her from straight ahead, as air was pulled from this tunnel like an all-out push of resistance availed the room's conditions. Thaliana raised her bow and released an arrow that quickly appeared ready on its string, as if arrows were timed for certain situations at their moment of release. She was a gambit not understood. James and Robert dove for the floor and covered their heads, as the Indian princess let a second arrow fly with quick release. The first hit its mark dead on. Buried in her victim's head, he fell and exploded into black dust. The second arrow hit the shoulder of another dark Angel, wounding him but not enough to take him down, the Dark Angels stood quickly to regain his stamina and balance. He pulled the arrow from his shoulder and scream in a rage that thrilled the mountain. He stood over seven feet tall with darker conditions, waving a sword back and forth, shimmering in his hefty hand, as he flipped and turned the blade and set his jaw to do impish things of the dark. He stammered back and forth unblinking. Her enemy was there to intimidate, to irritate, and to annihilate with a quick swish of his sword. Thaliana pulled a two-sided blade strapped on her side, rolled under the seven-foot Dark Angel, and sliced at his leg and the small of his back. An ululation of pain bellowed out. The Dark Angel took two quick slices through the air while leaping up at an angle to drive his sword swiftly down toward the Indian princess's heart. She moved and bounced off the side of the tunnel as swift as her adversary yet faster. A glitch of light rolled and spun at a speed not followed. The Indian princess was a flash of light, pushing and rolling, churning and twisting, without comprehension of flight. In the rage was no light, but the Indian princess understood this enemy to be well trained as a representative who'd lived through the ages of time. The Dark Angel leapt forward and tried to pin Thaliana against the cave wall, she somersaulted around with a speed unmatched as she landed ten feet away. She strung her bow and shot another arrow as the Dark Angel closed his wings and blocked her shot.

Her enemy lunged forward, extruding his sword in the rage as he encroached with a flash and sigh. Thaliana moved through the air with stealth like speed to undermine her larger framed enemy, as she planted a blow in the kilt of his side. He stumbled froward and fell on his own sword. Raining ash splashed on the tunnel's wall leaving an empty blackness floating in the air. In the distance, a trumpet sounded, as these warriors of another world filled the tunnel with a black metallic smell. They turned to adhere to the sounds above. The Guardian and her students of earth, with their wolf-dog turned back toward the water basin.

Thaliana quickly looked at the two men. "We need to find a place to hide. Follow me," she yelled, as she led the two men and the wolf-dog back toward the water basin, where they had heard the voice from the void of the light. They pulled through the water basin as she looked back at the three floating atop the water. Thaliana spun her wings in the entrance of the lower room, caving in rock and dirt to cover their tracks.

"Follow behind me," she said. "This water basin leads to another way out of this mountain." The Guardian pointed out, "Breath underwater like you would fresh air. My cloak of armor will keep you from drowning."

Robert looked at his son with a disillusioned expression on His face.

"Trust me," she said, as Thaliana dove beneath the water and pulled them along. She swiftly moved through the water at a pace faster than visualized as the current. Stirred by her wings, she gently led them with the waters hidden secrets.

Suddenly, Robert could see that his Guardian's wings lit up with a glowing light that became translucent of their surroundings. *This couldn't be happening,* Robert thought. Light and warmth and air were all a part of her comfort and leading, as she propelled them forward, deeper, twisting and turning through hidden channels. Miles of flowing water beneath this mountain gave way to a world gone unnoticed. They appeared to be swimming through an underwater aqueduct. For some reason, the three followers appeared not to be afraid as they moved through the channels of a different world than the one from above, as if they were being prepped for a place and time to come.

The Indian princess's movement was the flexing of power not understood. As she swished back and forth, like a giant fairy feinting forward into the deep. They were destined for this journey, without understanding why. Robert saw Thaliana's wings brighten with each stroke. Fish and mammals of the water were visually clear, as the blue brought forth the life of the deep. The deeper the water, the brighter Thaliana's wings lit up, as the remittance of power shown through the deep had its own reasoning of existence. She carved out a path in front while leaving the dangers of the Dark Angels behind. They were surviving beneath the water without air from above, as they began to acknowledge the Guardian's power was beyond boundaries set by this earth. The underwater aqueduct expanded as the world below made itself known. A world of life and movement soon to be exposed.

James acknowledged fish he had never seen before. Giant squid of enormous size, a halibut that weighed over a thousand pounds, as seen of his dimensions, turtles rising up under deeper waters, decapod crustaceans scurrying along. Anguilliform were spotted with bright colors of green and yellow, blue fin tuna, large cephalopods, everything committal from the world above. Mammals procured a common space as a world unaffected by the things above.

Suddenly, James comprehended that the waters were different than the usual ocean affected by sunlight. He would have to study this closer. Yet the waters below were of fresh water surroundings, of melting glaciers mixing with saltwater moving in from currents below. Having a degree in marine biology, and working on his doctorate, he picked up on the viability of the changing of life almost right away. Then it hit him, as life for his father and he were about to change. As a father and son had grown apart through the differences of age and the passing of time, they still had a common bond, like the fish of the ocean and those below remained connected through the tides of life. They all held purpose. The underwater aqueduct twisted and turned through a maze, as they began to move away from the darkness of the deep and moved toward the glistening of light as the opposition of the dark was noncommittal. Thaliana looked behind her for a brief moment as she turned toward the top of the water, as life and breath of the living lay close above. Robert, James, and Skittles had taken the water into their lungs without any panic or unrest. Light from above slowly filtered its way in their direction as the light and the liquidity of the water started to blend as one.

Where are we going? Was Robert's thought. The water felt neither cold nor hot or felt unnatural to breathe as liquid. They reached the top and broke through. The air and sky revealed their world as earthen facts of normality made both men relax, as did their canine friend. Robert heaved forward extracting the water from his lungs, as James and Skittles followed suit. On top, Robert viewed they were surrounded by a glacier of blue ice. The sun broke through the clouds causing the light to temporarily blind them, as the air and sky filled with the viability of life, as seen from the birds of the air, and the sounds of sea otters barking their calls in the distance, an eagle floating above, while hovering to mark her prey. The temperature suddenly began to drop as the three huddled together to stay warm. The clouds moved in again, and an unnatural presence filled the air.

Thaliana turned and looked toward both men and the wolf-dog. "Stay close to me, and I can keep you protected from the cold with my heat shield." Thaliana's heat shield began to consume the water around them. Her golden-plated armor turned bright heating her heat shields. For some reason, both men had already figured being close to her. She had protected them up to this point. Robert and James were still confused about all these conditions as if they could defy the laws of this natural world, not yet comprehending things from above. Their Guardian was not human as previously revealed. She was not bound by the laws of nature or Newton's law. She was only bound by the laws of a world they didn't quite understand. A realm from above was connected to share a common bond in the commitment of love, for the love of a father and love of a son. They were becoming devoted followers of this so-called Guardian. They were being taught through experience, without words, but in deeds of power not quite understood. She could fight or out-dual others of her kind, commissioned by a king, from position of power on high, standing tall although her frame said otherwise. She was misleading at times but never depleting of her cause. She dealt raucously with her enemy for they were many, but she never doubted her possibilities, for they were marked by a king of realms. These so-called Dark Angels were not of this world. They were from a place that would soon be erased from memory as most worlds show a beginning and an end, a place that held only the purpose to contain those of the dammed.

The Indian princess helped both men out of the water and sat them down upon the side of a large chunk of blue glacier ice. They were surrounded by cliffs of blue that rose two hundred feet on all sides, the longevity of frozen blue glaciers, stood out as the mighty mountains displaced history a precipice of delight, as the length and breadth of the mighty shown brilliance of a different light, leaving only forty feet of space hidden between the mountains if ice.

She spoke with a leading voice, "We need to go back to your cabin before they find us."

Robert whipped his head around. "My cabin is not far, a half mile up off the river bank."

Thaliana turned to acknowledge this new information. We'll have to make a run for it, before it's dark. They come mostly in the dark."

Thaliana focused her eyes on James for a brief moment, as she stood there in front. She reflected a feeling of assuage like trying to calm them before something of greater magnitude showed itself.

Robert glanced her way. "What's your plan? We can't stay Here much longer. We'll freeze to death."

Thaliana showed a bit of concern for their lack of patience. "Don't worry about being protected. I have a plan. Let me dry your clothes, and then we'll leave to your shelter."

Thaliana looked at Robert. "Do you have more weapons at this place?"

"Yes, I have a power bow with metal tipped arrows and a shotgun hanging above the fire place in the front room. And there's a box of dynamite in the cellar."

Thaliana stared at James. "Your kind of a large person, are you, not?"

James raised an eyebrow. "So, what's your point?"

Thaliana has a puzzled expression. Ignoring the comment, she said, "Can you bring yourself forward for a moment so I can dry your clothes." James stepped forward hesitantly, while wondering about her frame of mind. Who was this strange Indian girl that talked so funny? She being so small, not really intimidating, but somehow James and Robert knew her mission was quintessential to represent.

She reacted without his approval, grabbed James by the hand, and then engulfed him with her wings, covering his entire body. Her wings lit up with a brightening that brought heat surrounding them. James felt the combination of both heat, air drying the chill from his bones. His clothes became dry instantly, as he held on to Skittles. He looked like a fluff ball. This caused Robert to smile. A whimpering whine exuded from the mutt. She repeated her process with Robert.

"I can only take one of you with the wolf-dog. I'll be back for the other." She handed Robert her sword. It felt heavy in his hands.

Robert half-heartedly smiled as he glanced nervously at the Indian princess. "So how do I use this contraption?"

Thaliana was full of stress and worry. She turned her head back around toward Robert before lifting off the ground. "I find it hard to believe that you are chosen of a king. He must have sensed something in you that everyone else missed?" Robert understood her sarcasm but brushed it off without much regard.

"Well, he is a king of course, wouldn't be right if his subjects were smarter than he. We've never had to use swords against our customers in the supermarkets of America. This might be a traditional way for your kingdom but not of ours."

Thaliana turned her head toward Robert to catch the inflection. She remained quiet about the subject. She knew it would become futile to argue the point of her missing something that her king had seen right-up-front. The father and son were picked for a reason to represent a king in battle, but why? And why an old man, worn from time and altered by his experiences, positioned for greatness, when all the experiences he'd ever had fizzled in the memories of lost causes and forgotten celebrations. And a young man, who'd seemed softer than usual around the edges, picked to take part in a battle of the ages, how would They cope? They were an awkward bunch at best, but none too revealing, and not so appealing on first impressions. They were out in this wilderness hoping to find a purpose in their direction, yet what? The Indiana princess turned and grabbed James.

"Hold your father's pet, and I will carry you." James reached down and grabbed Skittles in his arms, firm and tight as Thaliana swooped both off the ground and flew skyward. They shot above the shear blue walls of ice. The air was so cold it took James' breath away, but once past the icy cliffs the air warmed to a comfortable level. The wolf-dog closed his eyes as they swished through the air. James could feel the strength in the small frame of the Indian princess. She flew straight up to clear the walls with quick agility, faster than a bird, faster than a plane, superhuman strength. She held him with strong arms of comfort. She represented a king, who'd looked past this thing called doubt. She was a quick stepper, a moving queen, fast and lean. She was strong and seasoned for all the right reasons. She was homed in, brought her tools of trade, set of fire, and pushed to the max.

James opened his eyes to see the sight of the vast wilderness from above it was inspiring, pumping his adrenaline to lethal levels, making his heart almost beat out of his chest. He screamed from the thrill ride across the sky. "Huey, heeee'…!" as if caught in the moment. Skittles remained with his eyes closed, his body stiff within James's grasp. He could see the cabin up ahead. Another car was parked along the gravel driveway. He thought of Amanda and knew she would be mad. James thought to smooth over this difficult situation when she was told of this imbuing story. Thaliana sat James and the wolf-dog on the porch without saying a word. James's hair was fluffed from the fast-moving air. He was full of confidence, as he blazed from the sky; he began to feel strong, yet where was this confidence coming from? He was just a professional student of the classroom, right? Taking one step forward to a higher purpose, but what? He had lost many hours of sleep from a racing mind, wanting to learn, to find answers about life. He pushed himself beyond his limits, like a marathoner cutting a pathway down some distant trail. He was standing up for a father whom he dearly loved, to make him proud, to outshine the rest. He would do his best. He was here to stay, and guide those in his gentle sort of way through what he thought to be right. He was a dreamer, a down to earth schemer, a heartfelt redeemer, yet he never came unprepared, or lacking. He was quiet at the moment and humble but sometimes caused trouble, picking things up from the rubble of leftover dreams pushed to the side. He was here for the ride.

The wolf-dog's hair was astatic on automatic like he had been on high heat in a spin cycle dryer. Heat and static electricity all played a part. Amanda came out quickly, seeing the two in disarray. She developed a distrusting glare, with a scowl on her face. The Indian princess took off midstream without being noticed. Amanda didn't catch sight of her flight. She had already gone.

The Guardian flew quick and steady toward the same flight path as she had come. The glacier's plenitude stood in the forefront of its icy conditions. From memory, the Indian princess had known that Dark Angels were her fierce competitors in battle, she thought, but something wasn't right about the up and coming fight that was about to unfold. She knew her king had reason beyond her understanding of pleasing those of the realm. A Fallen race that would give chase, those of a darker world not seen by those of earth, led by an evil heart cast from the realm of heaven's gate. This Seventh Realm of Heaven, were angles were better equipped and better prepared for a leader who sat through the ages of history. Those of position and rank had hidden powers that hadn't been mastered or learned yet by those of the Fallen. The Indian princess knew there would be changes in the future revelations, the removal of all advantage in battle conditions. This King gave power to the Dark Angels as well as to those of heaven's elite, and no border of separation had been given to such until now. The Indian princess landed back where the blue walls of ice stood as a reminder of things of a colder world, which left miles behind of memories of the multitudes that had lived in the crowded streets of the many. They were blurred in the ranks of numbers, numbly walking through the corridors of commemorations, time within time, as if lost. She could see Robert sitting and staring into the wild blue of the deep, maybe a whale or large fish of some sort would swim to the top and swallow him up? She plunged toward him and grabbed Robert off his feet, startling him almost to a standing position. He turned his head in terror not sensing her sudden movements as she spiraled back to the sky, making haste to the cabin, worried and wondering, caught in mid-flight with those creatures crossing their path. That couldn't happen, but would it? When she finally sat Robert on the porch, his face had turned to a sallow condition of misunderstanding.

"Are you okay?" she asked.

Robert's paling condition made him look exhausted. He'd been going beyond his limits of expectations. He rolled his eyes from dizziness. The acrobatic flight did a number on his stomach.

James looked the part that he already had a bout with Amanda. She was livid from his lack of considerations, sensing all things to be measured before seeking adventure. Robert busted through the front door and pulled the shotgun off the wall, with all the clanging and banging one does when in a hurry. Amanda whipped about, astonished, fit to be tied, and hanging on the loose end of denial. What was this old man thinking? The room was lit with a warm remittance of flame. The gentle lights of comfort reflected from James's eyes. His emotions were stirred as the reflections had shown. She had missed the part where James had explained about the Indian princess, with the golden glow of color dazzling off her wings of light. She was a force to be reckoned with, with her heavenly countenance staring out in the early evening harmony, a set of worry in her eyes. She looked as if her memories carried her to another place, a place of warmth and comfort, a place where beauty never faltered from the lack of bliss. Even after all the training and support, she now stood alone, waiting for the end of the world to stop spinning. What was next? Who would she call? No place to hide, no place to go. When Amanda finally acknowledged the Indian princess's, her face turned white.

James noticed the look and reminded her, "I told you we had a Guardian, but you wouldn't listen." He passed off a flinching expression of delight, as he looked back at Amanda trying to read her thoughts. "You should spend some time getting to know her," James said as if to catch her off guard. "I told you. She's not a part of our world." An unimaginable twitch of misunderstanding flickered in Amanda's eyes.

Amanda was speechless. This image of an immortal being here changed her way of thinking, but she was still mad about James's lack of communication. He leaked derisive words from his mouth.

'What's wrong, honey, have I misinformed you?"

Even after the sight of the Guardian on the porch, Amanda still found a reason to throw her angry stares. She was livid from being left in the dark. James walked over and tried to give Amanda emotional respect, yet she pushed him at arm's length.

"Why didn't you come and get us?"

"Do I really need to explain our situation with what you see before you?" Amanda had a misanthropy stare flash across her eyes. Robert looked over at her and couldn't believe she held to her agenda. Neither man had the patience to deal with her scolding.

"What's wrong…you don't believe us?"

Her eyes whipped back at Robert with piercing glare. "Don't tell me how I need to see things, old man. I don't need Your sarcasm. This is not your fight."

Robert grimaced in her general direction. "Why does everything you face have to be a fight?" Robert felt like slapping the immature woman.

Thalian interrupted their conversation. "You don't understand the situation, young lady. You should kindly take your children and leave this place for your safety."

Amanda's stare grew more bewildered by the moment. "They're not just my children. James needs to take notice of his own responsibilities." The Indian princess bowed her head and folded her arms. Her wings folded inward and disappeared beneath her mass like things of heaven were left in mystery. She walked through the threshold of the door. The hostility of Amanda grew thick. Amanda's eyes darted across the room and saw this Indian girl as competition, and not of a higher position of purpose.

'So…who are you? Amanda said with an untrusting glare.

"My name is Thaliana. I'm a Guardian sent from the seventh realm." She paused for just a brief second to consider the girl's dimensions of hostility. "Young lady, you need to drop the attitudes. The enemy is out there beyond the clouds. They seek his father's life and your husband's," while pointing with her eyes.

Amanda got a sheepish smile on her face. "Well then, we'll just leave, and let you get on with your little charade of importance."

Thaliana flew across the room, without the assistance of wings and grabbed Amanda by the throat and held her up against the wall while turning her head side to side. Amanda had terror take hold of her as urine trickled down her leg onto the wooden surface of the floor. James's eyes set in the flicker of emotion filled with misunderstanding. Amanda flushed a crimson color, as she tried to reach for her own throat, but was overcome with the Guardian's force from her vengeful words. James was dumbfounded by the abrupt violent move of their Guardian. She stood vehement as she glared into Amanda's eyes. Revealed from the Indian princess was the bright golden color of light. She held tightly to the girl with the attitude but did not crush her throat.

"Do I need to change your frame of mind before I continue my mission?" she paused.

"If you hinder my appointed plan, I will take you down to the bottom of the mine where there are much damper conditions. Those of the Fallen would have pleasure at tearing you apart While using your bones as weapons against their enemies." Amanda's eyes flashed a jolt of fear.

James ran over to grab Thaliana's arm-pleading. "Let her go. She doesn't mean any harm."

The Indian princess whipped her head toward James. "You have love for this one?"

James was surprised by the sudden proclamation. "Yes, please let her go."

"You've made a poor choice for a mate." The Indian princess insisted." I could change her attitudes with manual labor and a difficult life. That's how my king would deal with one so stubborn."

James paused to consider her statement. "No, it won't be necessary. I'll have a talk with her."

The Indian princess has a puzzled look in her eyes. "That way Never works in the seventh realm. Talking never accomplishes anything. The king would never allow it."

Amanda was still held in the air up against the wall, as her shadowing will begin to leave her. Thaliana turned her view to the young lady again. She gently sat her back down but held her deep stare toward the woman with the attitude.

" You should learn to control your wayward tongue before you lose your head. The Seventh Realm wouldn't stand for such insolence."

Amanda coughed and sputtered until she got her breath back. The crimson color slowly left her. She still had a look of indignation toward this Indian princess. Yet she wasn't about to lock horns with a Guardian, who did not have best interests at heart.

"Are we still going to have a problem with you? Amanda is your name, right?" In my world your name carries the meaning I dare not to say. Are you going to be burden to us? If so, I can end your miserable existence this every moment."

Amanda looked toward James as if he would defend her, yet he knew Thaliana had read her right on. Amanda had personal issues not understood by the Guardian of some place called the Seventh Realm. She had a different agenda that didn't include her own personal circumstances. She removed her hair out of her big blue eyes and held the tears back while trying not to show her emotions. Thaliana caught the gesture and knew the young lady had been verbally abused by her father, no longer of earth. She showed the worn scars of memories. She had lost her ability to trust, as all thistles and thorns of the world leave their mark, so did an uncaring father.

"You know it's not your husband's fault that you are in this way. He loves you despite your abusive behavior. You still have control of your emotions…don't you care that you intend to leave the scars upon your children but still continue your unbalanced ways. Don't you consider that self-defeating? Your husband has your best interest at heart, but you continue to torment him. So, what is the cause? Amanda turned her head to look at Thaliana.

"You don't know anything about my life, so why do you interfere with our situation?"

"Because your lives weigh in the balance of having each of you being focused on what lies ahead. Because the end is here. You need to prepare. They're coming for him." Thaliana looked out the window toward the sky.

Amanda was still focused on her fragile world of existence, now, looking out past the door, as if being led by the Indian princess's guiding words. "Who's coming?" she said.

"The Fallen are coming, and they won't take your fragile heart into consideration before cutting your head off and throwing your body to the wind."

Amanda's eyes blinked wide. "Who are the Fallen, and why are they coming here?"

The Indian princess glanced back at the young woman of the shadowing will and knew they all needed to know the whole story about why those Fallen of heaven were at war with those from above.

"Sit down. I will explain why there is war in heaven. A story of brothers sworn to secrecies yet torn apart by the hatred of seeds planted that fester in an evil heart." Thaliana motioned for Amanda to sit at the kitchen table while Robert made lunch.

James took a seat alongside her as all three turned their attention toward the Indian princess. They were told a story never heard before in thousands of years of history that had past. Even heaven had incurred division as slowly revealed by this Indian princess. James and Robert and Amanda listened while the Guardian methodically unraveled the past memories from heaven above, as pertaining to future endeavors unrecorded. Her words and thoughts shared of the most bizarre and lethal story ever told of love and commitment of two brothers pulled apart by a separation of those of heaven and those of the Fallen. A befriended evil had engulfed them, started from a brother's proud heart.

6

CORNELIUS

Thaliana paced back and forth trying to focus on what to say next to her new students sitting in front of her. Then it came to her that the beginning would be the most logical place to start, a story of profound meaning not written in books of earth but only in memory. She placed her hand upon her chin, and then began the bizarre account of the last ten thousand years, as those of heaven accounted for under the high echelons of government. Those of heaven hadn't been left out of the burdens that trouble a weary soul, as life had a way of bringing bad tidings to all at one point or another. Thaliana took a seat at the head of the table as she looked out across the meadow in the late afternoon sun. Robert continued cooking the afternoon's lunch and served tea.

"You know, heaven isn't a place among the clouds as humans would think. It's a world within a world, but different. Not anything understood from a human perspective, as things of my world was created from a celestial beginning. Heaven's beginning was similar to earths. It's not as if there was no evil or strife created in the realms, as all seeds that are sown have a beginning. Politics had played its part in the realms, much like here on earth. Structure has its shortcomings as much as it has a chance to bloom and become something beautiful, as all worlds have to deal with what comes from the heart. Even an omnipotent presence wouldn't exist in chaos without some sort of monumental peace agreements, and governmental structure. Thousands of years ago, of course, you have heard the story of Lucifer whose true birth name to be Helel Ben Shachar who was cast from heaven's realms. He was the most promising. He was heaven's morning star, one who carried light. He was the brightest I was told. The king was so proud of him, but then things began to change. He had cast his lots in with so many others from a darker side of existence. Long ago, when he first started meddling into the king's affairs, he noticed that change had caused him to feel more confident. He was noticed by his peers when he started doing things a little different than the others around him. This gave him a sense of power that he'd never experienced before. It caused him to want to live above others, who he'd considered inferior, because he felt they couldn't see the potential in themselves as doing things from their own perspective, instead of relying on their king. His heart had hardened and he had turned to evil choices from a different perspective by interfering with the humans. Of course, the king judged him for his self-important deeds and cast him from heaven to live all eternity in a place hardly mentioned with the realms. This decision was final, which reflected back to his other creations. Everyone, of course, was shocked beyond all measure that Helel Ben Shachar so rightly named, fell from grace. Of course, there were many who were saddened by the first eternal soul separated from above. Some understood why, but others didn't. And as so, these changes took place in the hearts of those who knew him. Even the king felt the sadness left in his decision. Helel Ben Sachar, whose brothers were appalled by this decision and would one day take such measure, forever being imprisoned, to not ever experience an ordinary world of the living again. His punishment was not talked about. It was a difficult ordeal for those knew him to comprehend his demise."

Thaliana stopped, because she'd remembered the enticing smells of food, how their bouquets had a strong draw, but she also needed to prepare her words carefully as both men's eyes were fixed on her every word. And Amanda's face paled to a sallower color.

"May I?" Thaliana reached down and took a piece of meat that Robert had fried up in a skillet. "This is very good." She sat again, and took several bites before continuing her story.

"Besides the many that were cast away from his presence, there remained those of his brothers that stayed behind to hold position and seats of leadership, knowing they could not help him in the future, if they were cast to the wind as it were. So Helel Ben Shachar understood he had to leave behind many that he'd developed strong relations with through the course of time. They spent many centuries in the back borders of heaven keeping a low profile, trying not to upset the natural order, holding to the fact that one day they would see their brother again. Of course, many had regretted not going with their precious leader, mentor, uncle, or whatever he was to be to the many. As they say on earth, blood is thicker than water, and it holds true among those within the seven realms of Heaven. Their leader, being a great grandson of the late departed Helel Ben Shachar had held something in secret. He sought to get even one day with our king. Such dangerous feelings and words said from a boy of angelic beginnings. Who knew not what he was saying, as most boys of their youth tend to lean toward the flames before they know their surroundings become too heated. His older brother tried to convince him that the past had nothing to do with their part in the realms now, but he wouldn't listen to words of wisdom. He only believed what his uncles had told him of the past and wouldn't let it go. Instead of trusting in rules and regulations, he let his heart take hold of deep-harbored visions. He made his own way. He let seeds of ill will fester within his heart.

"As you already know, we were created as you were. We're just at a different level. We are only dissimilar in power and physical conditions that go beyond human understanding. We are an elite class of angels, yet this wasn't enough for those of the Fallen. They thought too much of themselves, and the powers given had been all consuming. We have our limits of control given by our King. For eternity is not what you think it is. As you, we've taken to the human side of creation, and life above is not understood as mystic clouds that rise in the distance, as stories told of the realms above are only explained to you as mysteries. Those of an elite class of heaven had to prove their worthiness to inherit position, as things not written have no bearing on rules and regulations. So, history in heaven remembered, plays a part of what's to come. Our rules aren't written like yours from below. The king has learned from too many hard-fought years that rules and religion have lost many souls. Humans have influenced change in heaven's realms quite efficiently. Even though the king wanted to replicate many forms of government as those of earth, he had a change of heart. The world had become fettered and chained to the will of the Fallen, and conflicts experienced of earth have reflected as a mirror in the faces of those above. Earth has become a testing ground. Those leaders chosen were given position in government only after stringent guidelines of servitude. These angels now have steps of government and attend to military service, just as man has developed here on earth. The only difference is, crime is dealt with on a more immediate level of platitude. So, the realms of heaven's government are tightly dealt with. Politics has its place but is frowned upon by our King, because they have become too complicated. Multiple levels of government have become ridiculous, 'too many chiefs and not enough Indians,' as my father used to say. Each realm was classified from oldest to newest, the oldest being those who have been in heaven the longest. Now, merit and intelligence are not the only conditions." Thaliana paused to let this sink in.

"I lost my life when I was nineteen years old, so I'm one that is attached to the present realm, the seventh. What has caused most of the turmoil among the ranks of heaven was the change of his purpose. The humans showed my king that humility and a contrite heart moved others to do wondrous things. His justice now is not based on age and wisdom but by the conditions of one's heart. Of course, the humans were used as the example. The King has come full Circle. He has decided to create a new class of humans to help change the outcome of what's to come. He refers to them as the 'pure hearts.' They call themselves the Circle. They have purpose in what's to come. They're on their way back from a journey from a distant star."

She glanced across the table and looked at both men to get a reaction.

"Most of the elders, who've been there the longest, have been living in fellowships based on merits for thousands of years. Now they've had to adjust, put aside personal gain and glory. The King, at first, considered the humans to be the least of his creations, but now they're used as a prime example. Of course, the elders disapproved, because they have the most to lose. The first through the sixth realms are thought to be those who have looked down on the younger generations. The Seventh Realm of

Heaven is considered his greatest creation, yet those of the other realms have been banned from moving from realm to realm. The elders seek their own personal justice because they feel they've earned the right to hold title. They seek to show the King that might and glory hold a higher purpose than humility. The elders are sending their very best against us. Pride and prejudice have pushed them over the edge. They have gathered against the King to wage a war not recorded in history books like you have here on earth. Their failed brothers, the Fallen, were sent to roam this uncharted space between the living and the dead. This place is set out between the boundaries of time but of no physical condition. This malign habitation was created to keep them from terrorizing the world and those who live here. This is where your journey begins. You're to help the Circle. They have brought with them a few friends along for the ride."

The Indian princess let out a breath of air slowly. She glanced into the eyes of the three adults who accompanied her story of heaven. They looked stunned.

Robert didn't quite understand what they should do. "Why are we a part this?"

"I'm not completely sure, but I can take a guess," Thaliana returned.

"I don't understand what is so important about my son and me?"

"Their leader plans on using you as a bait to tempt the King into battle."

Robert glanced at James. He'd seen the look of terror in his eyes before, but this was different. A shuddering chill went through him. James has a distant stare in his eyes. He wondered how safe his family would be; he had to send them home.

"Is this some sort of game?" Robert asked.

"I don't think so. I know the King has his purpose in making these changes."

"But what can we do before all this takes place?"

Thaliana stared past Robert's look of concern. Past all the memories of history come and gone, without hearing all the silent words said and knowing that the chaos to come was almost upon them.

"Have a little faith in yourselves. There's not much time to think about the situation. You must prepare."

Somehow this didn't help Robert or James feel any better about their situation or even give them any bit of hope toward the subject.

Thaliana continued telling them about the Seventh Realm of heaven. "When I first entered heaven, I was very impressed with all the beauty, the useful things that our King had made in all his creations. Nothing was short on perfection, but with time, a material world became ordinary again. The eyes and ears of the many had become complacent. Most of the elders have lost their focus. Of course, I had my own realm to worry about, without considering ideas thought of from abroad from realm to realm. I loved the beautiful little cottage by the lake. I had a boat by the shore. It was all I wanted, nothing extreme. Most others became unrealistic with all the newness of everything. After a while, everything became obsolete. They were bored. They wanted the chaos back into their lives. It gave them a chance to feel again, to get their hearts pumping, as they had said, the thrill of hunt, the challenge, the chase. It wasn't enough to have the biggest palace to live in or beautiful attire or close friends to adore. They were always trying to outdo each other. In the end, it became a tragic predicament.

"Then Cornelius, their leader, the one that started all this chaos, came up with this brilliant plan of drawing everyone's attention to this battle, an idea that pulled them toward this chaotic end that left my King's will out of the mix of his original plan. Cornelius's plan was a ploy to draw the King's attention away from the end of this natural world, to give them an avenue to stop the boredom or find success without involving the King's help. The battle of all battles, set in a neutral zone so neither side would have an advantage over the other, on some off beaten path out in this wilderness, which you've come to know as your home." Thaliana raised her hands as if pointing toward the cabin she stood in along with the others. "This was where I grew up too, which brings us to our present-day situation. We're the last hope, the only barrier blocking the way for these Dark Angels to find victory. We're the last straw before everything begins…" Thaliana couldn't finish.

She looked toward Robert to see his stare of incomprehension.

"You have become a key element in this game of chance. You're a chess piece to be played out at the right moment. Those of the Fallen will come here. Cornelius will be pulled toward this area to fight because that's where you will be. It has not been by accident that you've been drawn to this area. He has his reasons to have placed those seeds in your heart, as they have drawn you here for an eternal purpose. This area has its problems and advantages. It's not easy to access too. It's well hidden, and the weather is more than unpredictable. It's far from any type of military support or accompaniment that the government might try and use. Speaking from experience, it's in an area that retains some of the most challenging land that has ever been lived on. The forest will hide most of the armies that come here, and the glaciers, the rain, and the fog all play their part. They will not show any mercy to anyone standing to challenge them. I know you have learned the layout of the land over the last five years. Your knowledge of the area will be a key in battles strategy. We're counting on it to help us prepare."

Robert's face had turned a paler color of white. He didn't know what to think. He walked out on the woodsy porch looking past the cool evening air in the lower meadows. A wolf slowly walked past in front of the property at a distance. An eagle could be seen flying high above the trees looking for a small squirrel or a field mouse. There was a slight breeze passing through the tops of the tress, something was coming, and nothing or no greater force was ever going to stop it.

Thaliana came out on the porch sensing an uneasy feeling within Robert's expression. She looked at him and knew he was thinking, thinking of the whys and how's, and who'd done what? With a distant stare in his eyes, soaking in this story of heaven's productions were like watching rerun of a bad dream. Thaliana tried to lighten the conversation up.

"You know, the seventh realm is a beautiful place. The people there are good people. It's more than I deserve, maybe more than most deserve. This place here is nice also, beautiful in its own sort of way. The best part of the seventh realm is the structure of life. Everyone has a purpose of everyday. The children go to school as they do here. I have my father and brother and two sisters with me now. I'm the only warrior of the family. My father thought Jacana, my brother, would be a better warrior. But Gabriel chose me to train. He said I was more focused and quicker of my decision making."

Robert was worried. His mind was venerated by his thoughts and feelings for being considered by this King of realms, but why him, and why now? He had no particular talents that could be helpful, or did he?

Above, the sky showed darkening gray colors quickly changing the landscape as another storm was headed their way. Robert stared out across the land that was chosen for such a fight, a battle of those creatures who were not of earth. So many questions that day would go unanswered, but the problems of before that held meaning was like that gold below in the mine. He was ready for whatever was to happen in the near future. For what was to come reflected a pellucid expression in Robert's eyes, and he didn't know where to start or if he'd find success, because what was to come was still a mystery. And Thaliana's words were still fresh in memory. This story told was hard to grasp mentally that a kingdom above was considering him and his son as reliable resources. This Guardian was here to make sure his heart at the ripe age of fifty-nine would be up for the task at hand. She knew Robert, at another time. He once had that gentle warrior spirit as she'd shown, yet he'd lost is ability to look past adversity. But now, after her vote of confidence from a King, she knew in her heart that he'd be ready. For the changes to come were not directed by unlawful ways of thinking, but by a Guardian no less, from the seventh realm of Heaven. To be light unto their journey.

Robert had found his place in this world again, and to him that was all just fine. He went back into the cabin and grabbed the shotgun with a box of shells and headed back out onto the porch. He looked up into the sky with a heated stare. A flicker of rage crossed his eyes. He didn't understand these creatures, but he wasn't about to let them rain *in* on his parade, especially at the cost of many lives.

Thaliana flipped her view around and looked at the shotgun. "What's that for?"

Robert clicked the shotgun just before saying, "For up close and personal. I want to be able to look them into their eyes before life leaves them."

It was around six o'clock in the evening. With plenty of light in the sky, the sky looked as if it was full of birds; yet from a closer view, they seemed to have grown. The sky turned black as a swarm of something not recognizable, moved at a speed not comprehended by human eye, as if with jetting wings of creatures pushed the air from the sky. Robert drew in breath. Thaliana crossed her arms and bowed her head as her wings, and her body armor suddenly covered her frame with a golden glow as sharpened talons extended from her fingers. She was ready and steady and prepared for a fight. Robert ran back into the cabin to warn the others. Amanda and the children were led to hiding in the basement below. James brought up a box of dynamite just before closing the basement door and secured the cabin. Robert went back out on the front porch. He tossed one stick of dynamite into the air as Thaliana shot an arrow through the core exploding it in midair. These creatures of the sky dodged and maneuvered around it to avoid injury. And those of the Fallen flew in Circles above. They waited for their leader; for their purpose of being here was not understood. From careful observation, it looked to be about fifty in number that had filled the lower portion of the sky. The Indian princess showed concern yet for reasons not comprehended. These creatures of the night didn't give the impression to be in attack position. Their leader landed on the ground just in front.

A smirk of recompense broke out on the Dark Angel's face as he viewed this smaller representation of a King. He knew they would send his very best representation but this? What was heaven's elite thinking? The mammoth Dark Angel stood out like the leader he was. A chuckle of fermented air broke free from his mouth when he saw how tiny she was. He looked down and then back up at his captains and scoffed.

"Is this his best?" he shouted back to his captains. A jeering laughter moved through the group of his consorts. His attitude carried an omnivore's manner as if he and his contingent group were eaters of soul. Thaliana sensed their purpose this day was to let their presence be branded in memory as to reduce their confidence. Yet her confidence was surrounded by the teachings of a King well familiar to self-discovery.

Robert had loaded both sides of the shotgun. He was ready. *What is this thing that stood before me?* Robert thought. They didn't appear to be of heaven and surely not of earth. They were tall with a grayish color that lay within their skin, with blackened eyes that pierced the soul. Robert noticed right away that they wore armor set for battle, but for when? Suddenly, something large and unfitting flew straight at the porch, knocking everything over to clear space, including Robert. This second Dark Angel stood as an unrecognizable mass, he expounded a physical presence of dark shadows, long and quickly displaced movements, pushing past the comforts of friends. He had muscles bulging with sweat while showing a quintessential setting of his rank. This creature was marked for atrocities frowned upon by those left earth. He was here to make an impression, maybe do some damage as his character suggested. He looked at them like they were petty humans. Robert was pushed to the back of the porch and hit his head hard against the back wall. His shotgun flew from his hands, clearing the outside end of the porch as it went skittering into bushes, now out of his reach. This dark gray figure that stood before him was over nine feet tall with a wing span twelve feet on each side. An overcoming smell drifted in on the porch. Thaliana turned and gave this presence an opposable stare yet kept her composure, sensing their numbers overpowering to represent. The Dark Angel beetled his frame over the top of Robert as if to intimidate. His eyes moved back and forth. His hands were immense with long emblazoned black fingernails with protruding tips. His muscles gave off the stench of death. He was all consuming in manner and breath. His teeth were jagged with silver-tipped graying around their edge, the smell of burnt cinders of flames that could not penetrate his flesh revealed. They were from a place neither heaven nor hell, a place that represented retribution for the damned. His wings were pointed on the tips of their feathery flanges like bone shards. His armor made from material Robert had never seen before, with spikes and briars sticking out all around. It would keep others from impeding his own personal space. When he spoke, his voice was projected as if to match his size. He pulled a sword from sheath that still was remitting blood from another's ill fate. Robert's eyes filled with questions unanswered since the beginning, as if time stood still for this brief moment of recognition. Thaliana stood her ground without an ounce of acknowledging encumbrance. This impressed their leader standing before her. He smiled while turning to look above at his captains, like he was reciting lines for a play and wanted to impress. Thaliana pulled a talon sharpened blade from her armored kilt. A glow emerged from the blade, which flashed in the eyes of this creature before her. She didn't wait for his Dark Angel to make introductions. She flew over the top of him and buried the talon blade into the nape of his neck. he roared in pain. His echoed cry bounced off the mountain top. He tried to grab at the small Indian princess, but she was too quick for him.

Robert had scrambled off the porch and reached for the shotgun. The second in command stood over him pinning him against the wall. A wave of emotion pushed up in his throat. All he could think of was the safety of his family left in the cabin. Robert told James to stay inside and keep Amanda and the kids hidden. How would they stand up against so many? Robert pulled the trigger at the same time as this large figure jolted him up to a standing position and brought his hand across the back of his head, knocking him unconscious. The wound procured, to the Dark Angel, from the shotgun, started healing almost right away. the bead of shells pushed through the surface of the skin, and his skin healed up as beads fell to the porch's wooden floor. Their leader pushed the Indian princess back, pulling his sword just inches from her throat. Thaliana's heart sunk as she stood still.

"I am the leader of the Fallen. We are the Dark Angels created by him who reigns above, and I am Cornelius, leader of brothers, ruler of the sixth realm. Why are you trying to fight me? I have come to make peace with you, Guardian of the seventh realm." He spoke, of a position he no longer held as if to use it as a bargaining chip. Thaliana stood at the end of the porch just staring at this massive presence that stood before her. Her bottom lip quivered with emotion, remembering the human side of life from the memories of her youth. She was well familiar with his brother, a teacher, a leader of the most high, and a trainer of his military. She was waiting for his next move. Cornelius pulled the talon blade from his neck. The wound closed and healed almost instantly. Her face didn't appear to be surprised. She'd forgotten the powers of this darker side, of a world unknown to her. Separated from the things above in the realms of heaven, these creatures had changed into an abomination. They were deemed a part of the night, nocturnal, blood spillers, planet enders. Cornelius took a step back and saw Robert from the corner of his eye, his reason for being here.

"He is the one I come for!" Robert laid there unconscious against the wall with a pasty white complexion, as he laid there limp. The Indian princess got the gist of his words.

"Guardian, my fight is not with. You have a seventh Realm to worry about. My fight is with your King. He's the one That has made poor decisions for his kingdom."

Thaliana had a bewildered look on her face. She had known the reasons for this overture of introductions. This was only the beginning of something grander than she had understood. This wasn't about a battle of wits between men. This was about the showmanship of a heart full of revenge. She gave into his twisted way of thinking and let things rest for the day, another time to expound authority and wisdom. She had been bested by another. There would be another time at this place, and she'd prepare herself mentally; and one day shortly, she'd be ready. This was a day for learning and giving, even though her heart didn't quite know why. She turned to see his projection of purpose. Their leader's eyes focused again. He pulled his sword away from her throat and acted like he could be her friend.

Thaliana spoke before he could begin, "You have no idea what you're doing. He will destroy you and your Dark Angels, like you never existed."

Cornelius chuckled loudly while shutting his eyes. "Young warrior with such great faith in things do not speak of. Why do you bore me so? He will not be able to save his puny, pathetic humans. They have no real value left on earth. He only feels love for them because he sees them as his greatest mistakes, as if he couldn't live with the guilt of his creation. He doesn't wish to love these pitiable little worms with their fragile existence and hopeless cause. They believe he loves them as they die by the thousands in the streets from hunger and disease."

Cornelius looked at this young Indian girl commissioned by a King as she stayed silently still. The Dark Angels stood out in front of the cabin in organized silent ranks, defiant images of the dark. They stood still like statues carved from an ancient past, just waiting for their devoted leader to signal them to move forward but he wouldn't. he had another motive pushing him for another order, an order planned through the ages as brothers for brothers would seek revenge on those who had taken their' beloved kin away, and erased his memories, as if he'd never lived.

"The world is about to end, and you think the battle to watch is Armageddon. Those pitiful little humans. Don't bore me with such pathetic display of existence. He will slaughter his own in that field of remembrance. The real battle is with those of the realms. I have amassed numbers incomprehensible of what is to come. He has no idea of the depth of what I know. You should go back to your world. I will leave you in peace and your precious little realm if you stay out of my way. My fight is not with heaven but with the creator and his mindless levels of government. I will finish their dismal and boring existence with this battle to come." Thaliana stared up at the overpowering leader of the Fallen as he spit his words of bitterness through the air.

"My duty is not my own. I have committed my life to his purpose. He will not accept anything less than obedience."

"And you believe him, even though he leaves you in the dark about his exact purpose. What he intends to do in the end when this world is gone, and all his little puppets he plays with. You're just his pets, his corporeal amusement to keep him from being bored. Don't you see how he leaves nothing to fact? Everything is based upon hearsay illusions that none of his servants know of, except his son, who is too precious to get close to. They have no vision for such pathetic fragile humans, which have polluted this planet and filled it with defiling disease. It will never be the same if we don't stop him."

Thaliana stared into the eyes of Cornelius. She appeared to be confused by his misguiding words. "Your vision, old warrior, is muddled by your evil heart. You've let things into your soul that are considered defiling."

Cornelius turned his body around and glared at the countenance of this so-called Indian princess. "You have no idea what you're talking about, young Guardian of the seventh realm. You also have been deluded by his spell of captivation. Young girl. how can you judge me when you're still in the youth of your days. You have not a clue what's ahead of you, thinking your mystical faith can save you from a future with no depth to it, except his incessant will. Wait until the smell of death reeks within your nostrils and burns the very core of your soul, when the end comes. There is no anesthetic for a crippled soul, child. He has hammered into your mind commitment to him and your devotional worship, and this makes you cling to truths of empty words. How pathetic is this way of treating the ones who serve you with grand purpose. Do you even know his purpose of a future for this place, a place that is set for destruction because of his mistakes? These pathetic humans are not the real stage of his purpose. Are you blind to his reasons? Your sightless servitude is a waste of your precious energy, better off wasting your precious energy in serving me than a God-King that has condemned us all, without each of you bowing at his every whim of leadership. You also, in the years that follow, will find the empty demand that he holds dear in the front of your very noses. It's an empty mission for another of his delirious callings to fulfill his own heart with vain pleasure. Is that the King you seek among your people, one that professes to love his creation, but leaves you in the dark about his purpose, if so, you are blinder than I have ever been."

Thaliana was perplexed by Cornelius's words. She had no idea how to bait this creature to change his mind. What could she say to him, a leader of the Dark Angels without discrediting his position of authority? Considering her age and lack of experience, she was stultified to respond. She was new at this, and he, with his many years, was well marked for a calling she did not understand. He knew all the angles of deception. She stood her ground though on her true purpose of being here, only listening to his ranting in her quiet disproof of this leader gone awry. She could smell their tainted airs as if they were frauds. Cornelius was done talking. He reached down and grabbed Robert and heaved him up by the hands as he lay limp like a rag doll rolled up in his arms. Cornelius flew up straight off the porch with no effort and quickly was gone in the silence of the fading distance. His Band of Dark Angels followed closely after, melting between clouds of obscurity and the distance of height. They were gone in a fraction of time, a nanosecond, dissolving in the billows of darkening clouds above.

Thaliana stood in shock at Robert's demise. Her heart was sad and confused. Why was this happening? How could her King allow such atrocity to happen? But then, she remembered the faithful words of her teacher.

Don't put all your trust in your eyes and ears alone, trust your heart. She wondered if any of Cornelius's words held any value. She felt the heightening emotion, as a tear rolled off her cheek she reached for it. Her bottom lip was lambent with emotion.

James came running out of the cabin. he looked around, but no one was there except Thaliana. "Where is my father?" He asked.

Her eyes glistened with pools of sorrow. "They took him."

7

THE CONNECTIONS

The wind blew and the clouds rolled in, as the darkness of the sky was a warning. A storm was coming, and as the atrocities of the night would take hold, and the sounds of the land would be told, the battle of the ages would signal the end of the world. They had to prepare. The wind whipped through James's hair as he stared up at the sky smelling the dampened earth before rain. The trumpets would sound, and the dust would settle as the Dark Angels of the clouds would be there. As all those that live and breath in the air, there would be a time and place to face such creatures. James's heart was full of sorrow, yet he would never give up, as a son's love for a father could never be severed in a thousand years, and a thousand years were secured in a father's love for his son.

James blinked to draw focus on what to do next, knowing now his father was gone. He felt hopeless. He was too numb to reflect on what had happened. His sense of belonging was crushed through this loss. Where did they take him? How would he find him? Would he be lost forever? His stomach churned with a burning sense of tightness. He felt lightheaded as he grabbed at the railing just at the end of the porch. Slowly, a building rage and restitution against these creatures of the sky began to infiltrate his mind and heart. His eyes glazed over with an unchained hate that set his face into a bed of wrinkles of a distant stare. Thaliana looked across the porch. She was saddened, yet she didn't know how to bring comfort or relief to a man of the world unprepared. A knock on the wooden floor below reminded James that he'd forgotten about his family in the basement. He turned to get them. He went back into the cabin to open the door in the floor. The door in the floor was a way to his loved ones. They were waiting.

After seeing the stare of her husband, Amanda developed a worried expression in her eyes. James's wall of remorseful pain began to crumble. He knelt on the floor and began to sob while covering his head. Thaliana folded her wings inward and walked into the cabin; she sensed that they needed to talk. James's father was no longer there to give his assistance. Something had to be done.

Thaliana knew her faith would have to come into play to get her through these next few days. This was a test she had been trained for by her teacher, a test in this part of her journey that had come all too quickly. She had to be wise and patient for things to make any sense, and her mind had to be clear. She had been taught as a small girl from her Indian culture, how to deal with difficult hours of misunderstanding, as if life would bend from time to time, testing her character, testing her ability to remain strong, and her ability to remaining motivated. As an Indian girl preserved and lifted to a position of leadership, lifted above others who were bigger and stronger, she had been chosen above all to lead, to train, to represent the kingdom of the seventh realm. Her King had reserved the spirit of a young Indian girl who had lived a full life in a short time of nineteen years. This played a key role for a young girl who grew up in this valley. She was from here, from a thousand years before, walked these valleys and climbed these mountains and forged the rivers below. She developed an eternal image of a King who sat on high, watching and waiting, and knowing she would always give her best, for her time in this valley of the years before prepared her heart and mind for what was to come. She would remember her teacher saying, *plant your feet firm, and make a stand. Don't hesitate, and never show your enemy your fear.* She remembered first introductions with the two men in the tunnels. Thaliana never thought the gold would be the draw, but then from Robert's perspective, it did have its purpose. To a point it made sense, pointing them the way.

James knew his family couldn't stay. They would be unprotected and become a constant risk. His wife and two children stood hugging each other for a good while. The sense of their loss from an unearthly presence has left its mark. James knew they could not waste any more precious time that was quickly fading. They as a regroup, involved a new way of thinking, as his analytical mind worked best under pressure. James mentally began to plan and prepare for the future, something his father would have wanted him to do. He walked out on the porch to face the Indian princess.

"Can you train me to fight?"

Thaliana's face showed an inquisitive smile as her new recruit sparked something within her. "You're serious?"

"That was my father they took away. Yes, I'm completely serious."

Thaliana changed in the way that showed her concern. Her eyes lit up. "I will show you what I know, yet most of your skills will come from within."

James's expression of curiosity changed with a set of wrinkles. He knew being out of shape and spending the last nine years of his life in school left him feeling incomplete. As he did with his father and his schooling and anything else he put his mind to, he decided success was a matter of never giving up, never giving in. It was an endeavor his heart would follow to the end of time. Thaliana had a rising suspicion in the pit of her stomach that she would not be disappointed in training him.

"I would appreciate your assistance. I'll not disappoint," he spoke.

She smiled and put her right hand on his shoulder. "Well then, we'll start tomorrow. Right now, you need to find a safe place for your family."

James turned and looked toward the cabin door. "I'll put them on a plane for tonight."

It has been almost two years since the Circle had left in the starship, to the red dwarf star in the Barnard star system. Drew, Randy, Bella, Tommy, Toby, Torack, Jim Carson, Anna, and Dr. Zimmerman were a few members of a Circle of the gifted. They were only a few days away from earth. Torack was on the control deck with several of his Aquerian captains, making arrangements for the last few calculations for navigating their pathway toward earth.

Drew stepped toward Torack and crossed his arms while leaning over a front rail separating him from the command center seats in front. "We're all a little nervous about coming home," he said. The alien only blinked with a nod then smiled. Drew's face appeared to be a little flushed. He looked over at Anna. She was doing her nails, standing to the left of his shoulder taking in his posture, trying to figure him out. *Nice time to take to grooming,* Drew thought. Anna had cut her hair short and dyed it black, a popular style called in an A-line cut. She had taken to being somewhat abrasive toward others in her attitudes in a reclusive sort of way. She was still quite beautiful, and at times their bashful leader would be caught looking her way, but Anna would only smile with her eyes, as eyes can only say. She didn't see the point of throwing herself at a man that was still in silent mourning. Her life had turned upside down when no one had showed any interest in anything that concerned her, especially things of the heart. She remembered that little girl looking out her bedroom window, seeing the ocean waves crash on the beach, seeing her friends and family she missed them to the point she was numb. Her little girl ways and silent giggles faded in memory; she wanted those feelings back from those days of her innocence. She'd remembered the setting sun reflecting a night soon to come as the moon would follow, lying on top of the water, distant fairies dancing on the edge in their mock procession of giddiness. She would remember her room on the third floor with the cool ocean breeze baiting her senses. She had waited for the right boy to come along, yet he never did. Anna could not wait to get back into the company of Dr. Zimmerman; his presence was greatly missed. And the confines of being surrounded by books, somehow brought about a relaxed air of comfort that she had missed. She missed earth and the styles of dress. Her past had left this giant hole inside her that never could be filled. The confines of her heart had been lying in a dormant stare of being. Her way of behaving kept her feelings from getting attached to any one person, yet her heart was broken because Drew seemed lost, and she only wanted him to know that she would be there for him, if he needed her. And anyways, she loved him for being good to her in his quiet sort of way, the looks of love, the tender touches of fingers when doing small chores together, the placing of his hand in the small of her back to help her up when riding off from the stables. He was a gentleman with a gentle heart. *He didn't have to wait,* she thought. All the words were not said, but those big brown eyes had their way of sharing secrets that left her wanting. She just didn't understand why he was waiting. She was ready, if only he could be brave enough to speak, she would come to him and make her feelings known but when?

Anna looked up from doing her nail. "What am I doing something wrong to offend you, fearless leader?" she snapped out.

Drew raised an eyebrow. He was lost in his thoughts, focused on other conditions of the heart, not concerned with her sarcastic ways and misinformed stares. He was more concerned about his crew who were ready, to be back home.

"Are you okay?" He asked.

She looked at him like he had to be the dumbest. "Why would you even say that?"

Drew continued to look confused. "I'm just trying to keep peace between you two girls."

Anna rolled her eyes. "Well, try not to strain yourself. I wouldn't want you to pull a muscle from thinking too hard."

"And what's that supposed to mean?" Drew was at a loss.

Anna let out a huff of air and walked toward the door but said before leaving, "Maybe someday you'll figure it out."

Drew thinned his lips and shook his head as the door to his right closed behind leaving that conversation for another day.

They were all part of a special type of starship affiliation, a new race set apart from a regular fellowship, and nothing they wanted to do can change that. Anna cleared the door. As she flinted her eyes, she held back tears. She was a leader not known yet held in the confines of forgotten months of loneliness and unannounced reasoning. She had kept her real feelings to herself all along. This end of the world stuff didn't make any sense to her, and she only wanted a clearer picture of what this all meant. After finding out about where they were going, she didn't quite know what their part was in this adventure, but she was sure to do her part when called upon. There were other choices to be made, certain conditions overlooked like a lack of strategy. Why did Drew's wife has to die five months after getting there?" None of this was congenial to a cause. Now, deep in thought, she was never a dreamer for a back door schemer. She was just an unmarked girl with a tender heart. Anna's thoughts broke off when Bella entered from a side automated door and passed her in the hall. Transparent eyes flickered as the two girls returned artificial smiles. Bella entered the control deck and saw Drew in the distance staring out into space. He had a perplexed look on his face as if he had been punched. She looked back behind her, sensing maybe Anna had shared a few cross words with their devoted leader, then brushed it off. She went straightway to Drew and placed her hand on his arm. Anna had already left the room, so her latest competition would not hear what she waited a long time to share without mixed company.

"Drew, there's more about what I see…about the end."

Drew had already developed a curious changed expression of doubt. "What do you mean?"

"There's to be a major battle. They are trying to change the end, and there's more…" Bella's big brown eyes revealed a worried expression.

"They plan to take something from us…"

"What are they taking from us?"

"Someone attached to a Guardian…She's a princess. That's all I know."

"But why would they take one of our own?"

"I'm not quite sure. All I know is that those of a different world is referred to as the Fallen."

Drew had look of concern etched in his eyes, something that had been there quite frequently. "How many are there?"

"More than you could count in three weeks of concentrated effort."

Drew nodded his head. "But why now?"

"I don't know." Bella watched Drew's eyes, trying to read his mind. She couldn't tell what he was thinking but felt for him.

Bella reached over and put her hand on top of Drew's as he leaned forward from the main deck's window and was looking out at deep space. He could see Jupiter as a small ball with its brownish color of purple surrounding it, being the fifth planet from the sun. It was still a long way from the earth. Bella caught his stare of wonder. She knew by the visions they were heading into chaos, a place so unsettling in the back of her mind. She stopped and looked around, checking to see if they were alone. She sensed everyone else was at a distance. She turned to view their leader as a touch of emotion went through her and decided to unload what had been on her heart since the first time they met. Renee had died almost two years ago. It was just a careless, overlooked condition of security. This large bird of the air was passing by and took her. Bella's train of thought came back to the land of the living.

She glanced up into Drew's eyes and said, "I love you. I'm not sorry for feeling this way, but since we met, I have held this in my heart." She noticed right away he appeared to be in shock. "I really don't understand the way this has overwhelmed my heart, but since we're going to be tested by what's to come, I wanted you to know." Bella couldn't believe she just put her feelings out there without considering his approval. For a moment, she thought she'd lost him somewhere within her message, and it appeared his mind was somewhere else. And as the seconds rolled by, she sensed he was pulled off guard by her abrupt announcement of eternal love. She turned to walk away, yet he sensed her acknowledged rejection was too forthcoming. He saw the despairing look in her eyes.

"Bella, wait a minute, would you please?"

Bella turned to view an expression of concern on his face. "Yes…"

Drew paused before having the courage to see for his own sense of reasoning her quivering emotion set in her cheekbones.

"I love you too, but not like you mean it. We need to stay focused. Our personal agendas could get us killed." Drew didn't feel the same and apparently didn't know how to react. A quivering lip and water building on the back of her eyes, said it all. Bella knew she said too much and assumed he would feel the same, yet, Drew never said otherwise. His mind was focused on getting back home and nothing of the heart. He was still shocked, and lacking in words. He didn't know what to say to Bella to ease her pain. And his best friend had already left the control deck; only the Aquerae were in the room with them but showed no interest. Bella reached up and quickly kissed him, as a last resort of saying good-bye. Her words of any future would be closely guarded. Drew, surprised by the unwarranted kiss, pulled back…

James watched his wife's plane take off before turning around to see Thaliana standing at the end of the waiting room. Her face showed a gentle glow of understanding. She understood leaving loved ones behind had left a big hole inside the young man. His face had serious intent written into every moment he made. Thaliana stared at him without hesitation, wanting to know what was burning incessantly inside the fragile man. After the loss of his father, she wanted to make sure his allegiance was pointed in the right area of conviction. "We need to go. There's not much time," she said.

Thaliana and James walked back to the Jeep toward the end of the parking lot. Skagway's airport wasn't very big. It was dark already, so finding the cabin in the night would be no more of a challenge than a trip by day. Each curve and uphill turn seemed to tighten James's grip on the steering wheel, as if asceticism had set in. The air was full of a heavy thickness he would never expect. James knew his heart was geared from a father's constant prodding, to always do his best at whatever he attempted. He was driven like a maniac at times. His thoughts drifted back to growing up where everything felt normal. The trips travelling with the family, working on the cars with his father, it all appeared to have purpose. But now, what were the reasons? He still couldn't believe his father was taken. James broke off the memory as he caught the view ahead.

The forest, onward, was blacker than the darkest night, which caused a disconcerting fog to cross James's pathway. This was only his second time driving the road to the cabin and the first at night. An elusive eeriness became unsettling in the pit of his stomach. He wasn't the passive, loving little boy as in his youth. Fire and ice seemed to control his every movement. His memories burned inside him, leaving nothing but a glimmer of hope, something was missing. Thaliana glanced over and noticed the perplexed glare. She knew James needed time to think, a time to heal, a time to put everything back together before moving forward. The thought of seeing the Dark Angels left a morbid feeling in the back of his mind. These memories caused his skin to crawl and his arms to prickle. She comprehended the look yet held no clue how to interpret his feelings at what he had seen from the day. She knew how love was with family ties, losing her own family members one at a time. It felt like losing limbs but somehow still feeling them connected. There was this imaginary line drawn between the guilty and the innocent. Each had their place to go, leaving behind family, leaving behind moments that would never be forgotten. Why the turmoil? Why this internal strife? This was all madness in this mixed of world of the living and the dying.

Thaliana could see the cabin from the dim light of the porch up ahead. Skittles was waiting as if abandoned. When the wolf-dog saw the jeep, he wagged his tail. James had forgotten he'd left his father's pet behind, not having room on the trip to the airport.

"I forgot about the wolf-dog. He must be pretty upset that we left him."

Thaliana's expression didn't change. "He's okay. I took his scent out of the immediate area so the wolf pack wouldn't pick up his tracks."

James turned to see the expression in Thaliana's eyes. "You can do that? I mean, kill the scent?"

Thaliana flipped around to respond as she got out of the jeep. "Not exactly, more or less I covered his scent with that of the Fallen."

Skittles jumped off the porch to meet them halfway.

James bent down to pet the wolf-dog and gave him a hug, as if apologizing. "Don't worry, boy. We'll get him back." James talked as if to convince himself more than the wolf-dog. Thaliana reached for Skittles and gave a pat on the head as if everything would be okay.

Suddenly, the sky opened, causing an aperture, which separated the heavens from the atmosphere. Two enigmatic worlds trying to share the same space, for space held no equilibrium of understood life. A bright obscure light shown through the clouds, and a brilliantly glowing figure came down, reflecting off golden light. The light was so bright that James and the wolfdog turned their vision away to keep from being blinded. James held his hand up to block the intensity. He had a look of surprise but was past the point of expelling an indelicate demeanor. As he began to focus and see, this form was not of any ordinary creature. Both he and his Guardian saw that the image in front stood over ten feet tall, even bigger than Cornelius. This immortal's physical form appeared to be culled from a race unimaginable yet brilliant and resplendent. His wings were coruscated with sharp talons flanging off each golden feathery bone. His eyes were a deeper blue than the deepest of oceans. His hands were big and bold as if made for war or destruction yet held to a gentle control. His cheeks were slightly flushed with color. He emitted an indomitable presence like the stars and planets give form etching out this universe. He was covered in golden body armor with enormous breastplates, shin guards, and shoulder pads with spikes pushed up through the pads. This made James smile, wondering if this giant angel was prepared for a sporting event, and his position held was team captain. He had a sword strapped to his back with a blade that expelled a shimmery celestial shine. His hair, in thick long curls of velvety strands that draped over his shoulders and around his back and his neck, bore a chain of gold with the symbol of heavens realms etched into an ancient writing. His voice remitted an echo that shook the ground. He stepped forward and went to one knee, viewing his previous student.

"Quite an entrance, my good teacher," Thaliana said. He treated her with kindness and gentleness like a delicate, freshly bloomed flower. He turned to view James who seemed quite small for a position he wasn't yet groomed for.

"Be not afraid or discouraged by my presence, for my King has sent me with a gift. He knows of your troubles that follow. You are not to fear those of the Fallen. Their limits are given of a king's indomitable will and presence. He has sent me to advise you. I offer a gift. Come closer."

James did what he was told and moved forward. He looked back at the Indian princess wondering if this mighty figure in front was confused, picking the wrong student of war, yet he was the only one around. Besides this princess, who held her position from a royal beginning, he wasn't saying. He was nobody of importance in his own frame of mind.

James's body shook in misunderstanding as a representation of a King of realms. His mind couldn't absorb what was about to happen. He couldn't fathom simple people, like himself, being chosen without holding position of his earlier life. As others who had been chosen could find strength in the simplest of things, as the seeds of life planted grow from seeds to ferlies, which become monumental to the heart of a King, as the soul given imparts life, thus hence forging a pathway for those seeds to grow. The soul is the captor of marvelous, as once tiny insignificant seeds become the towering redwoods or specks of hope that sprouts from the first acknowledged deeds done, for inspiration derived can be the seeds giving back to the whole.

James looked up into Gabriel's eyes. He saw beauty and wisdom reflecting off golden light. It brought a deep sense of peace about him. "Sir, who seeks my presence? And what's this purpose?

Gabriel looked at James, a bit shocked by his questioning.

"I come from the presence of a King of the Kings. He is the father of all fathers. He is brother, forged of brothers. He is leader and teacher. He is the only King who dwells in the heavens."

James has a confused look about him. "I don't understand your purpose here, Gabriel. Why me?"

"You will stand in battle to represent all Guardians, as a son was given in an example of important leaders to come, you will stand for your father as he stood for you. Those Fallen from heaven will come to make their point, but you will be the one who will set him free, for the King of all the Kings gives purpose in the right for a father to love a son."

James's ears couldn't fathom the words being said as he lived this unrealized dream. He definitely felt Gabriel had the wrong person.

"Are you sure about your choice of representatives?"

Gabriel heard the hesitation in his voice. "I'm sure you're the one. Come forward, young man, and take this gift, given by my King."

James stepped forward, as close as he dared, and got down on one knee. His body was trembling. He wasn't even an A student, and some well-respected King was breaking rank and choosing him to lead. *I'm not a leader.* James thought. Gabriel lightly laid his sword on James shoulder.

Suddenly, a feeling of strength and knowledge and power ran through his body like a freight-train. Acknowledgement of what he was feeling was of an unfathomable happening. His heart filled with desires he once felt as a boy in the innocence of youth. James could feel the connection between his spirit and the divine presence of something most strange as he began to relax his shoulders and breathe in the air. He could feel his body changing as an unnatural purpose overwhelmed his normal way of thinking. Meeting the Indian princess for the first time had caused him to feel the same inscrutable feeling. He was homing into the gift not of earth, which wasn't taken lightly by this creature standing before him. He looked up at Gabriel, a chutzpah character, deeply concentrating on his present work. When James looked down at his own body, he saw something amazing. He did not recognize his usual self. He had grown to be a cherubic physical entity, with imposing presaged strength. He had wings that brightened off golden light, and his hands and face and his immortal grace were beyond any earthly sight. His body was a body of a Guardian. Skittles backed up and barked twice while wagging his tail. The wolfdog was not sure what he thought about all the new changes. This was different, one being pushed toward the age of immortality, one step forward to success. Thaliana's eyes widened. She had no idea this gift would be given, once hidden now revealed.

Yet Thaliana grasped this mystery that lay ahead would take time to absorb. Gabriel stood to his feet as did James. He pulled an object beneath his breast plate.

"Take this weapon. Its powers will protect you," he admitted. His voice boomed; an echo resounded off the mountains in the distance. James was handed what looked like something from the Indiana Jones movie in *Raiders of the Lost Ark,* a particular item in the likeness of a whip but much longer and made from a golden material that glowed, masterfully designed from materials not seen of earth. This angelic whip seemed spongy at first, but on closer examination, it was hard at the handle with finger holds for a grip. James grasped the whip tightly with his right hand. He fully extended the whip. It developed very sharp edges as he pulled the whip back, sharper than the sharpest of razors. When retracted again, the small blades appeared to fold inward to the inside of the chord. The whip extended a good fifty feet on full extension. James took the whip and flashed it toward a giant ponderosa pine that lay at the edge of the forest. The whip pulled the tree to the ground with a mighty crack that echoed a deafening sound. Gabriel looked over his shoulder and moved aside for this tree to drop in front.

"Be careful with this weapon. It has a destructive nature. Your thoughts alone are enough to command its powers. This weapon, brought from a place from the one true God, worked with hands of immortals, for your emotions alone will ignite its destructive force. Do not take this lightly."

James blinked surreptitiously to clear his head, for this gift was imbued by the hand of a God, and he was new at this position of leadership.

"Sorry, I'll be more careful with this here weapon," he said, making minor adjustments of what was to come.

Gabriel glanced back for just a few seconds longer as he gazed into the young man's eyes, acknowledging a speck of curiosity, for his king had chosen but a boy who was soon to be out of control. There were great responsibilities with a new title and position.

Gabriel has his arms folded across his chest as considering this gift and its inundated form, and then thought came to him.

"Your father is in a place between worlds. My King has his eye on him. He cannot be killed without bringing total ruin to his holders. You seek a young man and his fellowship that are not from here. He has been given free passage to another world by my King. He travels with a host of young people called the Circle. Find them, and you will find your destiny lies with those and their teacher. He travels afar from a distant star in the heavens."

James looked at his body. "What about how I look? It's not going to appear very comforting to present myself in this manner."

Gabriel stared at this awkward young man who was full of questions.

"You can change by thinking only to be small and your wings will disappear and your body will be reduced to your regular size. Your Guardian can show you other secrets attached to this gift."

James turned his eyes toward Thaliana. She nodded as if she understood what Gabriel was saying. The stoic teacher of Guardians looked back at Thaliana for a brief moment before taking to the sky. The brightening of lights receded as he gathered in mystic clouds and was gone.

Thaliana looked at James. He was still angel-sized. "This place is marked by the King's elite. No animal will get near this area now, not even the wolf pack. They would be too fearful."

James took the whip again and slashed at the air. The sound cracked loudly as if lightning and thunder hit the clouds.

"Put away your new toy. There is work to be done," Thaliana spoke.

James became like an obedient servant. He turned his attention toward his teacher. She had a peculiar look aimed in his direction. "Cross your arms together and close your eyes, and at the same time in your mind, think this phrase: be calm. And your body will respond, and you will become your original size.

To become large again, cross your arms together, close your eyes, and think of being big again. You will become as you are now, and your strength will return. Always keep your mind focused on the work at hand, or you will lose the privilege of this power."

"So do I have a different name than before, or am I just plain James?"

Thaliana walked in a Circle around James like she found humor in his outward manifestation.

"Your name is James. What's not to like about your name?"

"Oh, it's not that I don't like my name. I was wondering because Cornelius is the leader of the Fallen, and the Gabriel is captain of the guard. Well, I thought maybe there was something your King would better recognize me by…a title, you know, in case some other angel has the same name." The Indian princess broke out with a smile while she shook her head. "I don't think the King would mind giving you such a title, but don't let it go to your head. Just remember, you were given this power because my King saw something in you that sparked his interest. Don't make him regret giving you such a position. I'm here to keep you in line, for now. Later, when the dying comes, we will fight side by side with me in these fields before us."

James's expression turned sallow considering the statement when the dying comes. He has never seen blood before, not in this manner. This confused him about his true reason for being a Guardian. James reached down and picked up that ponderosa pine that he pulled to the ground. He wrapped his large hands and arms around the center and put his back into the effort, without struggling. Then he dragged it where the barn lay unfinished, thinking, to save it to finish up a job that his father had started. The image was similar to the fictional character of Paul Bunyan standing as a force to be reckoned with, because of his size. He turned back around after finishing this easy chore. He walked toward the Indian princess standing on the porch, showing a hesitant smile to her new recruit. She was worried about eternal conditions that had nothing to do with this immature boy.

She knew what he had been through so far was quite an adventure. She waited for him to reach the porch, wondering what he was thinking. Thaliana comprehended all the changes would take time getting used to. Skittles leaned against her and whined while nudging her hand. She reached down and ran her fingers through the top of his ears. Skittles lowered his ears and wagged his tail as James met them at the bottom steps.

"So, what do we do now?"

"We train and wait for the Circle."

James considered her statement. "What's so special about this Circle?"

Thaliana battled her eyes strangely knowing he would question everything. "They're the reason why you're here. We are to protect them. They were chosen by the King for a mission to come, for safe passage. We'll have to defend them. They're from a place far from earth. They are a Circle of members chosen to walk in a world between the living and the dead. A great gulf lays in the balance of a place where man nor beast have ever been, a place where the mind and body of the damned are separate from life, a terrible place where light as we know it doesn't exist, for the darkness rules there with creatures of that place. No forms of the living, except the Circle, have been there. Those that dwell there were created from a world set apart from the realms. The Circle have a better understanding of the dangers ahead, for what walks and crawls and slithers in that place will infest a world if given the chance. The Circle that represents the King is not ordinary beings that walk the earth. They've been specially trained by a superior race, as each have been given a gift for the breath of life in them is swayed like the turning of tides that move mountains. The Circle will help you in coming against them. For now, making this area ready will be our agenda."

"I don't understand? What do you mean…make ready this area?"

"The forest, the rain the fog, the glaciers, and the tunnels beneath this mountain will be your advantage. Shortly, my King will send legions of angels that will come to test their strategies, their plan of attack."

Thaliana looked above her, the cut of the land, the fiercely jagged mountains topped with ice and snow. The land held many secrets. The deep gorges, the narrow mountain passes, all played a role. A cold chill went through her, those distant memories being pulled from the frigid waters as seen of a little girl. She'd remembered what death felt like on that day, lost so many years ago. An encumbering truth made her shudder from what lay left to learn in the cold silent wills of the damned. They were pushed by the madness of the dying, no life of the living to advance or to be unfurled. She could see her father draped over the top of her, breathing life back into her once limp body. Strong warm fingers pressed against her lungs pushing water from her. She remembered seeing his face, then he was gone. This was something she'd never forget. This land had the roughest terrain she had ever envisioned. *It would be quite the treat in trapping these overzealous members of the* Fallen, was her thought. Yet she knew not to be overconfident. The pride before the fall, so eloquently quoted, not just for the benefit of human ears, it was a flicker of wisdom for all ears to hear and hearts to know.

James appraised Thaliana as she looked deep in thought. She stared out into the dark shadows of the night. Her mind drifted slowly back to reality. He broke off his stare when she moved toward him. James had remembered that his father had the basement full of tools and remembered seeing a small skip loader that could be driven out a back hidden door.

"We need to get started. There's lots of work to be done." And of course, he had his studies to do. Thaliana nodded in understanding his frame of mind.

"So, what's my claim to frame name going to be?" he barked out.

Thaliana raised an eyebrow. "So, we're back on that subject?"

"We'll, yeah…you never answered me?"

She was still confused about this strange man intent on changing his name.

"Well, if you insist. I'll give you a title, if, you forget all this playing around and get on with business from now on." She closed her eyes and folded her arms across her chest. *Why was this boy turned to man so insistent about changing his name?* she thought. She kind of saw him as a big adolescent, who at the moment stood nine feet tall. *A big baby…* was her second thought. This caused her to smile, as he noticed she had her wheels turning.

"How's the name Lacobus, Latin, meaning 'one who takes the place of?'"

James, not realizing this name had the same meaning of his present name was left in the dark, but he liked the Latin meaning for it made sense. Thaliana tried to remove the smile that had crossed her face. James didn't miss it, but this new title sparked his curiosity. He liked this name that gave meaning to a title as if to represent a portion of honor. *Guardian Lacobus. Had a ring to it.* James thought.

"I think it will suit me just fine." James looked down at Skittles, continued crossing his arms, closed his eyes, and became his normal size, even the whip became smaller. He walked back into the cabin and started preparing dinner. Thaliana was glad to have the company of the wolfdog, and James, as they began to settle *in* for the night. The cabin felt cozy and warm in the comfort of new friends. James's father did quite well in building this home of ponderosa pine. He acknowledged his father's character in every nail and chiseled groove of craftsmanship. A glazed finish setting on the table tops, the soft features of the kitchen cupboards, the light pinewood floors, the exceptional contours of the bed frames it was all fabricated from his father's ideas of an old man's comforts. A pleasant feeling crossed his mind knowing this home was manufactured from his father's creativity. He felt a peace come over him. He could smell the cedar, and the pine, watch the sparkle off the cabinet doors, showing a craft profoundly perfected. The thought brought a lump of emotion up in James's throat. A hint of light shined through his soul. He had to find him, no matter how long it took, he would never give up.

After dinner, the two companions took to the fireplace and got lost in conversation over delicate confidentialities that seemed important. The light from the fire reflected off Thaliana's face. She began to talk of her experiences about her home. She looked at James as they sat with hot tea for warm comfort at the close of the day. She glanced back into the flames.

"In heaven, you would have to earn those wings. They're not just given out like candy to children. The King expects perfection in all our members." She looked across her shoulder with inquisitive eyes of light judgements, "How long before your studies are done in this place?"

James looked up from the fire, trying to pull himself from a distant place.

"I have only thirty days before finishing my doctoral studies, and then I receive my title. I was in an undergraduate program that my mentor from Ohio State University set me up on. Why do you ask?"

Thaliana looked up quickly with an expression so vivid. "So you know of the Circle from Ohio State University?"

James seemed confused for a moment. "No. they are not familiar to me?"

Thaliana turned toward James trying to retain his full focus. "You have a connection with this professor, Dr. Zimmerman?"

James measured her words while staring into the flames. "Dr. Zimmerman was one of my mentors for my first four years of college, but how is he involved in this?"

Thaliana's eyes widened. "He's the key to everything about the Circle. He was their teacher."

James got up and stirred the fire, and then added two more pieces of wood.

"So, you think Dr. Zimmerman took a special interest in me for what? You think I'm connected somehow to the others?"

Thaliana adjusted her legs as she turned to warm her right side.

"I'm sure, but somehow this is not just by accident that you went to the same college and had the same professor. Dr. Carl Zimmerman knew of the connection, obviously, or you wouldn't be here. Nothing about this place is by accident. There's a plan in place that involves us all."

James turned his head slightly in Thaliana's direction. "So what's my part this."

Thaliana got up and poured herself another cup of tea from a tea kettle sitting on the top of the stove. She didn't really know what was to come for this young man, but off the subject, there were other important oddities to consider.

"I believe you need to finish your studies. That would seem to be the most promising solution. The King would always insist the best of students to put their studies first, for without strong leaders in government and strong men and women, the alloy of leadership begins to fall apart. For the inner workings of solicitude for family structure are torn apart as the bonding values of cohesiveness become emaciated and the acuity of the masses are blurred by the lack of focus. He doesn't want you to stop doing the right adjustments for your life, even with the end of the world coming. It wouldn't be right to stop believing in your dreams, for dreams show purpose, and purpose aligns the body and mind to complete the soul…" Thaliana stopped there because she wasn't quite sure she should say what had crossed her mind at that moment.

James has a puzzled expression written on his face, wondering what she was dealing with eternally.

"So, it's settled. I finish my studies, even with what's to come."

Thaliana crossed a thin line of understanding by a tender smile and a slight nod. James watched her for a brief moment, her long black hair that glistened in the fire light reflecting off flame. She was beautiful, yet her beauty was only the beginning of a well-managed girl. She was an immortal who had geared her way of thinking to an eternal purpose beyond the limits of her once human soul. She was carrying a burden on her shoulders that he wasn't quite sure he could follow. She released her hair that was tied back with a red band and let it fall around her neck and shoulders. She moved her eyes toward this man and saw that he noticed.

"What's the look for?" she said.

James blinked as if trying to recover by flashing glitches of memory. He put his head in his hands and closed his eyes; this incredulity in his head was hard to imagine. He needed time to think. His head was spinning from all this informal information that had involved his heart; they were all to consuming as frictions could lead to folly.

"I'm worried about my family being home alone. I'm not sure what will happen to them if those of the fallen spread to other parts of the world."

Thaliana raised her head with a cautioning eye. "I don't think we'll have to worry about that at the moment. They're not taking part of the whole world just yet."

"I know…but we are not limited to this small space of land, and they could be thinking of other areas where they could go."

Thaliana understood his meaning but knew what was to come soon would be directed toward life above. She changed the subject, as she tried to ease this boy's pains of trouble.

"I had to earn wings by many years of study," Thaliana spoke. "I didn't think the work would ever be completed. It took a long time, and it gave me a sense of value that I wouldn't have had otherwise." Thaliana paused to make sure she had his attention. "The seventh realm was for his most gifted at first, but then our King began to see that it caused separation between his elites and intellectual minds that he had handpicked through the years, but now it's different. Those who had rejected his plan saw this as a good reason to start turning others against him. They didn't like being put into a realm where they were looked on as being inferior. The King was always trying to improve the value of life from one realm to another, some didn't agree, others didn't care. Yet the seventh was way beyond comparison. That's when those from the darker side of the realms started to complain. You can only imagine what happened next. Cornelius began arranging these quiet meetings with others like him. His great uncles who were the brothers of this creature that our King had cast into that darker place where light doesn't dwell, held there until the day he would be judged for what he had done, his medaling with the humans. He didn't think that the King would take any interest in such meetings held in secret, since they were considered less important than his present projects. Cornelius couldn't see past all his own selfish desires to begin to understand that the King wanted all of his creations to share in the gifts provided. He lost his will to be patient and to wait on his plan and purpose. The King was trying to teach these power-starved angels to be humble, but they became defiant and disobedient to what he wanted for them." She glanced at James to make sure he was still listening, to make sure he hadn't dozed off. She then took another long sip of tea while Skittles came close to her and nudged her hand. She looked down at the wolfdog, and then back up at James.

"He has your gift too," she said, looking toward the wolfdog.

James turned his head and raised an eyebrow. "What...like turn into something?"

"Yeah, something like that."

"What do you mean?"

"He's the same as you. He's connected."

James transferred his gaze at the spoiled wolfdog, as he heard a whimper and saw a wag of a tail. "What? You mean he can have wings and grow big to be like me?"

"Yes, in a way…but different. He's what we refer to as an Honorite. I've never had the pleasure of owning such a beast, but I heard they're like having a best friend. He'll always be there to protect his master, as in watching your back. As I am your Guardian to guide, he is here to protect. You know, your father did not find this wolf-pup by accident. He was led to him. Nothing in life is without meaning as we all have a journey to travel. Even this wolfdog has his."

"But Skittles is not my dog. He was my father's."

"It doesn't end with your father. You're still connected by family, and the wolfdog knows his purpose and sees it in us and our ways of doing what a good heart can hold. He knows it's the mark. That's why he has taken a liking to the both of us." The wolfdog got up and nudged James's hand, then he barked once and sat in front of him and wagged his tail, like saying, hey, listen up.

James wrinkled his face while looking down. "So now you're special…huh?" Skittles barked twice and nudged him with a cold wet nose, which left something behind. James wiped it on his pants. This caused Thaliana to smile.

"He knows to sense danger or be put into a situation to protect, and then he will turn but the quickest way would be for you to cross your arms and then say the word *Honorite*, in a loud ominous voice." *Then it had just dawned on James, why Skittles had no problem killing the Alpha the day before. He was the protector, right?*

"He will diligently respond to your command as you see fit. Never have him do anything unworthy of a good man, or both of you will lose your abilities as immortals."

James turned his view back toward the Indian princess. "I would never do such a thing. Why even suggest?"

Thaliana's stare was somewhat piercing. She remembered him looking at her. It made her wonder. She knew he was different. He was a man of integrity but remembered he was still human.

"Temptations are still a part of your natural life. From past experiences, I've known that human emotions can change a man's heart to do the worst of things when feeling hopeless."

James considered her statement and knew she was talking about conditions of the heart.

Thaliana turned again to warm her left side from the fire.

"Good intent doesn't always win over. Experiences of a patient man seeks a path hardly known."

"And that means…?" Thalian looked up at him knowing he sensed her reasons were more personal, about secrets she herself had desired and lost. He looked at her with a deep penetrating stare. She knew what he was thinking and changed the subject.

"It means you can't always have answers to questions that are inscrutable of meaning, better left unsaid than lead a man down the wrong road. You must accept choices for what they are."

"And you're okay with that?" Thaliana knew where he was going with the conversation and avoided the directness of his meaning. She just shook her head and dropped the smile while gazing into the fire.

"Do you always speak in parables?" he asked. James knew she was hiding something that had left a few scars on her own personal life that she wasn't willing to share with someone she just met, even if they were tied together by some eternal covenant, fitting of a king, yet the wrong side of the tracks, as he was just learning conditions of an eternal nature, a road riding a fence he'd never crossed.

James interrupts the conversation, for the night was getting late. "We should retire for the evening so to meet another day and be fresh." Thaliana perked with that thought, knowing James and the wolfdog would have a tough day to come. She looked above to see the loft, but James stopped her from moving in that direction.

"You can take the room. I'll sleep in the loft." James saw that the fire was dying down.

His eyes became heavy with sleep as he turned once to look at the Indian princess. She got to her feet, walked over to James, and took a necklace from around her neck. She then reached up and placed the necklace around his neck. This caught James off guard. He felt the warmth of her breath and sensed the beating of her heart. She had the appeals of a beautiful woman as he had noticed. The expression in her eyes was one of love but not of a physical kind. The love she reflected came from a deeper meaning, as her eyes pulled him in. He'd envisioned that her presence alone was a draw of a King who exacted authority, understood something unique in a way that could change the face of a world. He looked down at the necklace she had placed around his neck. He knew that her reason for giving this small gift was twofold in meaning, even though he misunderstood, she wouldn't tell of her reasoning.

"Wear this at all times. It bonds us together." It was an ornamental golden image of an angel with a sword held high. An insignificant engraving with the word Guardian was in scripted of an ancient language he would not understand. James measured the gesture of kindness and knew this was something she was commissioned to do, yet something more underneath was left unsaid. As she walked toward the bedroom, she could feel James looking at her. To him, she was more beautiful than most women he had ever seen, yet he knew that part of her conversation about temptations also included him being spellbound by her heavenly beauty. He reached down to gather his wallet and keys before pushing past the ladder of the loft and remained quiet about what was said that night. There was a lot to think about, heaven and its seven realms. Beauty and splendor wrapped all into one. James's life was about to change, a change he couldn't begin to fathom. How important his role was in all this end of the world stuff. A King was taking an underdog and putting him in the spotlight to be tested, a test without knowledge or know how. Like the Indian princess had told him, don't expect to know everything up front.

James began to dream, and in his dream came what followed.

He was standing in the middle of this great forest surrounded by tall trees, animals of the forest were around him as if waiting, waiting for something of mystery that had held their attention. James reached out to touch a doe and was able to pet her soft skin. The dream felt real to the point he could feel the doe's breath gliding gently over his hands. Suddenly, the animals of the forest started running toward a beach, which was ahead through remitting light of a distant shore. James was led by this large number of forest animals as he began to hear distant waves breaking on the shore. James wasn't aware of why he felt the need to get to the beach, but something within him pushed him urgently to sprint. Upon arrival, he saw something most peculiar that blurred his visions. A gentle fog had rolled in covering the water, hiding something behind the waves. Just before that, people were standing in line waiting for their turn to be led forward to a place that didn't quite make any sense. Dark Angels had overtaken the beach and we're leading the multitudes slowly forward to something hidden. Only a few people were let out of the procession, but it appeared they were all rooted to their place, as if incurred for reasons, hidden in a clouded form of mental submissiveness. Fog inverted the water just in front as a deception wasn't made known until the very end, causing the crowds to remain calm. James ran to the front, wondering why so many were held in this gulf of misunderstanding. Once stepping forward, further results were to be known as several of those creatures with blackened wings were stamping the hands of a few waiting in line. After passing the front, he noticed people were being manacled to each other in a place that deceived his vision as nothing of this natural world could be procured by human eyes. A structured guillotine, as seen from pictures, was firmly planted over the water, yet not noticed until entering the water's surface. Heads and bodies were separated by this guillotine piled up, then dropped into a pit that seemed to be swallowed by the water. A pit so hot It burned his face. Two Dark Angels were standing close to the water's edge to make sure the line steadily moved forward. There were only a few that were let out of line, but the rest were led to this guillotine. The people standing at the water's edge waited like innocent children, as if everything ahead would be all right. They were in a stupor of conformance, impassionate, held in a mental trance as children were of trusting parents— all moving forward without being mindful that they we're facing the end of life.

James jerked awake suddenly, with perspiration beaded on his face and neck. His clothes were soaked with sweat, his heart was pounding, his tongue went dry, he sat up in bed and coughed— like he wanted to expel something from the dream that had entered his body, yet nothing came from him, except hot breath, a bad case of the shivers, and a repulsive sense with the loss of memories. Terror gripped him as this dream left something behind, even though James knew the only part left behind was the impression of the envisioned. This ascendancy of control was beyond comprehension. The pit of his stomach forced him to vomit. Those visions of death, of piled bodies discarded, left chills on the back of his neck. James glanced down at the necklace placed around his neck. He knew great responsibility came with accepting such a gift. He wondered what he'd gotten himself into. His tongue became swollen in his mouth. Terror had a new title that crept beneath the fog that lay devote, for death had a face that crawled under the skin leaving nothing of memory. Skittles woke and came to his side. James was about to explode from the lack of air. He came down from the loft and ran to the door. He burst through the front to get his composure back, yet standing in front just past the porch in sullen stature were thousands of those creatures remittent of the Fallen…

8

THE CIRCLE

The starship landed without any major complications. Torack thought it smarter to use a cloaking device to keep out of the government's line of sight. They had only prepared to stay ten days at the most, and the Circle have their work cut out of them. Drew led the others to trail after him, breaking clear of the door in the early morning air. Torack had landed the starship undercover bestrewn of objects that led to this cave.

A few hours from then, young Bella had taken to the parlor, sitting for quite some time. She seemed to be in a stupor. She had had these vivid dreams of creatures with wings that encircled the globe with ominous intent. She was nervous about what she had felt envisaged of their hidden message. Bella sat comfortably in a large eighteenth century arm chair with red velvet cushioning in Dr. Zimmerman's peaceful parlor. A quiet, reclusive aura seemed to engulf her. Dr. Zimmerman looked toward the perplexed girl as she seemed lifeless before him with her glassy stare, her uncomfortable aura, and the unhinged expression written in her eyes. She had her legs crossed with her eyes unblinking as she stared toward the courtyard. She seemed in the most uncomfortable position, from what he could tell. She had changed from the jumpsuit she was into something more of the Austin, Texas ambition. She had worn her usual western wear with a type of cream-colored cowgirl boots and blue checkered blouse, with a rhinestone belt buckle. Her hair was pulled back in its traditional ponytail. She didn't look scared or angry or any of the infrequent pragmatic emotions that she so often displayed from her past. Her face remained neutral yet added several wrinkles to her constantly perplexed predicaments of understanding. She would drift off somewhere now, and then from the standard of thinking. Her mind had wandered from time to time on the vivid view of her dreams, no one close bye, no one at home. Yet her place of restitution was seen by the expressions deeply etched upon her face. From what he could tell, she was daydreaming, escaping impediments of reality, crossing over to the other side, slipping to the darker side of situations, like an aged doctor pulling antidotes from a bag to perform a medical magic trick. He could see her nails bitten down to the quick, which reflected nervous tension. Bella had never learned the gentle ways of what a finishing school good teach. She seemed like a lost child from what Dr. Zimmerman could tell, possibly because of so many changes, too many implementations of death, constantly pushing back emotions, giving in to thoughts on the other side of reality, missing the normality of living as young ladies would do because she had been driven across the universe to distant stars. She didn't seem so prone to cry objectively as she'd done in her past. There appeared to be rules that governed her every move.

Quickly, Dr. Zimmerman broke her train of thought. "So, young lady, what difficulties face you this morning that holds you looking mystified in your troubles?"

Bella, still held by her spell, didn't acknowledge Dr. Zimmerman's direct questioning until all eyes turned toward her in a compelling stare. She blinked twice while moving forward in her chair as she called on to the ill-timed acknowledgement of her Circles unwarranted stares.

"Oh, I didn't realize you were addressing me, professor. I've had more than I could take troubling my dreams lately and find them to be quite unsettling." Spoken as a true visionary.

"Well, young lady, I do not wish for one of my own students to be in such a state, pray tell us your discomforting vision and maybe we can sort out the complexity of its meaning and draw our own suppositions of our present conditions."

Bella seemed a bit timid about sharing her dreams but felt she was in the safe company of those who were equal and assiduous as she was. "Well, to be direct to the point, I'm not quite sure how to word this vision, but I sense it to be a cautioning for all of us?"

Dr. Zimmerman looked around the room, sensing all eyes were focused on the subject at hand. "Tell us about your vision," he said." We are more than capable to decipher it's meaning to be sure."

Bella glanced back at each Circle member, concluding that each had known her for quite some time, and their judgments thus far would be far removed on discovery of those particular settings on her heart. She began to feel tightness in her chest, even though she knew each had the best of intentions. This was a day of reckoning for the lot of them. It was a day where dreams had become a reality. Bella then glanced at Drew, remembering that short first kiss from a few days ago and then turned her focus to the subject at hand. She wasn't sure if their incredulity would offer a way out of this abject situation, such as dreams may come forward from memories unspent.

"So much has happened in such a short period of time. It's kind of trite to have these repetitive dreams of such conditions that can't be quite understood, but I will give it my best shot," she said.

Bella took a deep breath and let out a huff of air, while twitching her face in a consorted kind of way, then placed both her hands above her right knee, straightening her back to improve her posture as only a lady can do with crossing her hands. This happened to be the position of her point of discovery. Then she began as the words caught on from her shaking beginning.

"I'm not sure where to begin, so that being said, I'll try from what I think to be start." She glanced toward the professor as if most of what she had to say would be directed at him.

"When we started getting close to earth, the dreams or visions started coming to me then and have progressed since."

Dr. Zimmerman interrupted her for a briefest moment to ask, "What do you mean by progressed?"

Bella turned her eyes into the direction of the professor again. "Well, I mean they become stronger impressions. These tall, dark, methodic looking creatures Circle the globe searching for people, or are gathering them together for some type of event, for what seems to be the finale of the end."

Dr. Zimmerman responded, "The end of what, my dear? Can you expand your statement, young lady?"

Bella's eyes began to get watery, and her voice began to quiver. The unsettling words brought emotion to the surface. "I'm not sure, but maybe some type of genocide or ritual, sacrificial in a way?" Everyone's stare appeared to be unblinking.

"Something is awful about what I see. It doesn't quite make any sense. These creatures with darkened wings are picking or choosing from the crowds, certain people. They're stamping their hands with some type of mark, and the air is full of this awful smell that chokes my throat. This odor seems to be rising beneath a pit. Not a normal type of pit, because it's not any pit I've ever seen. I get that impression that odor is death making his mark on those left on earth, but something else..." Bella paused and placed a fisted hand over her mouth to push down a hard lump of emotion.

"These creatures take control of everything. They line the shore with hundreds and thousands of people, close to the forest edge."

Bella paused again, before taking a deep breath. She could feel a morbid sense of lost. She continued, "They are beheading most of the people and piling their bodies into a large pile. They burn the heads and bodies in the fire, but it's not an ordinary fire but a fire from this pit. This fire burns so hot it burned my face and hands when I walked there in this vision." Bella stopped for a second and slid off a pair of gloves and removed a scarf around her neck. She presented her hands as an evidential metaphor of a dream that left behind physical conditions that didn't make sense. Her hands and part of her neck showed signs of redness, and a few blisters as if she was placed inside of her dream and felt the aura of its purpose. All members of the Circle showed signs of bewilderment. Dr. Zimmerman stood suddenly with an exasperated acknowledgment.

"Was there a mark of some kind, like a tattoo?"

"Yes, I mentioned that in the beginning. They were stamping the people from the crowds."

Dr. Zimmerman stood in silence for a brief moment as he pondered the vision in his mind. His eyes were set in a state of wonder.

This is the mark of the dammed...the end of the ages... preapocalyptic. These are words spoken of... the extinction of the human race – the slate wiped clean. The professor looked down in the young woman's face, with a raised motion of an eyebrow.

"Did you see where this event would take place?"

Bella shook her head while looking directly into the professor's eyes. "I believe somewhere in the southern region of Alaska, the last unspoiled frontier of the world, in an unpopulated area, hidden from the world with the worst of elements."

Dr. Zimmerman turned his vision outside the parlor window and then explained, "This is not the same battle that's mentioned or written long ago. It's a battle between those of heaven and a different kind of beast never mentioned."

The Circle looked surprised. They understood Bella's vision was a forewarning of something to come.

Bella shot a glance back at Dr. Zimmerman with peaked anxiety. "So, what is our mission now?"

Dr. Zimmerman turned from the windows view. "Save as many lives as we can. We don't have the power or resources to match a battle with those creatures. As your dreams showed, they will control the end."

Bella's face turned white. "But Dr. Zimmerman, you don't seem to understand. These angels or beast, whatever you want to call them, they don't just destroy what's left of humanity. They come after us. Don't you see? This is our fight too."

Dr. Zimmerman's skepticism was forthcoming. "We're meant to be here, not so much to fight back to warn." The erudition of the professor's calm was something needed. He looked with fervor as a father of students.

"Yes, I believe we need to warn others. But more likely, we need to make a stand at this place of battle. There are key Guardians there that have a direct connection to this place. For we fight for the right to live. We fight for the right to let these creatures of the heavens know we have a right to be here, more than they comprehend. The Guardians seek our protection, and we theirs, but yet there's more." Everyone turned to view their teacher. "This King of theirs they talk of has his hands in the mix of what's to be settled, and he knows all, he sees what we see. I believe that he approves of this, and what is hidden will be revealed, for our allegiance of this battle must be a part of why you're here. I sense. this being the main reason why the Circle had to return. The Circle is the key to the Guardian's success."

The parlor was filled with voices of confusion as each member of the Circle considered this new information. Drew's mother and father had been missing since earlier that year, because of a tsunami that hit the California coastline. After most of the students had made their calls back home, only Tommy's brother, mother, and father, and Jake's parents were still alive. Bella's Uncle Buck was still alive, but her father had been killed in an earthquake that hit two months earlier.

After Dr. Zimmerman saw where this was going and decided the Circle would be safer seeking the company of the Guardians as soon as possible. "Calm yourselves and hold your voices for a minute, all of you!" he said. Dr. Zimmerman waited until he had everyone's attention. "I see the best to our knowledge for us is to seek this place out from Bella's dream." Dr. Zimmerman turned to look toward Anna and Drew.

"Anna, I need for you and Drew to go find a map of the southern region of Alaska. Look up that town of Bella's dream and pinpoint where we need to go. We need to make haste."

Anna rolled her eyes knowingly, spending any time with Drew was to be a bit of a challenge but try as she may. She walked past Drew and showed a flicker of doubt toward this troubling young man with a bit of annoyance she cast a reflection. Drew was still in mourning, according to his best friend and nothing otherwise had been said, but he understood the look that followed. They walked out of the immediate area and headed toward a storage room on the backside of the first floor, out of the view of others. Drew wondered what this strange girl was about to do. Anna's eyes turn up to look once again at this awkward man child with the overwhelming oddities. He'd been mourning a wife who had been gone for quite some time now, and it was time to move on. Nothing could cure a broken heart better than another's love. He looked like a lost little boy waiting for the right person to come along and solve all his miseries of a discontented heart. Dr. Zimmerman saw the flicker of doubt in the young man's demeanor and was not quite sure sending these two off together would be of a grateful mix of company, for a boy so easily led by a girl with her well-formed opinions was about to be set up for the fall. Anna blatantly walked through the professor's old estate corridors like she lived here all her life, moving things about, opening cupboards and drawers as if leaving Drew out of her little adventure. She mimicked Watson trying to keep up with the famed Sherlock Holmes with her organized skills. The professor had kept such oddities of particular value for safekeeping, and had such valuables as maps and scrolls not left out as clutter. Anna shifted all her weight toward Drew as they stood inside a closet, and then she closed the door. The girls' sublimity of fulfillment was usually unfriendly but had suddenly laid a gentle head toward Drew's right shoulder, as if to draw an interest.

"So did Bella kiss you a few days ago in the control room?" Anna looked up with her big sad eyes.

He was mystified by her quick assumption. Drew tried to avoid the question by talking in a different direction. "Don't you realize we are facing the end of the world, yet you two don't seem to understand?"

Anna still had that pouty look about her." She told me that you kissed her. Is that true?

Drew recognized that he got himself into a tough situation with both young ladies. He had missed Renee so much that he craved the attention of another, which sent confusing signals in the direction of both females. He didn't quite know what to do.

"I'm sorry, Anna. I don't want to cause problems between you two. I like you both, but I don't want us to be distracted. We're in a difficult situation right now, and you don't seem to get…"

Anna, took a step toward him, and grabbed Drew's shirt while pulling him close, before he could fight her off. She swung her arms around his neck, and kissed him, and held on to him in a gentle loving way. Drew was surprised by her quick assumptions of a young man's heart, yet he pushed her away, and a strong emotion of sorrow began to overwhelm him. He stared into her eyes while the tears began to roll down Drew's face. Anna had him more than broken and confused about the sudden kiss. For the first time, Drew broke down and cried like a little boy. Anna was so shocked she didn't know what to say, but she knew he had never really let go of Renee. She was still attached to him in a way she'd never understand, unless she had gone through the same ordeal. Drew couldn't get his breath because the sobs overwhelmed him like a curtain of grief, so final, so internal that it ripped at his heart. He tried to force the emotion down, but his mind and heart seemed to be cemented together in a way that left him as a broken man from his memories of another loss. Renee had been so graphically taken from him, without a moment's notice, she was gone. Drew didn't understand that there was an eternal plan for the young man's life beyond what he could ever fathom. This caused Anna to feel guilty as she reached for Drew and put arms around him. Anna finally let go and cried with him on the floor of the closet, sensing his pain like nothing she'd ever felt before. Drew reached out to her and pulled Anna close while burying his face on her shoulder. Anna didn't know what to do for the young man who had stolen her heart the minute she first met him. But she knew Drew to be human just like the rest of them. The curtain that had taken him through the last few years had finally fallen.

Drew wanted to leave the closest but considered embarrassment if the others of the circle would see him this way. Instead of leaving, Drew contemplated just to wait for a minute. Yet Anna knew she had overstepped her boundaries of the boy's heart. Anna started to leave, but Drew grabbed her arm and pulled her in. Her heart was set a flame. Warm lips, poundings of her heart, she couldn't take much more of this. Drew kissed her with such emotion Anna melted in his arms. She was stricken in a way she'd never be the same after feeling this connection of young love. But Drew was still holding on to that flickering pain of his eternal heart. He hadn't let go of his wife who was now gone, their eternal commitment of love was still raging in the young man's heart to never be blown out by the future events to come. He finally pulled away and ran from the closet-confused, disillusioned, and distraught.

He shoved Anna aside and ran to the stairs, out of sight, to cover the realities facing him. Anna stood in the closet and wiped at her face to rid the tears that rolled off her cheeks and down her arms. She grabbed the map she needed in one hand and almost ran into Bella as she was coming out of the closet. Bella, who had further instructions from the professor, was sent to see what was holding them up. She came around the corner with a huff of air, with hands on her hips, all puffy and red. She expelled jealousy and mistrust of her competition as she walked on past her. Yet Bella saw something else in the young Anna's eyes that weren't there a minute behind them. She saw the swollen eyes and the redness that followed. Bella didn't know what to say, and neither did Anna as she passed her in the hall.

"Are you okay?" Bella asked.

Yet Anna never answered. She flipped around and past a sorrowful look toward her roommate. Bella's eyes saw the pain and hurt in Anna's character. She wondered if the bashful boy had gotten the best of her or vice versa. Anna turned her face to ignore her.

Her eyes reached up to take a look past the stairs, as she quickly noticed Drew disappeared down a hall. This was all too much for her to take.

As Anna passed Bella, she shot a wistful stare in her general direction. Bella could tell by the look something happened between the two that was overwhelming.

That's when Bella knew there was something developing between Drew and Anna. The two girls returned to the parlor with the map, yet Bella was somewhat on Anna's shoulder because she saw the girl was on the edge of a breaking point. Dr. Zimmerman saw the remorseful look in Anna's eyes too. The two girls pushed down their emotions while Anna handed the map she had found to Dr. Zimmerman. Bella had quickly pointed out that their destination would be in a small town of Skagway, Alaska. They were to come close to the Canadian border, easily found by Bella's dream interdictions. She had looked around the room and brushed her hair back with a wave of her hand as she shyly looked back at Anna. Anna didn't look Bella's way. Instead she looked out the parlor window wondering about Drew's past. Dr. Zimmerman look up to see the ego-damaged boy slowly drift back into the room with his face still lit with a bit of emotion. Anna saw the look of emotion still covering the boy's face too. She looked toward Dr. Zimmerman and knew he'd caught those ill-timed glances and sensed a problem blooming. The other members of the circle had so much on their mind they didn't read into the event of the moment. As time slowly passed, Drew's face turned pale as he looked Anna's way and sensed this to be a turning point between them. The confusing emotions of the moment remain hidden. Drew wanted to consistently do the right act but was sorely embarrassed for breaking down in front of Anna. He thought it best to keep his distance from the young ladies in the near future and confine himself among the ranks of his best friend, who had his back on the previous occasions.

Dr. Zimmerman stood in this Circle of young curious minds, changed by the reality of a quickly fading time, living a life abroad, learning to be flexible. It was all a game played out by serious attentions. He had been sitting for quite some time and felt prone to stand in their presence, to get their devotions in giving him the floor, as everyone turned to look at him. The professor brought them to silence with an unblinking stare as most scholars have that way about them. Each student became wide-eyed at his studious stare, and Dr. Zimmerman's eyes wrinkled with worry. At first, it seemed that he was hesitant of how to address them. But with his many years that had taught his wisdom with time and experience, he began with a delicate quiver of pain seen in the deep-seeded wrinkles of His face. Dr. Zimmerman knew what they were to face ahead would change them all. Responsibilities would follow them with the ending of the world, but how to explain the unexplainable, he wasn't quite sure. So, he kept it simple for now and left the difficult conversation for another day.

"This trip will include everyone here. You should prepare to leave for Alaska, we leave in the morning. All of you will meet out front or at 7 o'clock in the morning, don't be late." He insisted, as everyone went to their separate rooms for the rest of the day.

Drew and Randy shared a room that night and began to settle in. Anna and Bella were scheduled the room together, and Drew felt a fight brewing.

Dr. Zimmerman saw the looks that they gave one another and called the girls over for a brief conversation. He waited for the room to empty out before he looked down at both young ladies.

Both girls sensed a scolding, and seemed to be pouting about the predicament. He pointed to the seat in front, and the girls took a seat. Dr. Zimmerman looked at both young ladies. His face was perplexed from age, and the last two years had shown in his mannerism.

"Young ladies, please, you know my heart is with both of you. I wish that my wisdom and years could give you a little insight on what's to happen in the near future." He turned his attention to Bella. "Young lady, you know the days ahead are without mercy. If we survive the next couple of weeks, it will be because of our support for each other. Please don't let me regret putting you two into the positions that you hold. I'm nervous about the both of you sharing a room together. Bella, your time here is not about personal matters but about conjectures that we have not even begun to know." He turned his view to Anna. "And, young lady, you've a long life before you. Take it slow. Can I trust the both of you to keep your minds focused on the important roles at hand?"

Bella looked at Dr. Zimmerman and then at her roommate for the moment and considered their misalignment. "We'll be okay. I'm sorry for not staying focused. This won't be a problem," Bella said, but Anna had an unconvinced look on her face. She kept silent, knowing anything she would say would only be used against her, for both young ladies were dealing with incomplete hearts and family members gone, so insecurities were strong. Anna and Bella both had kept to themselves at their new world, without interfering with Drew's life, considering that he had been through so much with the death of his wife. Both young ladies saw an opportunity of filling in that empty space of Renee being gone, without considering the consequences of their own personal endeavors. Drew was vulnerable, left with a big hole of emptiness, and both young ladies were seeing a limited window of opportunity. Drew, leaving his little girl behind, had also left him feeling that much more vulnerable, uncertain circumstances; the end showing signs of everything falling apart. Nothing was certain anomalies of the future were unmarked. Bella, looked up at Dr. Zimmerman, and then at Anna.

"I'm sorry, Anna. I have no business interfering with our leader's choice." Bella held the tears back knowing this would only make their circumstance worse. She took one last look up at Dr. Zimmerman and turned and left for her bedroom on the second floor, an unfortunate incident was brewing.

Dr. Zimmerman, puzzled at Bella's quick departure, looked at Anna. "Are you two going to be all right rooming together?"

"We're okay. It's just something we never talked about at our new home. I mean, how both of us saw Drew before." Anna was well familiarized by the situation. A cursory expression of demure crossed her face. She had left Dr. Zimmerman standing in a state of shock. When Anna got to her room, Bella was packing for the trip to Alaska. She had an awkward pout written in her eyes. Anna with her black short hair was carrying herself quite well, as if she felt for the girl from Austin, Texas. She had a distrustful attitude but was slow to enter the room with no intent of starting a fight. She shot a stare across the room.

"Look, I am sorry about the situation with Drew. I know everything has been so confusing. Drew's been through a lot in the past year, and I think we both thought the same thing. It's not up to us what the unhinged man thinks. This situation isn't predictable, like buying a used car."

Bella remained quiet for the time being. She continued to fold her clothes and put them in her suitcase.

Anna rolled her eyes and took a seat. "I know you have feelings for Drew, but you have to realize that I care for him too. If, sometime down the road, Drew chooses to be with you, I'm okay with that. But if he chooses me someday to be a part of his life, then I would want you to give me the same respect back without fighting about it." Bella sat down on the bed for a brief moment and looked up at Anna.

"I wasn't aware that you cared for him."

Annas face grimaced. "Bella, how could you not recognize that I had feelings for that man? I was always around him, doing chores for him and Danica, staying up late at night, helping him with that baby of his. How could you not?"

Bella's face wrinkled with lassitude. "You never said anything about loving him."

"Bella, how could I say anything? Janet being her closest friend, it was an infringement on her friendship to Renee. Look at the situation and tell me if it would be right to say anything in the midst of everything that had happened to the poor man."

Bella turned her eyes back at Anna. "You could have said something to me in private."

Anna's face became perplexed by her assumption. "You don't get it, Bella. I didn't ever make plans in the back of my mind if Renee didn't make it I would move in and complete the boy's heart. I accepted the fact that he was married, and that was his life. He loved Renee. It had nothing to do with me. You make it sound like I needed to plan better to have made this work. Love is not a game, Bella, where you get to pick and choose which cards you draw. I made a mistake and fell in love with the big dork, but I'm not willing to sacrifice our whole plan by doing the wrong intentions. And both of us chasing after that broken spirited man can't be the right way to face what is happening now."

Bella's face drained of her natural color. She sat on the edge of her bed and silently cried. "I am sorry, Anna. I have let my weaknesses get the best of me. If we're chosen to be the leaders of a new world, and we start out like this, we'll only start another world off on the wrong foot, and I don't want to do that." She got up and put her arms around Anna.

Anna felt Bella to be sincere, so she didn't continue the discussion with her about their love for the same boy, whose heart has been changed by his circumstances. The girls prepared for their trip before getting ready for bed.

Drew and Randy were packing for the trip too, but something was different about the young man across the room. His best friend since they were small boys was wondering about his condition. He knew Drew was thinking about something that didn't appear to be quite normal. Randy sensed his best friend was holding something inside that he felt possibly ashamed of or embarrassed about and didn't know how to bring the subject up. Randy stop packing for a second as he looked at Drew.

"Dude, what's ailing you? You've been quiet since we've got back to the room."

Drew shot a quick stare back at his lifelong friend. "You don't really want to know."

Randy looked up again. "Actually, I do."

Drew shook his head while rolling his eyes. "The girls… they're starting to fight."

"What do you mean?"

"Bella kissed me a few days ago after you guys left the control deck of the starship."

"She did what?"

"She kissed me … but the worst of it is that… I let it happen."

Randy had a peculiar look on his face. "Do you love Bella?"

Drew had a worried look on his face. "I miss Renee so much. I said something I shouldn't have said the Bella. Well, I meant it in more in a leadership type of way."

"What are you saying, Drew?"

Drew pause before he continued. "I told Bella I loved her back, when I didn't mean it the way she took it."

"What in the world you were thinking?"

"I don't know … she told me she loved me first. I felt obligated in a way to say the same. I don't know. With all that's happened to me in the last two years with Renee and the baby, and my family being gone, I've been an emotional wreck."

Randy shook his head. "Dude, never tell a girl that you love her unless it's something you really mean, especially someone like emotional little Bella Strong. She's so insecure already. This will devastate her when she finds out you were not yourself."

Drew was pacing back and forth before turning. "That's not the worst of it."

Randy turned and looked his best friend in his eyes. "When Anna and I went to get the map, she kissed me too, and the worst thing happened after that." Randy had a puzzled look on his face.

"What happened? I mean… what do you mean?"

Drew was embarrassed to say. "I lost it. I mean after Anna reached up and kissed me too." Drew stopped and looked at his best friend that he had known since the third grade. The look in his eyes said it all. Randy's stare began to read his mind and body language.

"So, what are you saying?"

"I started to get emotional. I don't know why it happened. I just had everything hitting me at the same time."

Randy looked at him with a serious stare. Drew looked back with the wave of emotion slowly coming full circle, yet he pushed it down.

Randy saw the emotion flicker from Drew's face as he reached to put a hand on his shoulder.

Hey, it's something I've been holding for so long. It just hit me."

Randy's face turned serious. He put his arms around his best friend and squeezed him tightly, and then held him at shoulder's length.

"You know, I'm really proud of you. You're only human like the rest of us. Two beautiful girls after you and your worst torture of the evening were to lose your composure. It's okay. Wake up! Anna is the better choice for you than Bella, not that this needs to be something to worry about now. Just take my word for it. Bella is way too sensitive for you. Anna is strong where you aren't, and vice versa. Just ignore both for now, so they don't start any problems while we are facing the fire in the next few weeks. But my choice for you brother, is Anna. She's smarter, quicker in doing the right adjustment, and she won't leave you tussling in the wind. Bella would put her own desires before you, and she won't let up until you're broken. Keep a low profile, and I'll watch your back. Janet would get a kick out of this one."

Drew had a look of panic in his eyes. "You better not tell your girlfriend. I'd die from embarrassment."

"There's nothing to be ashamed of for showing emotion, Drew. You've held all this *in* for the last two years. You needed this, my friend. Can't you see that?" Randy paused to get an answer, but Drew kept that part of his heart unseen.

Randy finished by saying, "I won't tell her for a long time, but someday, it will be a great story to share. But for now, it's our little secret." Randy patted Drew on the back again. "Hey, I didn't really know that Anna had a thing for you?"

"Well, I did. Something happened two years ago, that I never told you about, and everyone kept it a secret, because of Renee being so sensitive, and because of what happened with her. They kind of protected me from anything leaking out."

Randy shook his head. "What's this, confessional night, airing all your demons before the great battle of heaven and hell?"

Drew knew his best friend would support him, yet Randy would still share his opinions, even if not accepted on his terms.

"Well, yes, I guess that's what I am doing. Sometimes I believe that's why it's good to have a best friend, just in case you don't see what's so clear to be quite the way you should see it, we can let the others know and gain a better perspective"

Randy looked at him, surprised. "Drew, I get what you're saying, but I'm surprised you would hold back from me and not tell me something as personal as that. I mean about another girl when Renee was still around."

Drew showed uneasiness in his stare. "Randy, it wasn't like that at all. It was just bad timing, and she was scared of that place."

"Whoa, big boy, start from the beginning. I don't like being left in the dark about dirty little secrets. Besides, these are juicy little morsels that you have left me in the dark about for way too long."

Drew had a vitiated look in his eyes as he stared at his best friend. "I was supposed to bunk up with Tommy the last night in the Smyth's Family Mansion in Bristol England. You know, back in 1891. There were six of us, two in each room. What first started all the confusion was Jake and Angela had already decided to share a room together."

Randy sat on the side of his bed with one leg crossed over the other with a smile on his face like he was hearing wonderful truths that were feeding his grateful soul.

"Please don't look at me like I'm doing you a favor."

Randy laughed. "But you are, my dear boy and blessed friend, these are morsels to my ears. You're the one that's been hiding secrets. I tell you everything about my life with Janet. 'No stone unturned,' those were your words I believe you said so many years ago. Go ahead continue your beautiful little story of glory. I'm all ears."

"Hey, don't be so full of yourself. I'm trying to make amends for myself, and you're exploiting my good deed."

"No, I'm not. I am basking in the unsettling truths that my best friend has finally shown his true colors, and I don't feel so impelled to stew in my own guilt. Just let me enjoy my little moment of pleasure. Your pain will soon depart from you. Continue." Drew wasn't sure how to take his friends daunting attitude but sensed he owed him the pleasure, so he continued.

"The first time I laid eyes on Anna in the library of the student development center back in college, I was struck by her beauty. Renee stomped on my foot for even looking at her… well that was my first mistake with dear Anna. My second was, we slept in the same bed our first night in Bristol, England." Randy covered his mouth as if he was one of the girls, all wide-eyed with pursed lips like he was making fun of the latest gossip.

"Dude, stop making fun of me, or I'll not tell you."

"Oh, you'll tell me all right. You know I won't let this ride until it's all out of your system. Just keep it coming."

Drew shot an unmannered stare at his soon to be ex-roommate. "Anyhow, all the others knew of my predicament and keep it to themselves, the girls included. I'm not sure how I got home alive without Renee ever finding out, but somehow, I did."

Randy's face lit up with a giddy smile. "So, did you guys do it?"

"Do what, you mean have sex? No, we didn't. I was too scared to try, and having a second chance to live again, I figured God would have struck me dead on the spot if I would have tried, plus she ended up in my room by accident."

"What? What accident?"

"I was waiting for Tommy to come in to the room, and instead, three minutes later, Anna comes in and tells me some lame story that Bella wanted to bunk up with Tommy, so there she was all cozy and cuddly looking," Drew said.

"So, what did she do next?" Randy said, with a quirky grin.

"She started getting undressed and was standing in funny looking frilly underwear that came down her knees all cute while staring back at me. Daring me to make a move, I guess?"

"So, what did you do, my sinful boy?" Randy expressed with mouth open, hands, raised with wrist bent back, as if he was one of the girls.

Drew looked at him with a distasteful stare. "Come on, don't do that."

Randy blurted out a little giggle. "Continue your little story of bliss. I'm listening."

Drew shook his head like he got slapped by one of the girls. Whatever…anyhow, to shorten this up, I didn't have the heart to take it any further. I was petrified of her. She was so beautiful. She made me feel like I was going to lose it."

"So, what happened next? Randy was pushing him.

"She walked up to me and put her arms around me and then tried to kiss me."

Randy started laughing.

"Shhhh…quiet, dude. You're going to wake up everyone."

Randy covered his mouth while grabbing a pillow and burying his head into it.

Drew waited for a good minute before looking toward his friend in complete humility.

"I'm not going to finish telling you if you're going to continue to act like a child."

Randy unburied his head and got his composure back before Drew said another word.

"Anyhow, she's holding on to me in the most unprofessional ways." A line of stuttered giggles eludes Randy's mouth while Drew is tries to ignore the continued interruptions.

"She pressed her soft, warm body against me. I knew she wanted to be close. I thought I was in some type of twisted nightmare. My hands were shaking, and my heart was a mess.

I could feel a raging emotion coming up in my throat. She has this way about her that's so attractive. I mean, not just her looks. I don't know why I was so hesitant at first, but I was. When I came to my senses, I pushed her at arm's length without really understanding our connection, being naïve and not paying attention to her body language because I was lost. I told her she needed to be thinking about our mission and not some personal issue, which caused her to back off, and then she went to bed."

"And that was all that happened?" Randy asked.

"No, there's more." Randy rubbed his hands together like he was anticipating more juicy details.

"She woke me up a few hours later and slid in under my covers, then I pulled her close, and we feel asleep." Drew explained.

"That's all that happened after that? I mean you didn't do the dirty deed." Randy asked.

"No, I wouldn't have gotten that far. I kind of sensed that she didn't want that. She just wanted to feel like I cared for her, some instinct, something you can't explain with simple words. It was like she could feel what I was feeling. It was mutual. She was an attraction that tested me, a test I was soon to fail if she'd tried any harder to sway me. I was as vulnerable as much as she was. All I know was that she and I were connected on a different level that I can't explain, almost like we were meant to be together. But because of everything else that happened in my life, it was wrong to even try. Do you get me?"

Randy had settled down to a point where he knew this was the real Drew that was sharing what was inside of him; he was being up front. He was exposing his one weakness, having a love for a girl, who had stood in the background, waiting for the right opportunity to make her feelings known, while yielding her heart as an open book.

"Yeah, I get you. That's why we're friends, and that's why we'll always be friends, because I do get you. Now let's get some sleep and remember what I told you about Anna and Bella, then leave it to fate." Both young men slipped into their beds quickly, turned out the lights and fell into a restful slumber.

9

SACRED GROUND

James walked with beads of sweat covering his face and back. His heart mimicked a thumping he was all too familiar with from crossing the paths of those dark immortals in his dreams. His chest heaved heavy from the ghostly shadows imprinted on his mind… tall, dark, imposing figures, stoically standing, dashed by wind and rain. James turned his head angled toward the clock sitting on the nightstand. He blinked to bring the numbers into focus. It was just past eight. The dream of wind and rain had left behind clear blue skies just beyond the window. The earth and air had been cleansed from the other day, ceded assumptions that all conditions brought about cleansing.

Skittles was gone…not where he had left him from the night before. He could hear a succored humming from an unknown angelic place, as if a quietly sung song gave order to a new day. James felt out of his normal element, far away in a cabin hidden way out beyond the borders of any normal type of living, set in the secluded backwoods of unfamiliarity, with no city traffic lights defunct of meaning, no, mounting moments of street noise blaring from over populated city streets. Only calmness in a clairvoyant type of way was expelled from earlier morning submissions of quiet stirrings. The chirping of birds flew passed the window. James reached to rub his eyes, after pulling himself up out of his nightmarish stupor. He put on pants and shoes, then shirt and jacket, and made for the ladder hanging just below. Someone was already up and moving about in the kitchen. Thaliana kept busy preparing a simple meal of meat and eggs with juice and coffee. The aroma filled in the cabin with drifting memories, practiced and perform from an Indian girl's earlier traditions. James took a deep breath as his stomach growled and his mouth watered. He thought back to the captivating dream. It left an unsettling chill reaching deep within him. James got cleaned up before confronting his soon to be teacher in the kitchen. Within minutes, he was sitting at the table examining a young Indian girl cooking and humming a song that brought the morning along, as she leaned into toward the stove flipping eggs in a skillet. A ponytail showing black shiny hair, tanned curves of a tender neckline, a petite gentleness only shown by a girl of her youth, James swallowed hard and blinked to clear the visual, trying to focus on his conditioning of the future, and not so much on this beautiful flower in front of him. She had tightly fitted deer skin clothing covering her petite frame, showing beauty and grace wrapped in perfect features. She wore the same headband laced with greens and reds with the feather sticking up from the back of its frame.

"Good morning, princess." James, proclaimed, startling her a bit "Smells heavenly."

Thaliana stirred the mystery meat in the skillet, rolled her eyes before looking at his conditions. From where she was standing, he was an underdog. He looked inexperienced, out of shape, misinformed, undertrained, left out of the loop of what to do next. This was her first trainee, and she didn't quite know how to begin. He looked like an ordinary man from her point of view, but also that could be the problem. He had the wrong look on his face, like all men look stultified before figuring out the smartest one in the room was always female. Thaliana turned to look at him again because he had that lost little boy look on his face as if showing what he was thinking and about to say something stupider than anticipated. Thaliana was hoping she was right about all this, giving special gifts to a half-backward old-fashioned young man living on earth, full of mistakes, full of quirky antidotes, and misguided stares. Besides she was one of the heaven's elite, and to her he was just a human with all his awkward ways. A man child looking like he might be after the big chief's job while not even having friends. He was lucky, was all being at the right place at the right time. She might be homed in, doing the right plan for him in the right manner, to giving *in* and showing him the big picture of what was to come. She must put on her good shoes to make the right impression, as her mother used to tell her. The boy couldn't afford to make mistakes under her training. He would shape up, or she'd quickly ship him back where he came from.

Then her eyes met his. "And good morning to you," she said, in passing off a hesitant smile.

Thaliana had prepared enough food for three. The table was set with two plates with simple knives, forks, coffee, mugs, and juice glasses. He pulled the chair out away from the table and sat down. She wasn't sure if he would be the right kind of man to make a suitable partner swishing swords at bad guys who would look like they were wearing grey pajamas with indulged egos, flying about polluting the air, while creating a fuss. Once James was sitting, Thaliana brought over coffee. The arousing scent of special grounds drifted through the air.

He looked at her as if he still couldn't believe that she was really here; she, being sent from a place with realms. What's up with that? Maybe he was still dreaming or maybe experiencing an alternate universe, and he was like Buckaroo Banzai flying across the eighth dimension battling interdimensional aliens called the Red Lectroids from planet 10, as if to play the same movie over and over again. He reached for the coffee mug and sipped while watching this striking Indian girl move methodically about in the kitchen, each movement planned with precision, each preparation detailed so perfectly, and every gesture always in kindness, yet something was missing. She seemed to be well-trained or well-versed on her mission but leaving out details for what was to come, like she would let him know at the right time. She appeared to be more impeccable at each passing minute, but why did he feel like she had been holding something back, and why was she so quiet? James figured she'd been quiet for a reason, a reason that made him feel nervous to the point he started playing with his fork and almost dropped it on the floor. They were stuck with each other, he had figured. You know, trainer and trainee sitting across from each other, nowhere to run. He felt lacking in his manners compared to her facing the fact she was from a realm, for God's sake, and he was born in a town called Hemet. Just saying the name sounded like a stray battered poodle with a hair-lip trying to bark. He thought about how much time he would bury his head in books and now was faced with a beautiful Indian girl showing her talents, but then where did he fit in? The school-crazed youth, had accidentally cut in front of the line just short of the pearly gates, and then some larger- than-life uninformed guard inadvertently sneezed while tapping James on the shoulder to come on in. He then slipped on by, into a world for those of the gifted, like a church mouse who went in unnoticed and ended up with the largest piece of cheese fully exposed. This thought caused James to look down and cover his face. Then he smiled to himself and then laughed a one line "ha," causing the Indian girl to turn her head.

"What's so funny?"

James, caught off-guard, looked up. "Oh… sorry… nothing… you wouldn't appreciate my warped sense of humor, anyhow. That smells delicious," repeating himself, as if trying to change the subject. At least in his own opinion, he had developed a sense of humor. James tried to pursue his own psyche that such a thing wasn't possible, finding a Guardian from heaven's elite here to answer his every beck and call, but was she? He had begun thinking the beautiful Indian girl was only here as a temporary physical presence. He would imagine, since there would be no witnesses, again disappearing at a moment's notice and be gone compared to a computer-animated character in a world of laptops. She was a figment of his imagination, with a lack of appreciation. She couldn't really be real. Come on, who really looks like that? Somehow, she blipped off his computer screen and had become a part of the living, like a magic trick that was too complicated to understand. And once awaken, she would be like that memory. James sat quietly within a moment of peacefulness, a bit bemused by his situation, waiting in wonder about what would come next. He thought for a minute, in this rustic cabin of open-air skies, away from congested cities. James like it here. This was a place he could unwind the knots in his neck, put on his comfortable shoes, watch the smoke rise from the chimney, draw energy from the slowly moving sun, and give in to simple chores of like taking naps. Maybe waking up on the wrong side of the bed as if there would be no price to pay for negligence. Nothing could take away that good feeling of simple moments apart from stress, quickly acknowledged deadlines, and overanxious teachers that pretended to be your friends. It was good to sit for a moment and take in the air without a single care. It caused a smile to grow, as he looked out the front window. He had figured since he was here, he would stay. Nine years of chasing dreams would be forgotten in this serene place of relaxation. James, in the past, had felt to be more of an understudy than he thought others would be, knowing that smart people were usually much harder on themselves, causing sleepless nights, with added age, changes of physical conditions could be typical, to look past the years of substantial flaws in hoping they would disappear. He took the right road with the wrong reasons in mind as he looked forward to spending a little quality time with a father who was now gone. He'd turned down a road not realizing the lapsing of time and did a turn in a different direction, which led to nowhere. Who was he kidding? Not having a clue or plan for why he was here. He wanted to stand up and scream like this might clear his memories and then move on. Maybe his father had only gotten lost, soon to return. His reasons for being from another place and another time were as if his dreams were his real life, and everything else played second fiddle. And as soon as acknowledged, he'd wake up, and everything would start over for another heartless mission to take hold. So, what was he doing here? He was meek and lowly at times, and still young in his prime, but what did he miss? He only wanted to get on with his life. Wouldn't be right to think spending a little time with his father to be an abnormal facade of living, but now, caught in the mix of changing his destiny, and wow, a King from storybook heaven acknowledging him? What was so special about this overspent student and his father? He felt like he woke up from a bad dream and noticed he was orphaned, like all little boys without a home would roam the countryside looking for just one soul of a discontented heart to love them, no connections of a civilized world to conform too, no bed or fireplace to warm up to. He was that little boy.

They were way out in the middle of nowhere according to James, the edge of discontent in space, a place too far from anything considered a normal home, a place where home didn't exist, because this was a place that wasn't suited for the delicate or the innocent. It was a place set past the lines of safety, which was quickly shadowed by darkness when the nights took over, and the gloomy fog rolled in. No witnesses to view those of an immortal kind accept an occasional squirrel or wondering fawn. James was worried. He couldn't quite understand some mystical King leaving all attributes of fate in the care of his hands, especially after being a professional student. His way of thinking might have caused him to slip off the deep end. He had too many overexposed brain cells pushing past the limits of over amplified numbers on a fast track of sleepless nights, and weaknesses, as his mind raced without reason or cause. He was burned out dressed out of context, was one card short of a full deck, last to know, and first to forget. Then figuring out to be a misfit, and then this Indian girl came along. And now, his father was gone, pulling him so far out on the edge of oblivion that he had no knowledge of where he had gone. He was definitely out in the straits of no man's land, like all his natural senses would lead the poor, the blind, and the destitute toward the edge of nothingness. James had been living in a world with his head buried in books, studying ancient artifacts caught by anglers of the deep blue sea, and now he was supposed to be commissioned for something much greater than flipping pages and memorizing quotes of distant scholars who have been dead in the grave for decades. He appeared to be a meager scientist wasting away in a lab, giving *in* to bad dreams of distant thunders that only would strike within the dream, as James sat at the kitchen table, soaking up memories of gloried moments lost from before, after being fed politics and traditions by teachers unknowingly. Had he missed his calling? And this Indian girl expected him to accept everything as fact, like a lamb led to be slaughtered, and yet his whole life has been reared on conditions too bizarre. He hadn't grasped any concept of how to accept plans for what they were, for dealing with issues and problems had not been solved by trusting some distant protector prodding him along. Problems were solved by James's own sense of reasoning, by long hours of critical thinking. He used pragmatic logic and schooled revisions by overzealous zealots with trying positions as all projects measured, all conditions considered an avenue until proven wrong. But this obvious young princess wasn't buying any resistance, as she stood on an imaginary pedestal with softened skin and shiny long black hair, definitive tanned surroundings, wearing clothes of her culture's past. James sensed her fragrance, carpels of flowers with gentle remittance and gingerly moments, with dedicate conditions, as he waited for an eternal bell to ring or give its last toll, so life could advance for those who were willing and move on to a life of the next world, as many elders he'd seen let go of life, to move on to other happenings that showed no evidence of strive. For life has been difficult through years of friction, who was he kidding. James tried to show a hint of acceptance. She wouldn't bend to his lack of reasoning. He would have to wait to see the result to come. Being well schooled had given him a sixth sense about certain areas of concern from a visual perspective, not waiting to be slammed by her mental rejections. Yet her presence was a little misleading. Like all scientist questioning everything unsolvable, James held his questions in reserve for the time being. He turned his head toward Thaliana and repeated a compliment while denying himself his inner feelings.

"Umm… home cooking…"

Thaliana turned to take in the young man with the mischievous glare. From her angle, his hair appeared to be slept on like a rooster splaying his spiny comb. She smiled when thinking it made him look out of order from his usual perky self. She knew the typical male ego couldn't handle any quick judgments of a physical nature, knowing and learning that from having brothers and a father who was compared to a king. Thaliana creased one side of her mouth as she raised her right eyebrow and kept her physical findings at bay. Within her playful mood she smiled. "Yes, it does smell heavenly."

James acknowledged the smile and a sense of playful assumption with a confused look on his face.

"If you're still hungry, there's more," she said. James looked down at his plate trying to push a rounded smile out so he could continue holding her attention.

"Oh, I think this is more than enough for me. Maybe Skittles would like some of the leftovers?"

Skittle's, ears perked up with the sound of his name. The wolfdog got up from the floor and walked slowly over to James while clicking claws on a wooden floor. He nudged this strange man in his presence. James sat a pie pan down on the ground and filled it with meat and eggs. The wolfdog let a slip line of drool from the corner of his mouth, as the long line of saliva dripped to the floor, the careless canines wag of a tail of canine delights, and smiled as only canines do, with open mouth, eyes and teeth shining, with a sense of hunger as his main motivation. Skittles looked back at James with an anticipatory glance. He seemed thankful for his portion of abundance, as food for thought had its traditions but nothing to do with wolfdogs. He then turned his head to look again at the steaming pleasures. One minute later, the pie pan was clean; and the wolfdog showed content, with the dish and a splatter of leftover food around the floor. James reached down and ran his fingers through his fur, a gentle guiding of a tender way, this to be the start of a long friendship that was bound for bonding, in a strange sort of way, for a dog can be led if he's heartily fed to never stray. Then James looked back out the window as if the most important matters to come we're pulling and preparing his heart out past the meadow's edge, like life in the Fastlane was just up ahead.

Thaliana wondered what he was thinking.

Time went by, and the dishes were done, and everything was put away in its proper place. James got up and wandered out onto the porch, remembering the dreams of the night in his vision, wanting to know what caused those nightmares. The visions left vivid memories of sweat and palpitations, minor avoidances, and a pounding in his head. He was too old to be confused, too young to give up the ghost, too smart to be outgunned, for his company was of a heavenly host. He knew these dreams would have their time, but for now, there was a peace in this place, as the sun beaded warm across his arms and face, as the gentle breeze in the morning tickled the back of his neck and the air in his lungs calmed his nerves. He would find the answers to the questions on his mind, and he would know what to ask at the right time and plans unknown would be exposed as they were designed by his host. A trip for the dying. A walk to clear one's head, one breath short of consideration. A long trek up the mountains two steps too far off the edge, as answers go. And the dust would settle, and conditions unsaid would be shared, and the dreams envisioned, as the fog would break, and the sun would rise and the moon would shine in the days to come as the host of yonder looked on.

James closed his eyes and took a deep breath, thinking that the air would help him clear his head. He could start all over. If only the sounds of nature could remain, and the tickle of the scents, and the brightness of the sun, and the coolness of the breeze in the air, he felt alive and living like he had never done before, for the earth and the sky had presented a new way of thinking. This life he was living was about to be given, as Guardians would show him how to be, as long as he would be willing, she would lead in the right direction. His smile brightened up for the glory and honor were forthcoming of a King, like this young princess, following in the footsteps of her teacher. He would be ready to find his way through this maze as quickly as he could, while being the student once again.

Thaliana joined him on the porch. She had a gentle expression that James couldn't read. They sat in the two chairs that accompanied a small table of left-over wood. James and Thaliana turned to look at each other. They smiled but stayed silent. A calm, serene calling, touched the back of James's neck and caused the hair on his arms to prickle, a reminder of a spiritual setting, as if another presence was here in the distance of jetting mountains. The trees moved with a silky breeze pushing through the tops of the branches. Two small birds flew in and drank from a hummingbird feeder hanging from the porch's cover. James could hear water from a river in the distance rushing by. An eagle above had scored her early morning breakfast of ground squirrel. Off in the distance, James could see bright colors of purples and greens, and blues and oranges, lightly covering the slanted landscape, painting a rapturous picture of an Alaska frontier untainted by the world. A paradise of precision, a place pushed back in time, a world surrounding them by earlier cohesions. He averted his stares away from Thaliana. James briefly thought of the gold left in the mine. He turned back to acknowledge her diplomatic stare. He responded to break the silence.

"Is heaven surrounded with beauty like this?" She looked back from her distant stare, one eye closed with a high cheek, trying to block the early morning sun.

"The seventh realm is by far his best creation, and yes, to answer your question, beauty is a part of all days in heaven. It's better than anything ever seen, better than most deserve."

James looked at her squinting from the early morning sun too. They were sharing a mutual band of discomfort. He was curious why she would discount those of the realms.

"Why do you feel such things in heaven are undeserving?"

She looked into his eyes, which crossed a divided line of intelligent thinking.

"Well, because it's all but a gift, not something anyone could actually earn for themselves from service rendered." She held an inquisitive stare as if her cares were a greater precedence than the tenacity showing James a different meaning.

"Gabriel said it's a free will gift with not any attachments to its purpose." James continued to stare at her with one eye open. He knew she was holding something back, maybe from her other life, something unsaid? James tried to reach for an answer.

"So, you don't think the gifts are warranted by your King?"

Thaliana specifically drew focus on James's manipulating words, being one of an educated background and having been tested over and again.

"That's not my place to judge if my King has purpose or not but to just accept the gift for what it is and nothing less."

James was somewhat astonished at her lack of response to the question, but he sensed her eternal reasoning to be different than the thinking of a scientist, who'd based fact before fiction.

She seemed somewhat hesitant by the constant nudging, yet Thaliana still answered.

"You know, comparable to when you work for something here on earth, and it becomes yours, because of your efforts.

That's when it holds more of a value on a personal level, when you had to give your sweat and blood to attain it in the first place.

Now with a gift, it's different."

"How is it different?"

"Well, when it's given to you without cost, it doesn't hold the same value as so many trinkets given to my family and I. Similar to gifts from friends. I didn't have to work for it." Thaliana stared at James with an all-consuming glare. "Yes, I think I understand what you're saying. Like a child given a toy. Most of the time, the toy will not last. It will soon be broken and pushed to the pile of toys that use to be, but if the child had to go out and work for the toy and sweat to earn it by physical or mental effort, then this gift holds a truer value within memory. The toil of one's memory is too hard fought to forget."

"Well, yes, that's exactly what I mean," Thaliana responded.

"Maybe that's why my King requires us to earn our wings in as much to teach us purpose in the effort."

James sensed more than she was telling, as if there was something more personal beneath the surface. She interrupted his train of thought. "Are you ready for your training?"

James's right eyebrow raised in curiosity. "You mean my fight training?"

Thaliana stood up. She looked forward to the meadow. She measured the space with her eyes from left to right as she looked back at this awkward, boyish beginner.

"Yes, that's exactly what I mean. You hold title now. You need to be able to defend yourself." James stood and nodded in understanding, with a bit of nervous tension built up from sitting so long. Nine years to be exact.

With sweaty hands, he said, "Yes, I'm ready, readier than I'll ever be. Should I stay my normal size or become… you know…. the super-duper guy in the super sway."

This caused her to smile. She displayed two rows of perfectly beautiful white teeth that caught him off guard. Thaliana thought him funny and knew his frame of mind would help in difficult situations as all conditions of intelligence start with wisdom learned from moments earned. Hopefully, his ego wouldn't get in the way, one less problem to deal with.

Thaliana pushed out a deep breath of air to get her composure, as training was new to her as much as being a student of war was to him.

"I'm sure your human size would be sufficient, for now," while cupping her hand across her mouth to keep from giggling like a little girl finding that first curious boy in tow with affections.

"Later, I'll show you the simple rules of engagement in more detail, when you've mastered a few moves, and I see improvement." She still expelled a resolute uneasiness as Skittles jumped off the porch to get involved.

Thaliana took a fighting stance with her right hip faced out, one step forward while the left hip position behind. She began to move about in the front meadow with a watchful eye, trying to gear James up for an actual fight. James watched her moves and tried to mimic her changes. She pulled her sword and flashed it about. James took a step back, trying to avoid the direct path of the sword, as she knew, all good teachers speak while training their students.

James began to get this little smirk on his face, from her example, her retaining infinitesimal stature compared to those massive, darken winged creatures of the Fallen, how could she face up to them on her own? But then, she defeated two of them in the tunnels, right? James pondered his distant thought and dropped the smile. He didn't realize he was smiling.

"What's so funny?" Thaliana wrinkled her face in a way that exhibited a teacher's intuition.

"Oh nothing," James reported, "I was just thinking" She interrupted him before he could say something he regretted.

"Follow what my feet are doing without actually looking at them, and move your body as I move so you stay in rhythm with the flow of my body. This is so you remain aware of what's around you, the sounds, what you see, feel, smell, sense, hear and your acknowledgments of intuition. What's behind you or on your sides will become certainly clearer when first noticed, always being conscious of the physical presence, or actions of what's in front or behind, the movement of space between you and those around you are as objects that become a part of the air, a part of the blue of the sky, or the pine scent floating among the trees at the edge of the forest. Each having their part played out, for purpose doesn't stop with the human heart that beats with life but continues with every living thing that takes part of this world. Don't just rely on what you see but acknowledge everything about you. Don't take anything for granted, for what is taken for granted will be the end of you. The soul and mind that's contained in this body lives beyond its natural borders, for what touches the mind and heart borders on the edge of greatness, for greatness comes from a heart that thinks there to be no limits. The creator has placed astounding seeds in a man's soul, causing miracles to unfold. What sustains life is the miracle that also takes it away, wisdom is forged by the bringing together those anomalies not understood. So, life is for the living as death can be for the nongiver who is fruitless, like a tree planted in rich soil does not promise a rich harvest, for the fruit of the tree bears fruit from those strong roots that hold and bring stability and strength where none can be found."

Suddenly, Thaliana lunged forward with the blade while James reacted and took a step back to avoid her thrust. She missed him by inches yet on purpose.

"Yes, that's good," she said. "You feel what I feel. You see what I see, as your movements become a natural way of thinking. Empty your mind of everything, anxiety, thoughts of your past. Take in the air around you, feel the emptiness of the sky, the sounds in the distance. There should be flexibility of space, as distance of space only impairs the mind that wanders."

James got that stupid smirk again, like a clown showing his true colors.

Thaliana stopped her forward progress to ask, "Why the smile?" Thaliana developed a growing frown but understood the boy had quite the imagination. This reminded her of a boy she taught in school up in the cloudless beginnings of Heaven High, who was named Johnny from Golden Avenue. He always caused trouble like it was his middle name. Then she rolled her eyes just before pushing him back.

James blinked, surprised, while breaking a smile past quivering lips. He raised his hands in defense. "Look, I can't help it! Your movements make me laugh. I'm sorry, for what seems to be so clear."

Thaliana looked like she wanted to slap him. "Can't you take this serious... you won't get this if you're not paying attention."

James lost the grin. "Hey, Sister Sanctified, look... I wasn't exactly looking to change my life overnight." Thaliana raised her hand like she would pull him off guard. James shook his head while dancing around her like Mohammad Ali, "Float like a butterfly, sting like a bee."

She raised an eyebrow out of curiosity.

"Sorry," he said, "it's these shorts I'm wearing, and I'm not used to skinny jeans. My wife made me buy them. It's a fad. You know, fat people by skinny jeans to look slimmer, but somehow it doesn't do the trick." James pulled his tethered crease out where the sun doesn't shine."

Thaliana raised both eyebrows then broke out with a smile. You shouldn't be wearing skinny jeans if you're overweight," she said without a filter. "Try covering up. It's more pleasant for the eyes and easier on the stomach."

James got that smirk on his face again. "I'm glad you didn't say fat. I've been in the classroom too long, that's all."

Thaliana considered the overweight man child in the skinny jeans then laughed. "Sorry, it's just kind of funny."

"It's every fat person's nightmare."

"What do you mean? Thaliana said in innocence.

"Well, it's similar to waking up in the middle of the night from getting the shakes and then startling yourself by looking in the mirror and you see some fat guy with a donut in his hand and a cheesecake for a belly roll and then realizing it's just you slamming the carbs."

Thaliana put her hand to her mouth and covered up a smile.

James showed a hesitant grin and said, "I suppose that's heavenly humor for little girls with overrun egos."

Thaliana dropped the smile and smacked him in the chest. "Not funny. I'm not the one who eats jelly donuts, passing myself off as Arnold What's-his-name."

"You know Arnold?"

"Not personally, but wasn't he governor?"

"Yeah, but don't remind me, he helped put the whole country into a recession."

Thaliana smiled hesitantly. "Besides, Arnold What's-his- name, you start to see yourself changing, yet you've been so busy. You forgot to take time out for yourself, until years go by, and then one day you realize you're not the little boy you used to be. Some fat guy in skinny jeans took your place."

James lost the grin, and a serious look took over. "Yeah, how'd you know?"

Thaliana looked at James a little sheepishly. "I know how life works. I didn't spend all my days in the forest swinging from trees like an ape. We do have our moments in heaven."

"What… like at the heavenly celestial ball?"

Thaliana lost her smile quickly. "It's not like that. We have to work on relationships up there just like you do down here. You have this false sense about how heaven works." Thaliana was thrown back a bit. "It's not all parties and celestial marshmallows floating in the skies."

James looked up from the ground like she misinterpreted his thought. "I didn't mean it that way. Our world is ending, and you're trying to compare heaven as a place that has problems that are overwhelming, but nothing compares to the world ending as we know it. Heaven, I'm sure is nothing like earth."

Thaliana batted her eyes as if she was trying to bring herself back to reality. "Do you want to learn to fight or what?"

James's face turned back to the center of the meadows. "Yes, I'm sorry. I didn't mean to throw you for a loop."

"No, it's okay. We don't have much time left. We're on a schedule."

James's face turned serious. He moved as she moved, side to side, one step at a time, focused on her moves. Then James did one of those Bruce Lee moves. With his mouth open, he added a little acting with sound effects. Thaliana had no idea who Bruce Lee was and was somewhat shocked by this distraction. James pretended to go left and instead went right and almost knocked Thaliana off her feet. She developed an unnatural smile.

"Is there some skill you forgot to tell me about?"

"That's what Bruce Lee would do when surrounded by his enemy".

Thaliana smiled before saying, "Actually, that would be an excellent form, if you could forget that this is not a game. That form gives you more mobility and awareness of what's around you. I like this man called Bruce Lee. He has a style not seen before by the seventh realm."

James developed a grin as if to impress his recent thirteen- year-old girlfriend from middle school. "I guess you've never seen any old Bruce Lee movies, have you?"

Thaliana looked a little confused. "This Bruce Lee is famous from your days?"

"How could you know about Arnold What's-his-name, but nothing about Bruce Lee."

Thaliana stopped to consider James's statement. "We're made to watch politics of earth so we learn from your mistakes, but we're not allowed to watch old movies."

"That doesn't sound fair. I think you could learn more from old movies than politics. No wonder you guys are having problems up there. Maybe heaven could use a new entertainment director so your creativity get stirred up a bit."

"You think so?"

"Yes, I do. Who's running the programs up there anyways? Some old guy with bad teeth and a tainted image? Maybe someone needs to pull the rug out from under him, and tell him he needs Jesus."

"Now you've got jokes. Don't think the big guy in the sky would let that one go."

"Whatever. Take it easy, princess. Your horns are pushin' the halo too high."

An arcane glint cross Thaliana's eye. "Let's get back to what we were doing… before I change my mind."

"After you, princess, I'm all ears."

"You look to be a little more than that. We all start somewhere, don't we?" A flint of impatience showed on her face. James, without waiting, whipped around to gain some momentum and possibly an upper hand.

"So, who is this famous Bruce Lee, which seems to have you so spellbound?"

"He was the kung fu master of his time, but he's not around anymore to learn from, just his old movies he did years ago."

"Do you have the movies of this master of kung fu?"

"No, but they play them all the time on TNT or the classic movie channel".

Thaliana wasn't quite sure of his meaning. "Is he your ancestry of the past?"

James began to lose her from his exerts of all movies. "No, I'm not even Chinese."

Thaliana was completely confused by now.

James rolled his eyes. "I'll just show you some of the moves, and you tell me how to make the best of it." James shook his hands at his side and cracked his neck left then right. Thaliana wondered what he was up to.

She watched him as he did several turns with one leg half bent up into the air like a grasshopper ready to pop off one leg. Arms spread out in front with fingers swishing around as a distraction, turning his head side to side, showing his limited mastery of what he'd remembered from his youth. Even though winded, James did his best Bruce Lee impression. He added a little high-pitch Kwan as he moved to the beat of kung fu original. He struck high with his foot into a complete roundhouse with his right leg, using a high pitch kuaa sound. Thaliana moved back and fell to the ground surprised, by the graceful quick snap of his right leg.

A bit startled, Thaliana responds, "Okay, so you've got skills. You should learn his ways. I think they'll work."

James passed off a quirky acknowledgment, like he had a game, and rubbed his knuckles against his chest in mock protest of getting along. Thaliana looked at him in a bizarre sort of way. This man child was getting on her nerves.

"So, you think this Bruce Lee's kung fu would be good to use? James showed a slight glaze of wonder crossing his eyes not quite sure of her judgments as he placed his hands on his hips like he carried this stunt too far.

"I don't know. I've never tried to use these skills before." Thaliana sensed James was only acting and not really believing he could even begin to use difficult skills on an open battle field. She was sensing him to be a bit timid. Giving him further instruction was a must.

"You should try your heavenly form. If you think of this Bruce Lee art as a natural part of yourself, you might find success. Your skills, given of a King, will enhance your memories, enhancing battle skills, giving confidence where there is none. This will help you see a clearer picture of personal limits."

James developed that quirky grin again. "What, like a gambit from a comic strip?"

Thaliana had a serious look about her. "No, like Bruce Lee, except you have your gifts given in your title. Immortal powers magnify earthly training. Lacobus, Guardian of the Alaska Coast."

James liked the name given but wondered about this Indian girl commissioned by a king.

"What, do you mean. I'll be like Bruce Lee?"

"Well sort of, yet smoother, better conditioned with that immortal strength. You can't really perceive this from a human perspective. You will develop into what you need to be at the right moment. Trust me."

James shrugged his shoulders wondering what he'd gotten himself into, still somewhat hesitant. He bent forward with his arms crossed and closed his eyes. Faith had never been his strong side. Even though he had his moments of shine, what he felt inside wasn't to be one of those glorious moments. His father gone now, had taken his confidence away for the moment, and understanding still to be that fat guy pictured, so often reflected. Doing as he was told, James thought of being that heavenly creature incurred by divine intervention, and his body responded.

Might and glory and literal euphoria brightened the skies.

Skittles began to bark running back-and-forth, nipping at James's heels.

"Cut it out, you little flee, or I'll squash you like a bug!"

This caused Thaliana to laugh. Skittles was insistent about James the immortal making him his Honorite. Thaliana looked up at James with a bit of mental prodding.

"He's waiting for you. Turn him into your Honorite. I believe that's why he's nipping at your heels for."

James looked down at his adopted companion then shouts, "Honorite!" His booming voice echoed off the mountain. Skittles immediately transformed into this monstrous beast with wings, and sharpened talons, almost four times his original size. This creature's eyes glowed with a light blue-gray. His fur, a pure white coat, was visually transformed. His paws fettered brass, casting against transparent light. He had a thick body malefic of purpose as if this creature had the acuity of his position done, one from the realms. His teeth were jagged with hooked-like incisors set to tear tender flesh in a malevolent manner. James reached over and put his hand on top of the wolfdogs head. His wings stuck out with vehement pronouncement.

"All right, my good friend, show me what you've got."

Skittles, now Honorite, left the ground without a moment's notice, took to the sky with two flaps of his amenable wings. He reached the uttermost edge of the trees within a few moments. From earthly to heavenly form, he serrated the tops of the trees as wind rushed by. This beast of the air surveyed the plane before him, spread out in all directions as this view sated something deep within him. Not so much pride, but an elusive awareness that he would play his part in the battle to come.

No depth or height or greater warrior would keep him from doing what he came to do. Ahead, this Alaska coastline brought a revivifying feeling that pumped blood through his veins, brought his mind to drink in this wonder. For who could command the skies above to give such beast perceptiveness of a world above, as a ship sail tempered to a storm as it rises from bow to stern from swells untamed. He was free spirited soaring toward the heavens. He raised his voice to the mountain top; an ululation of celebration rumbled in this valley like a crack of lightning to scourge the earth below. He was a heavenly force displaying an immortal presence. A heart of exuberance was James's impression. He would be a Guardian of an elite set of angels soon, allowed to build his confidence. Thaliana's face flushed with color. James scored his wings and shot straight up to meet his Honorite above. It took his breath away.

Thaliana joined them by a few quick movements of her own. James felt a rush of wind pull past him. Thaliana took the lead. She did three difficult flips midair. James couldn't even imagine how fast she was going. She was a blur. She reversed course daring her new students to follow after, as she flew to the coast, she hit the water without a moment's notice. James and his Honorite quickly followed her into the depths of the deep with no fear of the unknown. They moved as a unit, timed through agility in the comfort of cooling liquid. Thaliana was a light in the deep as she led with purpose. The waters were full of life, as the abundance of fish were schooled in the current like notes written on inked pages in the rhythm of frenetic beats as the world below struck in a harmonic flow. They had developed an equality of vision, for the conviviality of life gave passage to the three. Their wings stayed dry as they took to the sky, never skipping a beat. Thaliana turned on her shoulder to smile and take in her two recruits scoring a path behind her. Guardians flying at the end of the world counting the seconds ticking on an eternal clock as the impunity of the three was about to unfold. Warrior princess, Honorite, and Guardian of the Alaskan borders held in the silence of this world unknown. James, Thaliana, and Skittles, ordinary names of Guardians, protectors of a Circle, ready and set to fight for the right to live. James flew back to the porch of the woodsy cabin, bringing his wings in. His Honorite stood on his right side taking in the beauty of the valley in a determinate fashion. Those of an elite class of immortals stood for the human race that was set for annihilation, for the right to come were held as mystery.

"So, when will we meet this secretive Circle?"

Thaliana turned her eyes toward James, showing a glint of concern. "Soon, they should be here sometime today."

10

THE GATHERING

A nna was one of the first to slide out of bed when the sun brought the first light into the bedroom from the second-floor window. She dressed and was downstairs before anyone else made it to breakfast, well except Dr. Zimmerman, who was already reading an old morning paper that had yellowed with time while drinking his coffee. He looked up over the rim of his reading glasses, with a tenderly shaded smile breaking across his lips.

"Good morning, young lady. I hope you slept well. Are you ready for breakfast?"

Anna looked at the professor and then responded to his morning greeting. "Good morning, sir. I'm not quite awake yet." Dr. Zimmerman set his newspaper down while ringing a silver bell.

"I am okay, professor. I can help myself in the kitchen. I prefer to get my own breakfast. Thank you. If you don't mind." Anna turned and made her way into the kitchen. Dr. Zimmerman waved off his female servant, as Anna began reaching for cereal and coffee. She added two lumps of sugar, a tad of cream to the coffee, and then poured milk over the cereal. She then made her way back into the dining area and took a seat. Anna closed her eyes for a brief moment, like she was saying a prayer. She looked up at the professor, pondered a bleak smile. She sat staring off in the distance as she sipped her coffee. Anna reached over the center of the table to add another lump of sugar to her heated comfort of caffeine. Dr. Zimmerman was watching every little move of how Anna was to eat her breakfast. He considered her still numb from the happenings of her family, tossed to the wind as if they had never existed. He felt for her. Dr. Zimmerman thought at one time he would see tears from the dear girl's eyes, yet something was missing, something detrimental was holding all the pieces together. She was apparently a dry water well. No tears. He assumed she was trying to hold herself together, for being of this Circle. If damaged, they'd all become unglued. He thought to cheer her up. If only he could light a fire under her, in an intelligent sort of way. Give her reason to go on, even though, those once loved were gone. She needed purpose in her life again, to swing the pendulum another direction, away from her fragile heart. With the curious acknowledgment, he stepped forward with words from those bits of wisdom accessed from memory.

"So, young lady, tell me about Orbitus. What is this new world like?" Anna chewed slowly before answering.

She looked up with a bit of sadness. "It's quite beautiful but lonely. It's too secluded from its people." Another pause. "I miss being in school." Anna went back to drinking her coffee and eating her cereal. She, with her short black hair, and a willful attitude, looked quite stunning. Dr. Zimmerman wanted the dear a girl to snap out of it. This in advertent melancholy was concerning him. She had stayed dressed in simple blue jeans and her favorite Van Halen T-shirt. He assumed she didn't want to face her old life again as those that were close to her were gone— too many memories of her father, mother, and little brother. From what he could tell, she still had the same face with familiar big brown eyes, soft supple features, sensible and bright. He had remembered her two years before. He had spent many an hour with her in deep conversation, conditions of common interest. She would listen to his opinions about almost anything. At times she showed no concern with the lackluster quality in character like her dreams would take her places. He knew there was something special about her. Her focus remained unattached as the professor continued his questioning. With age, she seemed to be more defined in how she moved her lips, how she formed her words, the way she moved her eyes. Her silence reflected intelligence. Through the last few years, she learned true grace was something hard to come by, for real beauty was something created from the inside. Concern was written in her eyes with the smallest of details. She appeared to have a softer approach on requirements of the heart.

Dr. Zimmerman didn't want to appear too pushy. "Are you doing, okay? I mean… in this new world?"

Anna looked up from her cereal bowl but not directly at him. "Yes, I'm okay."

Dr. Zimmerman reflected an infinitesimal glint of intelligent thinking. "So, explain this new world of yours."

Anna glanced up and broke off her stare from distant concerns and looked at him. She hesitated as a twinge of uneasiness filtered through her mind. "Orbitus is beautiful, like earth. Yet it has many dangers that we knew nothing of, until we had been there awhile. We have our own little neighborhood with in the city surrounded by the barrier from above… you know to keep things out. The Aquerae have set us up with our own community to live in, separate from their own. They're different. We do have our time with them, but most of them have higher training and are smarter than us. They're teachers, scientists, and families from, a place like earth, yet the way they explained where they're from, is nothing like Orbitus. There's this invisible barrier that completes our city, something like a dome, twenty-one square miles are our limits of space—well, I mean we can't go outside the city's borders unless accompanied by the Aquarae. Yet air and sunlight have no problem getting through." She paused and looked up again. "Since Renee was killed, they've taken stronger precautions. The skies are always changing. The colors are different from earth, vivid and drawing. Orbitus has shorter days, shorter seasons. The red dwarf star is not as bright as earth's sun. The air has a different feel to it, thicker, cleaner. We are stronger than we used to be. The planet has healing elements in its soils. Orbitus, in their language, means healing planet. No need for medications, except when wounded. Of course, we have the healing stones. Our bodies feel strange, not like before." Dr. Zimmerman raised an eyebrow.

"We can retain more mentally. Our minds work more efficiently. Our city was built at a higher level, above the cliffs tucked away between two mountain passes. It protects us from the strong winds from the north. The best part of living there is the water, so clear and clean, chaos and beauty all mixed in one. The oceans waters are unsafe to swim in, and currents are too strong. We're inferior in many ways to the Aquerian fellowship." Anna was hesitant about going on. "I don't always feel like we fit in there. It feels to be a place before our time."

Dr. Zimmerman's eyes fluttered to break the glassy stare from his vision. He looked over at Anna.

She met his eyes. "Do you think, maybe I'm not looking at this new place in the right way?"

Dr. Zimmerman chuckled transparently while his eyes lit up. "Young lady, change is the hardest to deal with, in adjusting there's no limits except what we put on ourselves. Most likely, you're missing people that were left behind." A bit of discernment crossed her eyes.

"No, sir, it is more than just that. I don't feel complete there. We have no history there. Our history is what makes me feel like I had a place in the world, but there you don't feel that. It's almost like living in a stranger's home. You know it's temporary, only for a while. My heart doesn't feel complete."

Dr. Zimmerman developed a puzzled look in his eyes while trying to understand her unsettling account, "And you feel that way because?"

Anna looked further into Dr. Zimmerman's eyes. "Well, after Renee passed on; everything began to change. I thought I could be of service to Drew and his little family. You know, they could have their place in my life, if only…" Anna couldn't finish her statement without giving herself away.

Dr. Zimmerman began to see in her manner and her voice her hidden meaning. A slight touch of reality touched the corner of Dr. Zimmerman's mouth. "I think you might have attachments to this little family?" Dr. Zimmerman assumed the obvious. "You love them?"

Anna was bewildered that Dr. Zimmerman would be so to the point on his meaning. She wasn't quite sure if she should say what she was feeling, yet her heart was set to break if she didn't. She looked around the room to make sure they were still alone. "Well, I guess that's rightly so. Maybe I do love them. That baby is so precious, and Drew is such a good father. He has a wonderful heart. He's the type of man that's easy to love."

Dr. Zimmerman chuckled. "Don't overdo it, my dear girl. He's just a boy."

Anna's eyes flickered with a touch of hope. "I wish he knew there was another way, if he could only...."

Dr. Zimmerman finished her thought. "Only what? Love you back?"

Anna looked at the professor, surprised to hear the words from his mouth. Suddenly, the dining room doors flew open, and Bella, Drew, Randy, Toby and Tommy made their presence known. Drew still looked half asleep. Bella had a scowl on her face. She displayed an air of discomfort. She was obviously upset about something said, as that scowl widened, she turned her eyes toward Drew. He tried to put distance between them. Bella's eyes remained unblinking. Drew showed anxiety in his every move. He remained quiet as he looked over to his best friend for moral support. Randy had a cheerful smile on his face, prepared for a new day. He was the first to speak with a jovial greeting, looking again at Dr. Zimmerman.

"A happy and joyous morning to you, sir. You look marvelous this fine day." Randy, for a moment, looked like he was going to jump in the air and do a shoulder bump with Dr. Zimmerman. The professor's bottom lip quivered with nervous tension. He appeared to be an overzealous youth.

"And a good morning to you as well, my fine gentlemen. Are you ready for this trip to Alaska?"

"Indeed fine, sir, indeed I am." Randy rubbed his two hands together like the true Irishman he was, as if he were coming in and out of the cold. "What's on the menu for this morning?" Randy's building temerity seemed to catch everyone off guard.

Bella didn't see the connection of gaiety from the irritating barrel shaped sloth. With her nose twisting in the air, she continued her informal of pugnacity. The pouty look was obvious. Randy saw Bella shooting her angered glare toward Drew. He then remarked in Drew's defense.

"What's wrong, Bella? Can't let things go, you act like this was all Drew's fault." Randy expelled a bit of resentment toward the girl. Bella's lack of camaraderie didn't fit the current conditions. Without a response, Randy continued his taunting.

"So…. are you letting this go…or what?"

Bella shot a heated stare at the emotional boy with his dukes up." Of course, you would say that. You're his partner in crime. You two need to be horsewhipped and left to bleed out! I hate you two for being so cruel!"

Drew looked up at Bella with the sad eyes. "Bella, I'm sorry. I didn't mean for this to turn out the way it did. You misunderstood. I meant the Circle is loved by us all. I didn't mean it in the way you took it."

Anna's interest perked. She was quite interested in what she had missed down the hall. She looked with concerning stares toward the boy misconstrued. She was curious what caused this tussle between the two Circle members of secrecies. Maybe there was a little hope for her after all?

"Just shut up, Drew. You're not the person I thought you were. You have a jaded heart."

Dr. Zimmerman's twisted face of wrinkles turned curious. "By God, dear girl, what are you saying? Is everything all right?"

Bella whipped her head around toward Dr. Zimmerman with the continue scowl. "Everything is fine and dandy, professor. Little boys who think they're men, they never know what they want. I'm through with them, especially the likes of those two." Her glare continued to cut a hole as her jaded pair of consorters only looked on. Randy returned the stare.

"Just let it go, Bella. He doesn't owe you an explanation. You started this mess. Drew only wanted you to feel a part of the Circle."

"And a fine job he did," she said, as her eyes reflected implacable measures. Bella, brought the attention of everyone, and the room was beating with life from the living as each member was watching every move that she made. Water splashed on the back of her eyes. To keep from crying in front of everyone, she got up and ran from the room. Anna turned to get up and chase after her, yet Randy stopped her with his words.

"I wouldn't do that if I were you. She's mad because Drew likes you more than her, and she doesn't know how to deal with it."

Anna turned her eyes to their fearless leader. "What did you say to her, Drew?"

Drew looked a little disconnected. "I-I told her that I loved her, but only after she told me. I didn't mean it that way it came out. I meant I love all you guys. You're like family to me. She surprised me with a kiss a few days back. She caught me off-guard. What would you do if someone was staring you down and expected a return answer? She's relentless with the emotions. She doesn't know when to quit. I'm sorry. She takes everything like it's the end of her world. I never gave her a reason to believe that our internal connections were more than the commitment of this Circle of members."

Anna looked at Drew with piercing eyes. "Do you love me like the others too?"

Drew sensed the women's reasoning had to get up and flown out the door. He hung his head and sat back down. He was caught. Anna showed disappointment in her eyes as Drew continued.

"I didn't mean to hurt her. She's the one that came to me, you know? I've not led either of you, girls in showing any type of interest, after Renee... I mean it didn't seem real that she died so suddenly. I wasn't prepared. Who would be?"

Anna's eyes continued to stare, unblinking. She knew he was right. His heart has been in the right place all along, yet both young ladies were looking past his heart's conditions wanting to be closer. Drew wasn't sure about anything. His feelings were still connected to Renee. Anna heard the sentiment in his voice. You could have heard a pin drop in the room.

Drew tried to explain loss without giving too much away. "My daughter needs her mother. There's this big hole in my heart... You know, I loved Renee, but now she's gone...I can't get her back." A tear rolled off Anna's cheek. She wiped it back. Drew looked nervous, but everyone in the room sensed the connection between the two for quite some time." I didn't know what to do. I know my daughter is precious, in a way I'll never understand fully."

The whole room was full of a sense of emotion.

"My daughter was a miracle baby. If my heart had been better prepared..." Anna could hardly hold her emotions back as she looked across the table. She saw that Drew's eyes looked a bit misty.

Anna finally spoke as she saw all members turned to look at her. "You're right, Drew. You deserve this time to heal and become a whole person again, but we all have felt your pain. I guess what I'm saying is, we all need time to adjust. Change of circumstance is always the hardest to bear. I mean we're only human. There's nothing to keep us from expressing emotions. It's part of living. It's a way of life."

Drew saw the stare in Anna's eyes. It left him wanting. Their stare toward each other became stronger as each second went by. Drew knew she was avoiding what she really wanted to say. His face become flushed with anxiety, a kiss in the dark, the pounding of hearts. She only wanted him to understand her heart, but he had to be the biggest Dork at times.

Randy saves the day. "Anna, the boy loves you. Couldn't you tell last night in the closest?"

Everyone laughed. Drew could feel a heated face, a quirky tightness of knots in his stomach. Anna across the table felt the same. Her stare was eternal as she looked up into his eyes.

Randy huffed out a sigh of discontented air. "Oh my God, Drew, just tell her…"

Drew tried to cover both his and Anna's embarrassment. "Dude, you said you wouldn't say anything."

Randy's face lit up like a shiny Christmas ornament. "I'm sure, she's okay with this," Randy said. He turned his attentions toward the girl with obvious emotions emanating off her face. She waited for Drew to answer this one hanging question in the back of her mind. Randy continued, "I'm sure she would appreciate you being up front with her. It would save a lot of time. If the boy loves you, would you want him to tell you?"

Anna had a small amount of hope glittering in her eyes. She looked back at Drew for a brief moment, wondering about his intentions. She then past a wistful stare back at Randy.

"Oh poo, you big lug, he doesn't need to say anything. I'm not expecting him to, just leave it be." Anna showed a bit of embarrassment for this acted out rendition of a bad situation.

Drew caught the look of her hurtful stare. He knew he had to respond.

"Anna, I do. I mean…Randy is…"

Dr. Zimmerman glared at the couple with frustration in his eyes while listening to this whole masquerade. The professor blurted out, "Just spit it out, my dear boy. It's the right thing to do."

Everyone laughed. This bewildering outburst, Drew had to say something. Stumbling over his words, he choked out.

"Yes, I do… I mean, I think of you… I mean I care for you, and not like a sister or a friend."

Randy interrupted him. "Dude, please grow a pair."

Drew took a deep breath. "Well, yes, I do love you, Anna." Anna showed a pouty frown, and then it turned upside down.

"Don't be so glum. It's not a crime to love someone, you know."

Everyone laughed.

Dr. Zimmerman began to coach the pair. "So, what's your answer, dear girl?"

Anna was surprised that everyone was taking their part in this debacle, like they were auctioning off cattle. She turned her stare toward the professor. "Isn't there anything sacred about privacy anymore?"

Dr. Zimmerman chuckled. "My dear sweet girl, if you love the boy, let him know for God's sake so we can all rest easy and get on with our lives. I don't have much time left in this world, you know?"

Most everyone laughed again at the expense of the soon to be couple, even Randy. Anna knew the boy had to get past this point of shaky conditions and share his heart, even at the expense of being embarrassed. Face it. They were family that was held to no secrets. But somehow, she knew in her heart she wouldn't let him off so easy. She wanted a verbal sign of his eternal commitments, in front of everyone. This was a defining moment for both of them, and Anna thought to give him a push.

"Well, he is somewhat of an awkward boy, but yes, I guess I do love him." Everyone turned to look at Drew waiting for his input. The others goaded their support by jarring claps and intermediate whistles. Anna thought they were all taking part in a sporting events. She tried not to elude the feeling of Drew's lack of commitment to her eternal conditions.

A nervous stage they had to overcome together. Vivid memories of the closet came haunting back to the boy who'd let it be known physically of his heartfelt intentions, and then a smile broke from Randy's face.

Anna showed a growing smile, even though she hasn't totally accepted Drew's true intentions. She stood to leave the room, when the boy kept his words silent. Then suddenly, Drew stood to stop her. As Anna began to walk past the tall thin lad, he quickly grabbed her, as a gentle hand swung her arm about. He reached to kiss her as Anna held a penetrating stare. Even though the embarrassment hadn't left her, she melted into his arms.

Jim Carson walked in on the kiss, a bit startled, showing a big rusty grin. He replied, "Do I get one too?" which set of another chain of misguided laughs. He pushed his card timing to draw further attentions. He reached over and tried to kiss Tommy on top of the head. Tommy swatted at him like a big pesky fly.

Anna reached up and ran her fingers through Drew's hair. "I've always loved you, you big dork. You were just too blind to see it."

Giggles and smiles accompanied them while Dr. Zimmerman pointed everyone toward the issues at hand. They spoke about what was to come. They spoke about the dangers they might face and their keen sense of looking out for each other at any cost. What worried the professor the most was when they had to face the heat of battle staring them in the face around the next corner? They all had to do their part, Jim Carson, with his gift of controlling the movement of physical objects. Randy had the ability of bringing fear to the minds of his enemy, affecting the memory part of one's thoughts. Drew could move in and out of hidden doors between distance and space. Tommy and Toby had their gifts of telekinesis. Dr. Zimmerman had his ways of seeing their future, like Bella, and a few capricious moments never shared with the others before.

Anna's only talent was seeing situations as they really were, on the inside. Past the lines of her internal commitments, she saw the potential of each individual place. This intuition she expelled was beyond the norm of each Circle member. Matters that could be revealed to her where others had missed, something that the others couldn't get past was her way of seeing the bizarre or weird, underneath cover. But to her, she felt it gave her the upper hand when it came to seeing people for what they really were, on the inside. Maybe that's why she had taken a liking to Drew so quickly and maybe why she felt saving the history of earth was so important. She had finally been given a chance to experience love for the first time in her life, with the help of Drew's closest friend and the taunting of the others. Drew glanced over at Anna without saying a word and took her hand, warm fingers of comfort, and tender moments she wanted to understand. The loss of Renee left an eternal scar upon the young boy's heart, yet Anna was there to fill in the gap to bring healing to the boy with a difficult past. This was her way of helping and doing her part. They had a mutual giddy smile covering their faces. They walked out on the back patio for a moment of privacy. Buckingham Estates was the perfect diversion from misguided emotions and moments of confusion. Drew reached for another kiss. Anna was lost in the moment. Hoping, wishing, for the best. Her heart felt complete at the moment. In a time of destruction, and heavenly secrets, they found love because of an endearing friend and the misguided words and wishes of others. This was a special Circle of friends and family who would join to support their leader, and this new love of his life. Drew placed his arms around Anna. She brushed the hair away from her eyes. She looked at him piercingly. A smile broke across her face. She was his, and he was hers, and they tenderly considered their time together as something needed. For love… this incomplete emotion tied them together as far as love goes. No place or person or special needs group was going to take away what had been destined. Drew pulled Anna close to him. Anna's right hand was wrapped behind Drew's neck, as she leaned in for another kiss. Her joy filled the gaps left behind from losing members. It was like glue that sealed their hearts together. This was their time of sharing, moments of love, and a time of eternal commitments.

11

HEAVEN'S ELITE

When the plane landed in Skagway, they were excited to find out what was so pressing in the land of Alaska, such a vast wilderness that had become the focus of great importance. Anna had fallen asleep on Drew's shoulder, and Bella remained at the back of the plane with Dr. Zimmerman. Tommy sat behind Bella trying to console her saddened disposition. Randy and Jim Carson sat up from across the row with Drew and Anna. And Toby sat by himself, yet every once in a while, he'd look back to check on Bella's condition. She saw his looks from time to time, from childhood interest, he was still watching after her.

It was time to depart the plane as they slowly shuffled to a shuttle that would take them to a rental agency, where Dr. Zimmerman rented two Suburban's from the earlier night. The drive through the mountain roads were somewhat of a challenge. The area to come had the worst of weather, as they were soon to deal with the constant muddy summer rains. It was seven o'clock in the morning as they started on the drive. Anna had never seen mountains more beautiful passed gloriously in the background. They had lost a day, one flight cancelled, taking a red eye that next early morning. A night spent in a shabby hotel in Seattle. Before she knew it, Anna was lest stiff with a few bags under her eyes, unfamiliar beds, and constant noise. She didn't sleep much the night before. She hadn't adjusted to traveling so abruptly, and understanding the comforts of life can quickly be stolen. Orbitus was lonely, yet the frequent peacefulness was a comfort to her soul. Traveling from place to place was draining. Before she knew it, they were on another plane, the third to be exact as she looked out the window and saw endless trees below them. Skagway was nothing like Seattle or Buckingham Estates back in Ohio, and Skagway was more like the planet they would be living on.

Blinking back to reality, Anna's mind moved forward. She rolled in the first Suburban in the company of Drew, Randy, Jim, and Torack with his Aquerian soldiers. Bella had visions of Thaliana and James for the last couple of days, wondering if this was all just a dream. Bella had made a direct connection with the Indian princess. A conceptual meeting to come. This unrealistic gathering might fall apart before all was said and done.

Jim drove the Suburban up front, and Tommy drove the second from behind. Torack brought three of his best soldiers along for the trip. Three of his captains stayed behind with the starship to keep the ship ready for a quick departure. Anna looked over her shoulder at these strange-looking beings who appeared to be misunderstood. They had striated cat eyes with revivifying creepiness. Torack sensed Anna's look but only smiled. She got the jest of his stare and turned her head back around, hoping he hadn't read her mind.

Looking ahead, she saw the early morning light give way to a cerulean sky after rain. Anna saw a beautiful open field sprinkled with a rainbow of colors. She had her window down and could smell a smoky wood rising up in the air. They had to be close.

Shortly, both parties would meet face-to-face, getting to know one another, finding out what each member of this Circle had to do. Anna was a little nervous about meeting angels from heaven. Maybe this Indian princess might have picked the wrong group of people for the job, bearing in mind, this dysfunctional group of young adults were not always up to par, or might not meet the standards for those of heaven, for they were full of inconsistencies. Most of the Circle members had never seen Alaska before, with the many acres of timbered land, and back roads that twisted and turned for endless miles. There weren't too many paved roads out in this wilderness; mostly dirt roads or fire roads went on forever. Alaska had over thousand lakes and ten thousand rivers and over twelve active volcanoes. This seemed to replicate Orbitus to a tee. Several brown bears had quickly crossed the road with two cubs followed after by a concerned mother. Jim Carson hit his brakes hard and swerved to keep from hitting the unannounced family. The second Suburban in the rear saw the bears and made adjustments. Around the last bend in the road, the first black Suburban's members saw the smoky cabin two hundred yards away. James was standing on the porch checking his gear while he noticed they had company. At the bottom of the meadow, the two Suburban's drove through muddied puddles of potholed terrain. Splashes of mud and crud and bumpy conditions caused a terrible ride for all of them. The noise caused Skittles' ears to perk up. James sat his gear down that he had been cleaning, and Skittles jump off the porch to check-out their latest arrivals. James, from earlier, set up four uniquely made military beds in the basement and remembered that the loft upstairs would sleep four, and the bedroom downstairs would sleep two. Both Suburban's began to unload passengers while James greeted them with water and sandwiches. Dr. Zimmerman was more chipper than usual. He was always at his usual best. With a flicker of excitement, he stuck out his chest. He tipped his hat in usual fashion to greet their host. James looked down and smiled but confused about his manner of dress. Top coat and hat seemed a bit strange. Obviously, the doctor was born in the wrong century. He raised his cane in James's general direction. Looking up at the cabin, Dr. Zimmerman liked the homey feel of craftsmanship. He knew the log cabin was built by the gentle hands of a man who had spent a lifetime perfecting his craft, through hard work and sensibilities. He could tell this place was marked for success. It stood out like an American flag standing for justice. This inimitable backcountry caused the professor to feel rapt. It was time to break out his pipe and kick off his shoes, and maybe air out a few days of walking. He wouldn't mind sticking around for a while and getting a few days of rest.

Oddly, James appeared to stare when he saw Torack and the Aquerian soldiers get out of the Suburban. It was a time when all of them would get acquainted with each other, with no actual communication between them from the past, only visions seen by Bella and Torack and the Indian princess. Being there were no phones out in this no man's land, they depended on the visions carefully placed. While walking up the stairs, Drew got nudged by the wolfdog taking up space. He looked down and saw the wag of a tail, a friendly gesture of kindness. He reached down and ran his fingers through his fur just past his ears. He would remember his days with his sheep dog, Captain Jack, a few years back. This reminded him of his missing company. He always laid at the foot of the bed while soaking up memories. Drew got a lick of appreciation and a wag of a wolfdog's tail. Skittles wasn't sure about this Aquerian fellowship coming up the steps. They appeared to be a bit odd to him, as Skittles sniffed at the air, making sure they weren't apart of some hunters' missed opportunity. He barked and looked back up at James. Torack hesitated to walk up the stairs.

James's nostrils flared while pushing out a grin. "He thinks you're closely related to fish. "Skittles licked his lips and whined.

James broke out with a smile. "Don't mind him. He already had breakfast." Everyone laughed except the Aquerian leader. After a personal introduction with Skittles, Anna introduced the others by pointing to the line of Circle and fellowship members heading up the steps.

"Hi, nice to meet you, I'm Anna." Anna said, while pointing to each member. "That's Jim, Drew, Randy, Tommy, Toby, Bella, our professor, Dr. Zimmerman, and our good friend Torack along with his Aquerian soldiers."

James shook hands with a half a dozen people, including the Aquerian fellowship. Thaliana shyly stepped outside with a slight hesitation. She put her hand out to make the last of introductions.

"I'm honored," Thaliana said. They all looked at her, wondering about this Indian princess claiming to be from distant realms. She didn't look any different from any other person. Torack and his Aquerian soldiers looked more bizarre than she did. She looked like a regular type of girl, not what they thought to be a leader of realms. Once inside, the group wasn't quite sure where to start, so James turned back and looked at the Indian princess. She glanced at James knowingly, sensing she would be the main speaker. Even though Dr. Zimmerman would have his part, she being a Guardian appeared more informed from a heavenly perspective.

The thought of being the main speaker seemed to frighten her a bit by the expression she showed, but no one said anything. Thaliana bared a tentative acknowledgment, with a slight hesitation in her stance. She took a deep breath and let it out slow, maybe having second thoughts. She couldn't quite understand her King having confidence in her. She barely filled her shoes, standing five feet four inches, a hundred and ten pounds. If seen by anglers of Orbitus, she'd been thrown back into the deep blue sea, too small to be considered a decent catch. For reasons unknown, she had all these eyes staring up at her. *What was my King thinking?* she thought. It reminded her how her earthly father would smile at her, when she could barely reach up to grab the reins of her pony. He had shown so much confidence in her, even though she could barely touch the bottom of the reins. Apparently, she understood just then, like her father, her King was teaching her how to be a leader. As before from youth of her father, with a guiding hand, treasured a touch of love in his commitments for a daughter. A lump of emotion welled up in her. She pressed it down to get her composure back. Then she noticed the aged professor sitting across the room. Silently rocking in the rocking chair with an expression of succor on his face, a glint of consideration for title. She was bearing arms of wisdom from a King at the highest of government, place unfathomable as far as humans are concerned. The professor looked content, measuring this Indian princess making new impressions on humans again. It had been a long time since she had students with open hearts in front of her. Dr. Zimmerman was reminded, through his many years, that first impressions weren't always redeemable of identifiable facts, that impact of personality had nothing to do with size as he would learn from personal experiences. She saw the intelligent look in his eyes and the expressions only revealed of a teacher. She saw the motives of his heart with that peaceful patience glistening across his face, which was a true virtue he would come to accept. He was a good man, a leader, one she could trust. Thaliana began to understand she was trained to be as her teachers were leaders and guiders of those of their youth. She was there to build upon her experiences that her father had started when she could barely walk, a toddler, a young teenager, a young lady, then moving on to be an Indian princess from the seventh realm then chosen by a King to be an immortal, a Guardian, one who walked and talked and held her head high. As all indigenous happenings have a beginning, she knew she was starting the cycle all over again, as a student to teacher, as trainee to trainer, back through the stages of schooling again, this endless cycle of moving new students through some type of system of leadership. She was being a light in a darkened world shedding a little light on the few.

Drew, from a short distance away, could see what was going through her mind by the movement of her eyes and how they were set. Everyone understood, even Anna and Randy saw it too. Everyone sensed something was different about this little cabin far out beyond human limits, hidden in the forgotten green wonders of this place, way out in the forest of this rugged country, hidden by trees and timbering land, yet somehow it still held meaning, something hidden by a King had left its mark. Maybe such a King would be sitting somewhere in the distance, taking notes, being patient has only kings can be, putting his finger on those that needed personal assistance and support, like this Indian princess.

Thaliana cleared her throat and tried to smile the best that she could. She began to share what she understood from her heart.

"I'm sure everyone is weary from your travels of the last few days. Please have a little patience for a while longer. This day will be about rest and getting to know each other. We have made accommodations for each of you," she said. She looked toward the Aquerian fellowship to include them.

"There's to be others who come here. We haven't much time to prepare. As you all know, and eternal clock is ticking the final days of this world. I will explain the best that I can about what's to take place in the next few days. I'll not leave any doubt of our purpose of being here."

No one was sure how to respond to the words of this Indian princess. She didn't appear on a personal note to be anything of a threat. She was humble, to the point, and quickly made her points of understanding. From across the room, she could feel what Dr. Zimmerman was thinking, knowing there was a time and a place for each diplomatic process. Thaliana considered all fellowships or people had their purpose, including their strange-looking alien friends. She realized their advance intelligence and technology would be of great service, for the purpose of a King was not written in any future heavenly books.

Thaliana looked around the room looking for details of her surroundings. It was quiet and cozy with a stone fireplace emitting a slow red burn. The kitchen table had a bouquet of wild flowers of purple and red picked from the meadow in front, along with a touch of baby's breath. The hearth mantle was adorned with several pictures of Robert's family when they were younger. He had decorated the cabin to give it a warm and welcoming aura. A chandelier hung above in rustic cabin like fashion. There was a bearskin rug spread out across the floor in front of the open fireplace. The ceiling above was sixteen feet high to accompany the loft with railing in front. A rocking chair sat next to the bay window, and an old leather coach lay up against the far right wall, with brown stuffing coming out of one corner. Placed on the chandelier were twelve candle holders glowing with trifling sparkles of light. Thaliana sensed this was the perfect place for a gathering of the gifted and those of their best of Aquerian fellowship. The cabin didn't appear to impress or win any awards for its beauty. She knew this was a place that reminded her of her youth. It brought a spot of emotion to the surface. It made her smile inside, knowing this place was perfectly planned out. Torack and three others were taken to the couch, others had filled in the chairs around the table, and the rest sat close to the open stone fireplace. Drew, Tommy, and the Aquerian soldiers had taken to the floor leaning against a far wall. Dr. Zimmerman, ready and posed as a leader should be, was sitting back just watching, waiting patiently, learning by listening. Then Thaliana raised her eyes and began her bizarre account of the last ten thousand years.

"Everyone here has taken that first step of faith with this acknowledgment of courage. You have done the right thing," she said. "I want to thank you for giving your time and energy this day and the days to come. Furthermore, all of you will look back one day and remember this place and understand why this battle had to take place. The window of opportunity for us is only in our favor for a short period of time. The Fallen won't know our true purpose until it's too late. Time management for the next couple of days will be very important." Thaliana looked around at each of her future pupils, each having their own unique personality and skill. She considered their chances of success. "We are all in this place for a specific reason. The mountains, the mine, the forest, and the water, and the weather conditions will serve a King for the next few days. Gabriel, captain of the Guard, will be here in the morning to help plan strategic battle strategy against those of a darker world, who will come and try to take this place. Their leader will then make his introductions on a more personal level. Like all politicians making a grand entrance, he will be no exception to this rule of expressing himself. He is an incomprehensible threat to the people of earth."

The Indian princess paused for the briefest of moments to let her words sink in. She noticed all eyes staring at her. "Those chosen few who hold the gifts by a King of the highest seat, called the *pure of heart,* as my Lord has proclaimed. You've been given an opportunity to start again on a new planet, far from here, far from the dangers of this place." She looked for each member of the Circle. "You're being here holds a key element of surprise. They will not realize your presence until it's too late. Those of the Fallen are unaware of my King's persistence. Something our enemy has overlooked." Thaliana points to James. "The one, who takes the place of the one before, has been given title. Lacobus, Guardian of the Alaskan Coast. They will help protect this place with his Honorite at his side." Anna felt a tad of deception brewing. Her eyes flickered as she viewed this Guardian in front, wondering about words unsaid.

"Furthermore, Thaliana said, "This place is a central point to draw them in." Thaliana thought to draw their interest by words of a story given of her youth.

"A boy marked to be a king, so many years ago, sought the heart and compassion of a brother in his youth, trying to find resolve, trying to find peace and hope in a brother's love, leading to a pathway of redemption, as each of us chooses a path in life. We stand, hoping the journey taken will lead to positions of glory, yet without the right guidance, positions of glory become antithetical leading away from light that can't be explained by flesh and blood. For each man, let it be known the right path to take is as that very thing buried as seeds in each one's soul. Some of us are drawn by the powers of this world yet others by the love embedded in character of each one's soul. It's almost impossible to tare the roots of such seeds from growing, unless a King's hand takes control. For why are we standing in this field ready to battle, waiting to take a path that can't be change? We are but brothers of brothers, and blood of blood, walking a pathway leading too far from home. What a man dreams he will become if those seeds grow and harvest into those elicit dreams transposed." Thaliana looked toward James knowing his love for his father was eternal. And mentioning the love between father and son had been the key for this battle all along.

"His father's body was taken because he's been marked. This Circle of members will lead you to the place where the damned are held captive. A world lies gulfed between the living and the dead, placed without distance or physical presence. My King is letting this play out. He doesn't want to interfere. He's commissioned those of the Circle to do their part. For a king's reason unknown, are built on integrity, love, and understanding of those brothers told, as this fight of brothers is way beyond the realm of what you should know. Battle with in war throughout history has served its purpose of teaching. Today is no different in what follows. The enemy will test your strength, your courage. He will exploit your weaknesses. My submission to you is to have an open mind. Stay focused on our purpose as a unit, our reason for battle in the first place, to represent a kingdom you've never seen by your natural eyes. Yet understand internally this to be something unexplainable, for a man's heart knows purpose without folly, for we are driven to our destinies without words or enlightenment until the very end of life, for life is not your own without strife, as the soul of man become complicated with the simplicities of life, as they pushed aside when the desires of one soul craves what's hidden in the dark. Those seeds are not the will of a father. They take the very life that's been given. They devour the soul from the inside out, leaving what's left in ruin. Train your mind and body to think as a warrior would. Keep your own personal opinions of reasonings away from your purpose. Let your gifts point you in the right direction. Do any of you not understand what I have said to you today?"

The room was quite to the point that silent breathing could be heard through the rhythm of the room's physical bodies pushed together from warmth and words more than bizarre.

Thaliana looked into each set of eyes. She was looking for any submissions of doubt among the gifted. Here was a battle of the ages getting ready to take place, not in a great city with history to proclaim as her glory, but a simple field of battle within the confines of nature presenting her quite bliss among warriors of the same mind and heart.

No city or persons would claim the rights of accomplishment to this battle except those of the chosen. Thaliana looked at the door.

"I would like to show you an example of defense, in case there are those of you who would doubt our abilities." She motioned for all whom had gathered to follow her out on the porch. Then the Indian princess released her wings as she passed the threshold of the door. Her body armor jetted out and covered her small frame as once before, and the sharp talons on her fingers grew out in golden curves. James and Skittles followed after and made changes to their own physical conditions. They were Guardians at present, as a feather marks heaven's elite. The Indian princess had a keen sense of intelligence as her mind had been opened up to its full force. It flowed from her pores like honey dripping from the honeycomb. A glowing aura of an immortal being was in their presence. She, as kings before her, expelled a character of willful beauty of being a giant slayer among men. She had spent many a day among heaven's scholars, rightly chosen by her King. They were enlightened by wisdom, trained by the greatest of warriors, by a kingdom unknown to this Circle of friends. Through captain of the Guard, his wisdom and tutelage had thought this smaller representation of a King well, for she expelled an assiduous zest for life, not by her own rewards, but that by her King. She was an Indian princess, a Guardian, a leader of the seventh realm.

The Circle watched in bewilderment as their Aquerae friends stepped back, making room for the Guardians as they flew across the sky. James pulled the whip from his side and stretched it across the meadow over fifty feet wide. As an imposing weapon of might, it struck the air and cracked the earth with a shearing bolt of light. The Indian princess cut across his path in a streak of light. Turning to James, she touched his shoulder to draw his attention. She exuded a connection of body and soul as the sky lit up with a brilliant golden light. The Guardians were understood to be from a place not of earth not held to the physical structure of flesh and bone, but held to a higher representation of a throne, far reaching of the natural eye, past the point of the imagination to understand. James yelled out, a cause of celebration that reached the mountains and beyond. His Honorite, his trusty companion, his protector, moved as he moved. He became a beast of claws, incisors, and heavenly form. With two swishing flaps of his wings, he was making history while shooting across the sky.

The Circle stood back, amazed. Jim Carson uprooted a ponderosa-pine tree with his gift. He threw it in the direction of the Guardians. James struck the tree with such force it splintered in pieces. An echo and a cry, a thunderous roar, traveled the distance of the mountains and back. Their bewildered audience took cover. Splinters we're flying as debris when shooting past the door. Bella dove to the porch, finding no safe place to be, no place to find relief. The air filled with an example of violence. Bella screamed while letting go. Drew grabbed Anna and slipped through one of his many doors to take cover.

After a minute, he stood to get his composure back and signaled for James to come near, as the winged Guardian approached and stood close to the porch. James saw Drew standing in the mist of splintered trees all around. Anna considered these Guardians making quite the mess. After calming, Bella stood and brushed herself from dirt and debris and a touch of attitude. *The nerve of them,* she thought. Drew had a plan and waved James close for their time of training would keep them from further holding back of the Circle's future success. James settled to the ground with a curious expression, wondering what this boy was thinking. He was stylish, a bit astatic, homed into a Guardian's way of thinking, super-sized to the third dimension, set to fight with wings floating just above his shoulders. He was on the short end of a long ride completing this task. Most of this Circle still looked a bit fearful.

"Yes, how can I be of assistance?" James asked. Drew had his left hand propped on his chin with arms across his midsection. He looked at James, maybe thinking he was a bit out of control.

"So, do you think someone could ride atop of one of your shoulders?" Drew pointed toward James's back.

James pondered the thought. "What…do you mean ride, like two on a motorcycle?"

A grin broke out on Drew's face. "Well, if it could be done."

Bella looked at the boy strangely deranged. "Are you serious?"

Drew cocked his head sideways, pondering Bella's statement, which ran a little deep for broken emotions, and then ignoring her.

Thaliana landed just in front, curious about the subtle conversation. She heard the question with a raised eyebrow, while understanding the boy's disconnected thought, after witnessing this moment of violence displayed just out-front. She knew what he was thinking before the question could be answered.

"Yes, this would give an advantage," she said, "but it would also be quite dangerous. Do you know those of such courage to take the gamble? Drew thought about it for a minute and then turned to look up at Bella standing on the porch. She appeared cross-eyed and fit to be tied.

Bella had already turned her stare with a wrinkled frown. "Drew, what…did you fall and bump your head? Everyone stopped talking and looked at her. She was wondering if this misinformed man child had lost his marbles. Bella reached over and smack Drew on the back of the head. Anna turned her stare toward Bella, showing a pouty adherence. Everyone saw the humor of the scene then laughed, everyone but Drew and Anna. Thaliana, trying to stay serious, smiled. She looked over at James and saw him amused by the confrontation like the rest.

Randy interrupted the laughter by a quick interjection in a best friend's defense. "Nice goin… Bella, leading with your feelings again." Everyone turned to look at Randy.

Drew brushed off the embarrassment with a wave of his hand. "I guess I had that one coming. Not thinking straight," he said. Bella perched a pouty disapproval. She looked out past the meadow like she didn't care of their opinions. She sensed her own unhinged moments of earlier. They had all failed at one time or another of making sense. They were full of awkward moments and insecurities, sometimes lacking any comprehension of the right path to take. Bella remembered growing up in a town of horses and Cowboys from a ranch of plenty of chores to do. She had missed the love of a mother who died early in years. She grew from a young girl into a woman, even though a bit disconnected. She was a different kind of leader without a unique set of rules. Who said they couldn't make mistakes or feel pain, or end up on the wrong side of the tracks trying to find their way in all of the confusion? Life wasn't always easy, or comforting, or conforming to some master plan. Sometimes life stunk and become hard to bear, but that didn't mean she would give up.

She looked back at Drew with a disparaging frown. A deep sadness followed her through this difficult path of life. "I'm sorry, Drew. I didn't mean to offend you. I don't have all the answers at my fingertips."

Dr. Zimmerman came out on the porch and put his arm around the girl. "Don't worry, young lady. We know who you are."

Thaliana showed a twinkle of water build in the back of her eyes. She knew what their teacher meant. Mistakes were a process of learning, doing the right adjustment, learning to say you're sorry when it hurts. This rare Circle of friends, weren't promised a yellow brick road, or the promise land or a rainbow at the end of a difficult life. They were only told that others would benefit from their efforts. They could never give *in* to those creatures of the sky or misinformed friends who were easily lead astray. They had never fit in anywhere…until they were put together. They were like a *puzzle*. They had to be figured out as they went along. Who wants to know that a King would pick them from so many others, set across the universe to distant stars? It didn't make sense at the moment. Flickers of hope crossed the young girls eyes as she was getting ready to watch the world's last flickers of light and hope for the best and give her opinions to help change the outcome of what was left. The right to live, the right to be challenged by those creatures disconnected. They wanted to delete humans off the face of the earth and leave no memory of them. Bella's mission was to stay focused to help the others as a unit.

Thaliana glared at this stranger than normal girl showing tautness then lightly touched her on the shoulder.

"Young lady, no one is going to force you to ride on the back of one of us. We have our own ways of seeing the world without assistance." Then Thaliana thought of the perfect example to explain their purpose of being here.

"History, from time and again, has shown men's worthiness in a battle of hard-fought condition, for learning to do the right thing at the right hour comes with great care, for men of battle are not easily cowed by the blood of their brothers spilled in submission. Rage and chaos meld in such conditions, revealing what man is capable of. For mistakes, covered from blood of brothers, dissects the heart to quickly discover a man's true intentions when the blood of those loved fills the streams and rivers, for what flows of color or country molds a brother into the worst of enemies. The time is now. We're facing a battle that leaves no margin of error. This is not a place for the faint of heart or the weak of mind. If you are to survive the next few days, it will be because of your pure will to live, your resolve to overcome your ability to see past all the hidden obstacles buried in places that you never thought possible, seeds that are buried in your very soul that pull out the best of what the human spirit can give. Today I challenge each and every one of you to give more of yourselves, give parts of your heart that you've never thought conceivable, dig down into the depths of your souls, and find those hidden caverns of wisdom and courage, pieces of you that have not yet been discovered, from character expelled where strength may come. Stand against an enemy so outrageous that the beat of the heart becomes hopeless in the grasps of this enemies' hands. My King has turned his back on this type of disappointments to find a better way, for life has a way of coming full circle. And this Circles intention will be measured by what comes from your hearts. Be not fooled by a quick solution for the coming conditions, there to be no easy way out. My King has commissioned this Circle to make a stand for all that sit in high leadership, watching, and waiting, for an internal reasoning is clicking a clock until the Winds of Time are quickly gone.

"The Aquerian soldiers will be at the center of this battle in the meadow. Gabriel will come with a few of his foot soldiers tomorrow and assist. After you rest this day, I would like each of you to spend time with each other and learn of each other's strengths and weaknesses that will solidify your bond. If you are to have the best advantage in this field, you need to trust each other. Let the blood that flows in the days to come, be those of your enemies unrevealed."

Thaliana looked out among the trees in the quiet ruins of jagged earthy mountains, across the meadows with the soft fragrant color standing in the quiet stillness of distance. She sensed peace dwelt here this day, even though chaos was headed their way. James and Skittles turned to their earthly forms.

From out of nowhere, Anna becomes curious." So, let me get this understood in my head. You're not an actual angel from heaven?"

James looked over, wondering where her questioning was going to end up. He looked at Drew before answering. "Well yeah, I'm here with her." He said, while pointing toward the Indian princess. Anna's eyes shot back and forth, wanting a clearer picture. "Well, a gift given of a king,"

James said, "because of my father being used as bait, I'm here to bring honor to the King, in any way I can."

Anna developed a smile on her face from James's assumption of remedial leadership.

"And you're the one to do that, bring honor to one's majesty's court?"

James saw that disbelief in Anna's eyes. "Not to one's majesty's court, but to the King's court." James looked unsure of himself. Who was this girl?

"Oh, I see to the, what's it called again? Anna was still smiling when she said it. James looked at Drew for a second and then responded.

"Is she with you? Does she expel this negative energy all on her own, with the chip on her shoulder to boot?"

Anna lost the smile. Drew was going to say something, but Anna interrupted him.

"It's not a chip, you overzealous bat. It's being careful." She said with a flare of emotion, James raised his right eyebrow in astonishment and then looked back at Drew.

Drew answered by responding, "She is a little rough around the edges but tender in the middle," emitting a short laugh and a pause.

Anna whipped her head around in Drew's direction, surprised at the response. "I'm not rough around the edges. I'm just careful at believing what appears to be so wrong. You don't know anything about the man, except by what you've seen out in this field. And from my point of view, he looks uncertain." James couldn't believe he was actually hearing this.

"Anna, can you change into a heavenly beast three times your original size?"

Anna glared uncompromisingly. "No, can you?" Drew knew he went a little too far with his unclear way of thinking.

James responded with a strange expression while folding in his arms. "Beautiful and irritating. Why don't you explain yourself."

Anna wasn't sure what to make of his statement. "So, tell us how you won such a gift from a King?"

"I really don't know, but I'm guessing it has to do with my father."

"What's so special about your father?"

James was fascinated by the over-inquisitive young lady with the callus character to boot, and she was calling the shots.

"He reflected something of the Kings heart. That's what I was told." James turned to look at Thaliana from carefully cohesive skepticism. Who is this girl?

Anna moves her eyes toward the Indian princess. James considered her with the unwarranted stares and awkward questions. Thinking about a little girl he knew in second grade, he wanted to pull her hair and push her down.

Anna showed an inquiring face. "Why have you really come here?" It seemed to be an appropriate question from her standing point. Anna wasn't impressed. "This is what she has told you?" She looked back at James. He wondered about the girl as he shook his head and lowered his eyes.

Thaliana sensed the doubt in Anna's questioning and knew with time she would see through the others in battle. Her doubt was not a lack of faith in reasons attained, but what followed.

Drew stepped back into the conversation. "I guess we'll learn soon enough about our angels or Guardians by what you are called." Then looked back at the Indian princess. "I, myself am full of questions, but let's take a walk," he said, throwing her off a bit Anna looked up. And being Drew was usually the one to stop heated conversations, he gently slipped between them.

Anna turned her focus for a brief moment, seeing Drew trying to keep this heated conversation for another day. This discussion appeared to be escalating. Anna tenderly smiled from Drew's, even temperance. The love of her life reached in giving his hand. Drew looked back at the rest as the Indian princess pondered in her motives as the couple left the immediate area while the rest deemed her questioning.

"We'll be back in a moment," Drew said. "We're a little weary from the airplane ride and need to air out our stiffness."

Anna gave a piercing glance back while being led by the love of her life, but not led astray. The land in the distance showed a presaged aura in the back of Anna's mind, yet so beautiful. She was thinking to look lost in one of her mystical fantasies. She knew her adroit conditions had her mind running in all directions. What were the true reasons for being here? It didn't pan out. They needed more time to plan-better conditions. And what was up with all this flying about? Her knight in shining armor was about to make a blissful approach toward swooning her off her feet. Accepting other conditions of relief for greater importance, she held back, showing patience from perseverance. She had thought back to that warm kiss that brought him to his knees. It caused her to smile. Drew smelled that soft fragrant perfume drifting close by. He reached for her from separating distance and graced her neck with soft warm lips, a warm gesture of love. Anna sensed him wanting closeness, yet his timing was a bit off by pulling her from that ill-mannered bout. What was he thinking? She looked into his eyes for a briefest of moments as she passed her fingers across his face. She sensed Drew's succoring character would be needed for a future endeavor. He acknowledged her expressions, soft and warm, a sparkle of love, tender hands, and future memories. They drifted close to the edge of the forest, not too far, but far enough to cause concern. Distant sounds of the forest moved in from creeping shadows unaware. Anna sensed they were not alone. She could hear the wind in the tops of the trees and the gentle chirping of birds. Then something strange shot passed her vision. This veritable land gave way to a world unaccustomed to the flexing of visitors walking as delicate creatures on her floor. Each indefatigable ghost lay in wait of this land, as if breathing. A life accustomed to flesh and blood lay waiting never depleting.

Randy looked in the distance as his favored friends took off for the edge of the forest. Jim perked up and noticed the disconcerting stare in his friend's face. Tommy walked over with Toby while the Indian princess made conversation with James.

"What gives?" Tommy asked.

"Don't like those two taking off like that," Randy said.

"Drew knows what he's doing…besides he had to get Anna away for a while," Tommy said.

Even though the light of day left behind a brightening pathway, it still remained darker at the edge of hidden tress. An eerie presence of elongated narrowing shadows brought Anna to look back at where they had come from. Foliage had filled in the gaps between the light from above and darkness from below, leaving an unclear understanding of life around making silent footsteps by thieves.

From distance, Jim saw them disappear while shadows of the latter part of the day began to take over. He looked at Randy and suggested. "I'll go check on our leader. It feels kind of weird out there."

"No…give them a minute…" Randy started to say, but then he heard the scream. Jim took off at a dead run as Tommy did with Toby at his side, and Randy at a distance.

Drew pulled Anna close. The warmth of pressing air hit his face, excitement of newness, pounding of hearts. Anna's conditions of holding back for so long had ended. She let go where secrets begin. No more need for emotional moments, no more hiding from friends. Neither one was thinking straight of the possibility of danger lurking close with the absence of their circle of friends. They were vulnerable in the worst of ways. Drew's heart skipped a beat as Anna was lost in love's second long kiss. Anna saw it first before she pulled back, the light in his eyes sparkled from a flicker of uneventful pain, creepy shadows reflected off uneven light. That's when she screamed.

A trilling scream came from the back of Anna's throat. "Drew!" He whipped his head around to see the biggest white wolf he had ever seen; well, the only wolf he had ever seen at close range with snarling teeth. And suddenly, a circle of unnerving obscurities crept in from behind. Silvery eyes exposed from a wolf pack of intruders bordered too close to home. Anna reflected intractable fear, unblinking. Drew was so mesmerized by silvery eyes and hot breath just inches away that he froze. Within seconds, they were surrounded. They were close to a den unexposed. Anna was nervous but knew they could be torn apart within seconds if they did nothing. Drew put his hands out and reached for Anna, slowly he said, "Anna…come closer… I have as idea." She quickly followed suit considering their malefic situation was mounting for moments of reparation, too far from the cabin by separation. Anna looked up and comprehended his thinking. She leaned in and reached for Drew's hand. Drew pulled her close and thought of the cabin. The wolf pack lunged, but nothing was there. Drew and Anna had slipped through a door and transported to the safety of friends. The Indian princess saw them appear in her head. She walked in on them in each other's arms. Thaliana glared at the couple as her incredulity overtook her way of thinking.

"I should have warned you before you took off on your walk. This is not an ordinary place for strolling on the edge of the forest. There are dangers out there that you know nothing of. You can't just take off on your own without the others with you."

Drew looked at the Indian princess. "I'm not a warrior, but I have few tricks up my sleeve."

Thaliana showed serious intent. "Yes, I see, but you won't always be so lucky."

Drew saw in her eyes that she didn't appreciate the cocky attitude. "Sorry, I wasn't thinking clearly. We'll be more careful next time."

Thaliana looked straight across the room to make sure she had his attention. "You should have known better. You're their leader. Choosing to make mistakes such as this is wasting our time."

Drew looked up at Indian princess and repeats himself. "I said we'd be more careful next time."

Thaliana's gaze was unrelenting, with conditions henceforth so incriminating. "My King would punish those who have done less. Make no mistake. You need to be focused, because those creatures of the Fallen won't do the same. They are focused warriors who have been training throughout the ages." Drew and Anna caught the quintessence of her lecture. They understood. Anna reached for Drew's hand. Her eyes pulled him in. Drew quickly looked back at the Indian princess. He knew she was pushing her limit and knew that this training thing would take her awhile in showing patience.

"So, why do you think all this is happening?" Drew asked.

She looked up suddenly, wondering why the question.

Thaliana had to think for a minute. This was the question of the ages…man making mistakes…someone behind him trying to clean up the mess. Then it hit her.

"I think, personally, people stopped believing in each other… to keep it simple. People don't see the big picture anymore… coming together as friends and family…doing goodwill toward to their fellow man."

"And why do suppose people are that way?" Drew kept prodding.

"Too many changes…too many religions…nonacceptance of others…too much politics not making sense…and the simplest of conditions like lacking love and compassion, while judging others to the extreme."

"So, how do we fix that?" Drew insisted.

"I don't know if we can…I mean love is like no other emotion, given to those of earth or of heaven. This emotion moves people to do things that are far from any normal circumstances. It can't be explained by the possibilities, unless…" Thaliana couldn't finish because she knew her King was taking people to the end of time because love had ceased, and frictions were at an all-time high.

Drew looked over at her, still curious. "So that's it…we just give up. We let everyone take what's coming to them?"

"Do you see an alternative?"

"Maybe this thing called love goes deeper than that?"

"What do you mean?" Thaliana asked.

"Well, I thought love is like eating candy in a way."

"And that means…"

It means that when we first taste it, the sweet part of it is so, overwhelming you're not sure what to do with it, but then something happens…"

"And what would that be?"

"Well, like sugar or something deeper inside us leaves cavities behind or leaves people feeling empty in a way, like empty calories. It's like planting seeds but not giving them water. It doesn't do what a balanced diet of vitamins, exercise, and other food supplements can do to make our bodies healthier."

"So, you're saying…"

"Go back to our original roots of how we had been taught."

"And how do we do that?"

"I didn't know, but we have to find a way, because the direction we're going right now doesn't look good." Drew said.

"Point well taken. It seems a little late in the game, don't you think?"

"Maybe so…but you can start by lightening up a bit on rules and regulations and try to see the whole picture like you suggested to me."

Thaliana had been caught by her own words. She knew this young leader had learned a hard lesson in life about this thing called love. She watched the young couple unblinking and wondered if she had the right frame of mind. She looked past the window as if looking for answers from building clouds overhead. Maybe the Circle was the right group to be here after all? Somehow her King was prescient of circumstances to come, that she would have missed.

Anna gently smiled as Drew pulled her close. Bella broke through the front door to see the couple in a warm embrace.

"You two need to get a room. I just ate about an hour ago and don't want to lose what I barely got down." Anna covered her mouth to hold back a smile with coquettish eyes in Drew's direction. Bella couldn't see the humor in the statement as she rolled her eyes with her usual mirthless conditions." What's so funny?" Bella asked.

"Nothing. What we do is none of your business. Unless there's something you want to share that includes us all?"

Thaliana looked sharply across the room. "Now there's an act of a loving gesture." She laid piercing eyes on Anna. Anna just stuck her whole foot in her mouth. Bella smiled but didn't say anything. Thaliana rolled her eyes and left the room.

"Whatever, you two. I'm tired and need a few hours of sleep," Bella said.

"There's an extra bed in the loft," Anna mentioned. The four boys are tenting it outside."

"I thought our Indian princess said it was too dangerous?" Bella insisted.

"They won't come near the property," Anna said. "The wolves sense the Guardians too close."

Randy crossed the threshold of the front door. He saw the expressions, as if female cattiness filled the air. Drew and Anna were nuzzling each other. Bella turned her head to avoid the gestures of love.

Randy interrupted them. "Hey, dude, the Aquerae are going hunting for wolf. Want to come along?"

Drews saw his best friend was just trying to pry him away from the girls. "No not really, but Anna's tired, and was thinking of going to bed. How about setting up the tent outside?"

Randy's eyes lit up with a smile. Anna reached over and hugged Drew for the last time and then gave him that long look of love before heading off to bed. Drew let go of sliding hands slipping through fingers. Her eyes lightly flutter before turning toward the ladder. He watched her ascent, enjoying every placement of her small hands and the rest that had followed. Randy put his arm around Drew's shoulder as he ushered him past Bella, who was more than glad to close the door. Randy remembered when they were just kids. He remembered seeing that little boy across the street playing behind his house, in the fields close to home, avoiding conversations at times, but always close to each other's side, leaving only in that moment of their make-believe worlds. They would pretend to be commanders of the universe, conquerors of distant worlds, and now that was actually becoming a part of their real lives. Randy, like that make-believe world with giving their best, as little boys do, roaming the neighborhoods. Drew dreamed of being a writer one day. Randy just wanted to survive his childhood. He remembered moments of solitude, of him and his best friend, telling silly jokes that didn't make sense, catching spiders, finding a dead rabbit over the hill and burying it like a pet, going to the beach every Saturday and catching the waves, along with feeling the salted air, watching football games of their favorite team, double dating at the movies when in high school, now a circle of friends. They would travel the stars in space. And they chased after dreams that could quickly be erased. They were best friends, through thick and thin, he would try not to forget. But whatever happened between them, he would be there right by Drew's side, as little boys to teenagers and now grown men. Their deepest secrets, their insecurities, their strengths, and their weaknesses were all a part of their journey. They were a pair that would stay together no matter what.

"I know that look," Randy professed. Drew squinted, with his hand over his eyes as he regarded the sun setting in front of them.

"What was it you used to tell me about Renee? Two things she loved better than anything?" Drew looked again at his best friend, not sure why the subject was brought up. He hesitated before looking back." Red skies and what? Randy asked.

Emotion pushed up in Drew's throat. Then he finished Randy's sentence, "And kissing in the rain."

Randy developed a big smile on his face while shaking his head and pulled his best friend close to his shoulder, a bond that couldn't be broken. "Can't beat that," Randy said. "Red skies and Kissin' in the rain."

A slow tear rolled off Drew's cheek. Randy tried to cheer him up while watching the sun set under red skies as he watched the clouds of the night roll in. Drew whispered under his breath as they made it off the porch and opened the box with the tent, "Red skies and kissin' in the rain." Randy looked over and broke out with a smile. "Hey, he paused, "It's supposed to rain tonight, but I'm not kissin' ya."

Drew reached over and gave Randy a little shove, faked kissing his hand and gently slapped Randy on the cheek. "That's as close as we get, unless you want the wolfdog giving you a nuggey."

"What a nuggey?"

"It's a… it's a wet kiss, mixed with bad breath, lots of pet hair, and whatever's left."

"No, thanks." Randy smiled and slapped Drew on the back as both lifelong friends unrolled the tent as their next adventure began to take form.

Thaliana knew she had to communicate with the Aquerian soldier's leader, to let them know what to prepare for. She was a tad nervous about confronting an alien fellowship she didn't quite understand. She hung out on the patio staring at the sunset, with her arms crossed, soaking in the warmth of the fading light with the perused expression. The days to come would be the hardest of her training. She wasn't sure of success. These young people were full of oddities that didn't match up to anything she considered normal, yet what was normal? And on second thought, she didn't have a choice. Run and hide was her third choice, count this as a loss or turn her head the other way. Who was she kidding? Thaliana left the porch and went back inside.

Drew looked out through the opening of the tent to see a fading glow of flickering flames. The cabin through the window looked cozy and warm, far better than sleeping on the ground with the usual sounds of owls and crickets chirping. A howl could be heard in the distance, the brushing of tress from the wind, the lurking of shadows crossed the tent. Drew zipped the tent door shut and laid there thinking.

Randy let out a slow breath of air. "How did we end up here of all places?"

"I don't know…I guess we got lucky." Tommy farted, and Drew raised an eyebrow.

"Not too lucky," Randy suggested.

Drew giggled, and Jim tried to smother Tommy with his pillow.

"Dude, stop!" Tommy yelled.

"You stop!" Jim yelled back. If I wanted to smell your butt, I'd put my head between your cheeks." Everyone laughed.

"Now my pillow smells like you," Jim said.

Tommy sat up and fanned his covers to spread his resent joy.

Drew unzipped the tent for fresh air. "What's this, high school camp? Dude, you and your flagellating farts gotta stop."

Everyone laughed. Jim reached up and pinched Tommy on the back of the neck.

"Are you serious? Dude, that hurt!"

"It was supposed to hurt, moron. You stink!"

"I feel sorry for your future family," Randy blurted out.

"I feel sorry for your current friends," Drew embellished. "What'd did you eat?"

"It doesn't matter what he eats. He's a natural gas bomb," Jim said.

"I can't help it. It hurts to hold it in."

"Dude, you fart again, and I'm shaving your head in your sleep. And you'll be missin' an eyebrow." They were all laughing now, even Tommy.

Jim reached in his backpack and handed Tommy something in the dark.

"What's this?" Tommy asked.

"It's a cork."

"What's it for?"

"Take a guess, moron."

"That's not funny. I'm not doing this on purpose."

"Don't take it personal then. My way of helping," Jim finished.

Randy smiled in the dark. After a few minutes, everyone settled down. That tent got quiet, and the slow rhythms of sleep shortly followed.

Anna was the first one up that morning. Getting ready for a new day was a great importance. She acknowledged the amenable ways of Thaliana in the kitchen already preparing coffee and fixing some type of meat that filled the cabin with savory aromas, fresh brewed coffee, a fire glowing red ambers in the main room. The comforts of home were all moments of preparing, like a soldier prepares for battle, or a strategist thinks of all angles of deception. Thaliana was setting a prime example of leadership. Anna came out of the bathroom drying her hair after a much needed shower. She was wearing soft dark black denim jeans and green T-shirt with a picture of the Aerosmith rock band plastered on the front. She was wild to some extent with a tender heart. Thaliana looked up over the pan at the short black hair, young girl with big brown eyes, perceptiveness in her manner. Anna was about five feet six inches tall, had the face of an inept beauty queen, almond-shaped eyes, narrow face with perfect curves of order. She was every guy's dream until they got to know her. She wasn't good at taking orders. She had her own way of seeing present conditions, and no Guardian or other would tell her the wiser. She was a package of fervor, not mean, cut lean, expressing an indelicate attitude. Anna understood truth to be like that gold those two men would seek to find in the mine. Now truth was a type of gold that wasn't usually something most men would seek after; she had the idea that it had to be something only a hungry mind or heart wanted to have or hold, like that gold. Anna said nothing before pouring herself a cup of black coffee and took her first long look outside the cabin window, which showed a beautiful morning of blues, greens, and yellows across the distance in an incandescent meadow. An anesthetized feeling of the past kept her silent. She was soaking up everything around. Anna stood leaning against the door jamb, enjoying the view. She had forgotten about how stunning the early mornings could be, especially in the uncharted pockets of Alaska. Man's last known challenge of uncharted history.

Thaliana had just pulled a pan full of hot biscuits from the oven. Anna turned back in the direction of the kitchen and said, "Would you like some help?"

Thaliana looked at Anna and smiled politely. "I think I've got it, but you can help yourself since you're up."

Anna's mouth watered from the smell of hot biscuits. "Well, maybe just one wouldn't hurt." Anna reached for a paper towel and grabbed one of the biscuits and decided making conversation with this peculiar Guardian might be encouraging, since she was up on current conditions, and the one chosen to lead. *Ha*, Anna thought. *She had looked too young.*

"Do you miss your own place in heaven?" Thaliana considered the girls questioning, knowing the young lady had missed more than everything about her own place of residence, since her family was gone. Then it just hit her, Anna had no home to go back too, and then she knew why she had clung to the young man so tightly. He was her only connection to this outside world, and her teacher. So many days gone, nothing to look forward to, then Drew came along. What was she thinking? She wasn't thinking at all. No wonder she'd confronted her so severely like she didn't exist at all. She realized everything about Anna was amplified, as if she stood on the top of the world looking down on all the problems that surrounded her, and nothing about God or king or anything connecting to her real world, which had become surrounded by loneliness and open wounds from lost family members. And nothing about love or goodness or hanging on to virtues were left in her. Drew had made a connection with the girl's heart. She stood alone looking for a way out. How could she have been so stupid? This young woman was picked out of millions of people because her King saw something in her that no one else got. She had integrity and a mind that ran truculent with desire, hanging her feelings on hooks that pulled at her flesh and smashed her soul, as she felt minuscule in the mix of everything happening.

"I miss the children mostly. They bring a lot of joy, and there's singing." Anna shot a focused stare toward this leader of realms, like she had struck a chord.

"What do they sing about?"

Thaliana was somewhat confused at Anna's attempt to make meaningful conversation.

"Well, about life, about love, and they sing on special occasion, like birthdays and championships… stuff like that. Oh, and they sing at baseball games."

"There's baseball in heaven?"

Thaliana was surprised at the question because she knew how popular the game was down here." Oh yes, there's baseball and much more."

Anna's face lit up with a bit of emotion." What about famous people? Are there any up there, I mean beyond the clouds?" Anna took a sip from her coffee mug and a bite from the biscuit. Thaliana observed her for a minute, sensing there was more to the abrasive girl than what she first thought. "I saw a man you might know from your time called Johnny Cash and his wife June Carter. Did you know them?"

"No, but I knew of them. They were before my time."

Thaliana had regarded this young girl who seemed quite the mystery. "Did you know Abraham Lincoln?"

"He was before my time too." Anna turned her stare toward Thaliana with a half-smile.

"Are we not going to heaven, I mean the Circle? That's if he allows such a thing to happen?"

Thaliana was surprised to hear Anna doubting their roles as the gifted. "I don't know what my King's plan is. I can only assume he will use you at this place where you've already been, a new heaven, a new earth, a place to start over."

"We're not all allowed to go, are we?"

There was a long pause for Thaliana gave her opinion. "You know everyone from your Circle were handpicked many years ago, even before you were born. You're meant to solve some great mystery. I don't know what it is yet or if I ever will, but it has to be quite important, or all this that's happening right now wouldn't even be happening."

That was news to Anna. She didn't think of herself with Drew having any key role in solving mysteries of the universe, but she did see the values of others like Drew, or Tommy, and even Bella, but herself?

She didn't have any special talent except being smart, and she was the only one who didn't experience a coma like the others. Thaliana saw the look in Anna's eyes.

"You know, my king never makes mistakes. What I mean is he found even something in you that he thought special enough to invest his time in making you," Thaliana said.

Anna's curiosity, perked up.

"And this battle ahead, we're meant to be here. I mean fight or be in the middle of this chaos."

Thaliana stood silent for a moment.

Anna suddenly flowed with more questions.

"Why would I be of importance? I've never done anything before that has stood out to others as anything significant. I'm just a simple girl with big dreams that never amounted to anything."

Thaliana had taken a serious tone with her. "But you're not this simple girl that you speak of. You're much more." Thaliana was confused by Anna's point of view of her own accords.

"So, you don't think my King is able to see your dreams. That could be why he has chosen you. What you feel in your heart has a determinate part of what's to come. Those characteristics that bring imagination to life that complete you. I believe that's what he's after. He sees the differences and strengths that you so apparently hold down. I'm sure that's what he saw in you."

A tear escaped down Anna's face. What strange words. She reached in surprise that she would show such emotion from these difficult words to hear. She just wanted to get on with life and end this strife. Now a Guardian from distant realms was trying to help her. Something touched her deep. Another tear escaped her and dropped to her side.

"Well, what should I do to bring everything into focus?"

"I guess never stop dreaming, never stop reaching for those things that you rightfully believe to be true, never stop believing in yourself. I'm sure my King would give you the same advice. Humans are not that difficult to figure out. They only need a little direction now and then to set matters straight. You know the right issue to do. I'm sure that's why you were brought here. You're here to give direction."

More tears rolled off Anna's cheeks and down her arms. She reached up to wipe the tears away, and then apologized.

Thaliana knew her words were making an impact on the girl whose world had been torn apart.

"I'm sorry for being so emotional. It's usually not my way. I'm usually, stronger."

"Oh, never apologize for tears. My King says tears cleanse the soul and frees the mind to do wondrous things that cause men to change their direction."

Anna looked up through the tears. "I wish I knew what to do. And I hope your King will not forget us. That is my true wish."

Thaliana handed a paper towel to the girl with the tears.

Anna looked up toward the loft and saw Bella standing, just listening to every word said. Bella looked sad and sorry for being so hateful toward her. A demurred expression shown on her face, about her own personal feelings. She made her way to the bottom and stopped just short of the overwhelmed girl. She looked at the tears on the table and on Anna's beautiful face.

"Anna, I'm sorry for being that way with you about Drew. He needs to love who could be right for him, and I know in my heart that it would be you, more so than me."

Anna and Bella embraced in at tearful reunion.

Thaliana got caught up in the emotion of this small Circle of friends and knew at that moment why they had been chosen. She was too tied to her own existence to the point she couldn't see the goodness in the others. She had become blinded by her own reasoning.

"Tears heal broken hearts, and free the mind to work more efficiently."

Both girls looked up through tearful eyes. They began to wipe each other's tears away with a paper towel, and then they laughed at each other.

12

GABRIEL

Drew and the boys, who slept in the tent that night, made their way out of the sleeping bags. Tommy had eaten something from the night before that gave him congestive flatulence. He felt his body couldn't subdue any more pressure. On further expansion, he decided sharing with the boys the night before. Drew considered throwing that tent away, but Randy said no. Jim Carson wanted to punch the floundering cowboy in the chest, of Tommy banishing breathable air. He flashed a disgusted look his way. Drew laughed along with Randy and suggested for Tommy to change his briefs before the girls got wind of him.

All the young men laughed as they made their way up the stairs. The girls were surprised to hear such laughter, released each other from their emotional moment of bonding.

Unexpectedly, the ground beneath them began to rumble. The noise made a thunderous quake across the meadow while shaking the front windows. The clouds parted, and three large figures dropped from the sky. They hit the ground with such force that everyone who was standing at the time lost their footing and fell to the ground. Drew threw open the front door and looked up. A paling glare brought him to pull back. Anna pushed back against the wall to get up after falling. Just beyond the porch stood three giant figures never imagined. All within the cabin quickly made their way out on the front porch. The three enormous figures stood over sixty feet tall.

"What are they?" Anna proclaimed as she turned about. The Indian princess glared at her in that general direction. Stoic creatures stood as solid gray and white monuments, paled in the color of stone, with wings folded in and swords reflecting imperturbability just before a storm. Randy pushed past the Indian princess to get a better view. His eyes bugged out on first glance. Drew looked over at Randy, wondering if what stood before them was even possible. They were sight for wandering eyes, a trio to be counted in the number of celestial beings. Each figure was set with wings of vast physical ostentation, recognized by sight of the Circle's miscalculations, as if the eyes perceived could not follow. Each point-tipped wing was invested with sharp talons of a hawk yet on a size no less than six feet long. Their bodies were set in a torpor, as if the cares of the world could not be shadowed for their only hope was to chart a course from a master's clairvoyant command. Their eyes were glazed over turning to white disks held in secret, as a presaged warning was set to take place, for at that moment, life in them seemed to be frozen. They were statues with square faces set to battle, lined-up, and, ready to raze. They were unconquerable soldiers standing stoically twenty-five feet out away from the cabin in a triangular pattern of war. Thaliana made her way to the porch and looked up, knowing these beasts were sent from above with a divine purpose in mind, yet why now, and why so abrupt? Something was missed from before, like a rising tide, bringing with it a wall of destruction, and the Indian princess had missed this forewarning secret to come. She turned and faced the gifted, exorcizing a worried expression glinted in her eyes. Despite their reasons for being here, they had an ineradicable purpose commissioned by the leader of heaven's realms. They were here to protect those of the Circle, but from what?

Thaliana looked back at the others, "Conquerites. That's their true name." Anna hadn't taken her eyes off of them since they landed. She was spellbound by their mass and their heavenly bodies giving off a portended feeling just by being here. The three cherubic beings stood without movement, with eyes and bodies set to take notice of anything moving, for their reasons for being here had not yet come. Everyone from the cabin held their breath, a signaling the end of the world appeared to be only a breath away.

Anna turned to the Indian princess with her face set in motion. "What's going on? Why didn't anyone warn us?"

Thaliana turned the view of Anna as she was jumping to conclusions.

"Please. Why are they here?"

"They are protectors of the realms. Gabriel's idea, I'm assuming. Our King would only dispatch them if he thought there could be eminent danger for the Circle." Drew didn't like the sound of what he was hearing.

"They're called battle shifters or planet changers, just a few of their names," Thaliana said.

Anna observed the Indian princess with a continued stare. "So, is there eminent danger for us?"

Thaliana caught on Anna's quick acknowledgment by not missing a beat. "They wouldn't be here otherwise. I'm assuming he's only taking precautions."

Anna was still deeply disturbed by the Indian princess's words. "But why send these Conquerites, as you have called them?"

"Something unexpected… I'm not sure." Thaliana smiled apprehensively. She didn't know why they were sent, but someone else had their reasons. These Conquerites were creatures presaged for an eternal reasoning, and not motivated by emotions or need. They are lead only by orders issued from above.

"My King has a higher determination with his time at present and sends his impenetrable soldiers to do his bidding. As seen from history, he lets man fight his own battles, as life on earth would be, as student to teacher, as seen from recorded history. Earth is as a training ground for those of the living. The angels of the Fallen don't know of them by being here, but they will soon."

"What's so special about these Conquerites?" Anna asked.

Thaliana raised an eyebrow, being a little perplexed that Anna would show a lack of gratitude for the presence. "They can't be killed," Thaliana said, "and usually they can't be seen, but my King thought that their visual presence might have a greater effect. They are unconquerable, according to the legends. It worries me my King would dispatch them so quickly."

"So, fitting a name," Anna said.

"Their only goal is to protect those that are within the walls and boundaries of a certain place," Thaliana said with raised suspicion. Anna was curious about their immediate purpose for being there now continued to remain unclear.

"Have these Conquerites ever been used for any other purpose before on earth?"

Thaliana wondered about this girl with her constant prodding. "Well, if you need to know, yes, but that's enough about the Conquerites. The day has come, and we've got work to do."

"So, what do we do now?"

The Indian princess began to know why a King who set on high would have chosen such a girl of annoyance. She was relentless. "You have this unsatisfied yearning for knowledge, and yet at times you have a held your tongue."

Anna's eyes formed a perplex division of understanding. She apologized for her persistent impeccable nature, not wanting to be fooled to accept anything less than perfection.

Thaliana looked over at this strange girl with her frailties and pale complexion, and then judged her for what she heard. "You don't need to continue apologizing for who you are. There's purpose in my King's reason to use a girl such as herself. I'm sure he has spent an extra amount of time in making you. In creation, there can be no error. Your presence here is very important to my King."

Anna looked around at the others as she began to gather her own assumptions about what was to come. Yet knowing assumptions can sometimes return back as redundancy. She would leave this open for future discussion.

"I only wish to know the truth. To find the answers that have eluded those most opposed of our current unknown conditions. At present, those creatures outside our door cause me to see them as a distraction."

"Well, you've seen how they look. They represent a portion of death we've not come to understand. They are destined for self-sacrifice for they retain no mortal soul. They've been specifically created for battle, and nothing else. They feel no obligation or tact, remorse or bitterness. Their mission is always the same, defend when necessary."

Anna's eyes flickered with a touch of light. "What should we expect of them when those of the Fallen come near? We are not soldiers. We are the Circle representing life. For death is a road for the dismembered and damned, a place so far from light that it imposes a King's purpose to be. Yet this Circle is bound for a higher calling, at which we do not know, for his timing and reasons are written in the stars of the sky. Yet my intuition tells me there's something well hidden from those scholars Fallen of heaven, for they seek only vengeance. With wisdom and perseverance, we will find those hidden secrets that save the soul, which are not too far precipitated, for man and the beast are hurried to lose one's patience, and therefore self-sacrifice would be something they have given, but not so of our company. Patience and integrity is a road we must seek to find a cure for these manifestations that come against your precious realms. There needs to be an end to them but with tact and planning to keep one from losing life, to be pushed into this fight appears to be what they want and not what should be done without considering every angle of this fight, before we give our blood for this King so willingly."

"Thaliana worried with hearing these words that expelled so vividly. She was worried that the Circle would serve an agenda that was not her King's design.

"Anna, what has brought so many details to your heart that you've sacrificed sleep for its cause?"

She looked across the porch with a disheartening expression and then to her peers. "I only seek the best way of preparation for battle to ruse our enemy for their improprieties will be their downfall."

"You will have your answers, young lady, but heed the warnings of what you learn, for your enemy to come is no ordinary soldier that walks the battlefield without compromise. There will be no second envisage for denial."

Anna's ears perceived her words with understanding. She humbly considered their demise as the weight of the world held detrimental circumstances. A purpose unfulfilled for a King was unknowingly moved forward by glory justified and the cost would be human life, a concession she did not want to keep. Those future sacrifices to come were for the recompense of just reasoning. History to come would be mapped out only as adroit reasoning void of rules or religion, as the incredulity of the enemy's heart would be forthcoming of a time without consideration of the end result.

"I have always been this way in life. I know it does seem the curse, but it gives me real purpose to know such borders of truth to be made known. Isn't that what all people should seek? As found out those hidden truths behind every wall, behind every door, or passageway, become the draw, because, without such truths made known; we fall short of being thorough." The Indian princess stepped forward and embraced the small-framed girl, who was about her size, knowing in her heart she was real to a point and trusting of no one. She knew she stood by her own personal convictions, which had become all-consuming from the mind of a King to a young woman, connected to a Circle by divine intervention.

"I see why my King found you to be so overshadowing." Thaliana turned toward Drew and smiled.

"Love this young lady as you loved the one before. You must be special to have a second chance to love again. Usually, my king doesn't see a second chance of opportunity, but I believe there can be exceptions to every rule."

Tommy stepped up to the plate." Are you referring to the stone tablets transcribed so many years ago?"

Thaliana whipped around quickly to see Tommy's face, where this awkward voice was coming from. "I guess you're alive after all?"

Everyone laughed at Tommy. The larger-than-life cowboy stuck with the southern grin. Tommy wasn't sure why he had the ability to bring laughter so quickly upon himself, but he sensed the close band that they all had the last two years as being a part of a unique group of people, those willing souls of a Circle embedded or rooted with trust.

"Well, to be frank, I'm a little like our dear Anna. I have always been an avid reader, and comprehend most of what I have read, but the mysteries written so long ago have meanings not quite understood, as parables go."

"Quite true, young man, but not to forget off the subject, for now, let me finish answering a question brought up about these three soldiers out front. These creatures, as you see, became a needed addition when certain misinformed angels had taken it upon themselves to turn other against our King. To express it in an earthly term, my king determined there to be dangerous connections of those who had turned to a darker side of life, leaving rules and regulations cast aside for their own personal glory. This could never be. The King had given rank to these beast as you see. Basically, they're just used as a deterrent, to keep the instigators or nonconformist in line. They were first viewed as an appurtenance to sway certain members of the realms that maybe living conditions weren't so bad after all. They were a military force that stood at the gates." Thaliana leaned over the railing looking at the feet of these monstrosities. "When the Fallen come, you are all to remain behind the protection of these Conquerites' shields. They will perceive any immediate danger that would try and cross these borders."

"Does that mean the Fallen will have no known way of eluding these Conquerites?"

Thaliana saw something deeper with in Anna not perceived by others. It wasn't that Anna didn't trust in her plan; she didn't have the ability to believe the Fallen to be complete failures at battle. She had seen something, past what everyone else missed. These angels, fallen of heaven, were created in His image like everyone else. They had the same capabilities and intelligence as all of his other creations. Yet, nothing from Anna's perspective should be overlooked.

Thaliana looked it up. "Gabriel will soon be on his way."

"When will that be?"

"Soon. Like I said, you've got to prepare."

"I'm down with that. Tommy broke in. Randy reached over and put his arm around Drew.

"I don't know about you, but when do we get off this rock and head for home? We're better off not even being in this fight, and it sounds to me like that we're not really wanted here." Drew looked at Randy and rolled his eyes.

"I'm with you, but let's do what we came here to do and then we're gone."

"Amen to that," Tommy proclaimed. "I don't want to stick around too much longer."

"We'd be in the way anyhow," Randy added.

Thaliana looked at the boys in the mix of emotions and unmannered devotions.

"Maybe Anna has a plan that we can accept, as a true legitimist," Drew said.

Anna's eyes turned to view her latest heartthrob. "I need to hear what Gabriel has planned before considering our own. Besides, when positions of authority start turning ugly, plans will soon fly out the window. No pun intended Thaliana, being a winged creature as you are."

"None taken."

Anna looked over Drew's shoulder to see a disconcerting stare in Thaliana's stance.

Randy, Jim Carson, and Tommy got off the front porch surveying their latest giant-sized soldiers just in front. The air felt different with these three unimaginable creatures standing facing out toward the silence. Randy reached up to touch the heel of one, and Thaliana stopped him.

"I wouldn't do that if I were you. You'd come to regret it. Believe me, their visions would take a hold of you and wouldn't let go."

Randy turned to assess Thaliana's solid advice. "Glad you told me."

"They have their own way of leaving their mark. I wouldn't advise any of you to touch them, unless you're appointed to do so, by me."

Suddenly, a sounding rumble shook the very ground underneath them as the clouds above parted and a surfeit of light exposed an angelic image lighting up the sky. After recovering from the sudden jolt of realization, all members of the cabin saw the most beautiful of sights. A cherubic form dropped from the sky and landed in front of the meadow in a trice of time. Randy and Tommy had to catch themselves from falling while the young Bella let out a scream. Anna's face was lit up like a ghost. What were they actually seeing?

Thaliana paid no heed from the sudden drop from the sky, for she knew what was coming. This angelic form wasn't here for a daytime stroll in the park but was here for representation by a King of realms. This inscrutable being expressed his might and power just from his presence, for his days had been long and his patience short because the time was drawing near to the hour. His assiduous sobrieties remained imperturbable to his cause. He stood abreast with sword and shield. He was a teacher, a leader, a true warrior of the realms. He had fought and taught and built up and tore down. He'd lived a long life and had his moments with strife with those that had fallen of his world. Where his blue eyes were willing, he'd raise his sword high. His form was revealing of an eternal welled feeling of the world would soon take flight.

Gabriel stood over ten feet tall with a body mass like that of a Greek God of Olympus. His stance held strong, and his attitude forbearing, for the fight to come would be forged by the mighty. He had high cheek bone and bore a red tint to his complexion. His voice was smooth with deep overtones of benevolence. He showed a flicker of mystery yet smiled when addressing his former student. He acknowledged the glint of respect in her eyes as he gave her a nod of approval. Drew, not being in his normal frame of mind stepped out and introduced himself and his fellow colleagues, as if his timing was congenial to this angel's cause.

"Hello, tall and handsome fellow."

Gabrielle pulled back and raise an eyebrow, as this puny representation of the circle held a fading claim of goodwill.

"I'm Drew, and these are the members of our Circle." Gabriel gave the impression of being somewhat surprised. He wondered if these small humans overlooked his actual size, maybe passing him off as insignificant. Gabriel remained humble in a gentle sort of way, to make Drew's acquaintance in the friendliest of ways, and held out his hand in a bond of friendship. The Circle's leader felt a radiant surge of power go through him. He looked up, in baffling surprise, for being so brave on first introductions. Drew noticed a weapon at his side that looked somewhat familiar. One from pre-Greek mythology called a Morning Star. Its total weight was about eighty pounds, except this one seemed modified from what he had seen from a high school field trip. An extending seven-foot golden rod, hooked to a twelve-foot golden chain, with a golden steel ball about the size of a softball with three-inch spikes jetted all around. Its usual form was swung in a Circle above the head. Something was different about this weapon of choice. Drew looked up wondering if this entity of heaven's elite would be so willing and then asked him what he was thinking.

"Can you show us the Morning Star essentially how it works?" Gabriel looked at Drew with a serious expression, but then he realized the lad was just a boy in years. Gabriel knew a short demonstration would set him straight about what they were up against. He signaled for the other Guardians to meet in the meadow. Thaliana, James, and Skittles jumped off the porch as the Circle watched at a distance. Of course, Gabriel was not serious about causing anyone harm, just a game of chance and movements, a demonstration of power. Drew and Anna's eyes grew wide when it started to look like a serious competition, as if codified conditions were taking form. James became angel size with his wings spread wide as Skittles followed along. Thaliana's body armor jetted all around. James and Skittles stood a good twenty-five feet apart. Giving Gabrielle ample space to swing the Morning Star above his head, he took it in his left-hand while looking back at the others.

He spoke for the first time to this boy of benevolence that stood by his side. Drew's, acknowledgment of heaven's elite placed his hands at his side.

"Your time is near," Gabrielle said, "as each one is marked for a journey. You are choosing a path that others dare not follow. For what their eyes can't see, and mind envisions are laid at the feet of the innocent. That other world never seen by your kind is soon to come." Gabrielle turned to look past him. "Along with your Circle of friends, the Winds of Time will take you there." Drew became lost in his meaning, yet Gabriel didn't wait for a return acknowledgment. He began to swing the Morning Star above his head. The weapon advanced in speed, crenellated of mounting power like a surging whirlwind eradicating weight and distance, mixing space with matter and erasing both. Gabriel swung this weapon with a greater force than ever seen by the human eye. The Morning Star whistled a warning, a high-pitched blast. It picked up speed as time went past. The wind and speed became forbearing, pulling everyone off their feet, a magnetic draw. A unique suction antithetical of gravity opened a black hole, an abyss pulled through the fabrics of time. The whirling wind draconian of unwritten laws, as a freak of nature set without boundaries or limitations, the whistling sound of the Morning Star tacitly brought to an aggregated level. Each member recognized this as a massive tornado.

Drew yelled out, "Stop! That's enough!" The power and force of the weapon alone was strong enough to cause damage to anyone standing close by. Suddenly, the Conquerites move their shields in a protective mode. Gabriel showed a punitive grin and backed off. Only the strongest older angels could wheel this weapon.

James looked over and wondered what he'd gotten himself into. He knew it was a weapon needing skills he couldn't fathom. Gabriel was a teacher for warriors of heaven's elite, immortals wheeled to do a God's bidding. He lowered his weapon of choice. He glanced at this young representation of man, regaled to set this boy straight.

"It's quite the weapon as you can see." Anna reached over to take Drew's hand and pulled close to his side. They were alarmed by what they had seen. The visual was so elucidating; it left those wondering what kind of King would use such accessories as this final resolution. Skittles whined while sticking his tongue out, dripping what was left of fluids on the ground. Anna looked up at the immortal as seen of intimidation. Even so, she was the only one brave enough to say what she was thinking.

"So, are you here to teach or just show off like a big boy with a big toy, like most men do?"

Gabriel raised an eyebrow and then looked at the Indian princess. "What's this?" he said with the simpering expression.

Thaliana's smirk turned at the corners. "She's like that. I mean the attitude is the girl to a tee. She means well, my good teacher. I'm still learning her abrupt ways."

"Maybe the young lady needs a few lessons of humility."

Anna brushed him off like this overgrown adolescent was a bit dramatic and then Thaliana cut in. "I think maybe you need to learn her way of thinking before judging her so harshly."

Gabriel sized up Anna's vagaries before making any further assumptions. "Well," Gabriel said, "I guess we're ready to get started."

Anna walked around this larger-than-life, angel and poked him in the stomach like he was the Pillsbury-dough-boy checking the rise on a certain cake. Gabriel was so shocked that he raised his arms and backed up while trying to avoid stepping on her. Drew's mouth flew open when examining Anna's improprieties.

"Anna, please… what are you doing?"

Anna turned to consider her appalled heartthrob.

"He's in charge of this whole thing." Anna shot a glare back at Drew, a degree of anger flinted across her eyes. She ignored Drew's comment as she studied this peculiar specimen of a King's elite. She inspected him like she was examining spare parts for General Motors and seemed to be a few parts short of a good car in lesser conditions.

Gabriel couldn't believe he was on display, comparable to an LG washing machine while the young couple with two brats was about to purchase. "How long are you going to examine me, young human?"

"Don't call me that," Anna bark out. She then placed her hands on her hips. "I don't understand," she said while whipping her head back toward the Indian princess. "He doesn't look the part."

Thaliana looked up at her teacher and turned back to look at Anna. She was quite spellbound that this youthful girl was giving this particular Guardian the once over, like she was getting ready to fit him for a suit. She still looked befuddled. This smaller representation of a King's choice had her hands braced against her hips. She hadn't made up her mind one way or another. Then she looked up with curious eyes.

"These Conquerites that you've brought here to guard this place, will they protect us even if our enemy comes up beneath us?"

Gabriel looked down and smiled acknowledging her question. "Well, I'd haven't really thought that they would go so far, but if you feel that the area needs attention, we'll look into it."

Anna shot a stare back at Gabriel as if he'd missed her point. "I was thinking take your soldiers to the farthest edges of the forest. Here and here," she said, "going east and west in the areas of here and over there," while pointing with her finger. Anna tried to sway her new recruit of the last fifteen minute as if he knew what she was talking about, but he didn't.

"Men…" she said while seeing the doubt in his eyes, "you're all alike." Gabriel sat back on a rock and scratched his top lip, probably wondering when this charade would be over. Anna reached down and grabbed a stick off the ground and drew lines in the dirt, in a bald area of clear grounds minus grass and weeds. Gabriel opened his eyes wider and looked down, a smaller than usual representation of a King might have something important to say. This caused the others around to pull closer, to view the few scraggly lines, she had scratched in the dirt. Anna looked up under a gentle cloud of dust that had kicked up from her new form of artistry. "So, do you get my point?" She asked.

Gabriel looked at Anna and laughed out loud. "I guess you've thought of everything, my small human friend. Why am I here?" He glanced back at his former student. "Where did you find this girl?"

Thaliana rolled her eyes before her reply. "She's one of the chosen. I didn't choose her. She was chosen by the King. It would be best you listen to her."

"And what strange purpose does she have among those of this Circle, for I sense she has no gift, like the others?"

Anna raised her eyebrows and shook her head. "If you're going to be difficult, I'm sure you can just wing it." Anna had her arms folded across her mid-section. I'm here so you don't overlook anything that will get us all killed."

Gabriel raised both eyebrows and put his hand to his chin. "How do you propose we will do that?"

"Well, for one thing, this Conquerites you think so highly of are going to scare everyone away. Who would even get remotely close if they see them? Whose idea was this anyways?"

Gabriel couldn't believe this small-framed girl was so brave with her words. And where did they find her? He couldn't believe his ears. "Young lady, if you need to know, it was my idea. And besides being in charge, what do you suggest, since you seem to know what's to come, and I don't." Anna looked up like she had stepped on his ego.

"My child," Gabriel said, "the world was not made in a day, but in seven. Come back on Sunday, and we'll talk then." The two other guards who had come with him laughed as the Circle behind stayed quiet. Gabriel looked back at the two guards knowing they reacted out of turn. They closed their mouths and dropped their smiles, as in a King had been deceived of knowledge.

Anna flinted her eyelashes up and down as if trying to clear a bad memory. "Who said bigger is always better anyways." Pertaining to his size, she looked at her Circle. "We need smarter not bigger."

Gabriel's face drained of color. "So, your point in being?"

"Fight the enemy where they aren't. I thought earth's history was familiar to those of heaven?" Anna waited with crossed arms waiting for a rebuttal of some kind.

"Are you familiar with the Sun Tzu and the Art of war?"

"Yes, I am."

Gabriel appeared to have missed something. Anna continued, "If they show up and see the Conquerites, they won't face us on the ground. They'll find another way in." Anna went back to drawing in the dirt. "My point is having the best battle strategies up-front. First, remember, the best possible way to start, involves reducing one's losses. I have information I downloaded and saved on memory. We can take a look at my proposals later. The three main points are one, to attack their strategies before getting close to the fight. Second, attack their alliances, so there's no surprise. And third, attack with soldiers as the last resort."

Gabriel began to see Anna's way of thinking, and so did the rest of his guard. "Okay, I'll make the Conquerites invisible so no one will see them." Anna thought this might bring merit to this after all, but then another issue needed addressing.

"I'm still unsettled about them finding a way in underneath this area."

"And what would be your plan, young queen?"

"Well, if there was one other way to get past these guards, I'd suggest posting several guards in the basement of the cabin, and something else? Take long jagged poles twenty-five feet long and drive them in the ground like so, at an angle to block them from coming up through the ground, an inverted upside down triangle as you can see." Anna went back at drawing in the dirt as if this had been a major feature in grade school, and she was just learning to try it out. Gabriel was curious about this human's perspective and decided judging her would be self-defeating.

"You paid attention in school. Who was your teacher?" Anna wasn't amused by the Gabrielle's teasing insight. She was looking at the big picture, which didn't include egos or little boys showing off their toys. She was serious, because this was a serious game, in this game of destruction. Anna shook her head and then looked up.

"It wasn't my teachers that gave me brains to think with. It was living with a family that couldn't learn from their own personal mistakes, mistakes that filled our lives with abstract living and moments of pain. I was tired of living in a way that kept us from having a good life, because I had a mother that couldn't see past the end her nose, who wouldn't listen to reasoning from a father who'd taken a backseat of leadership to keep peace in our family. I believe using one's head enables one to keep his head out of the clouds and better kept on his shoulders."

Thaliana sensed sadness in the way Anna spoke. Looking up at her baffled teacher, she blinked to draw focus. "I told you, she's different. She means business."

"Well, I guess she does," Gabrielle said while seeing a flaring flicker of pain, in Anna's eyes too. The girl saw past every angle of conflict, to see a world needing assistance. Gabriel saddened to see the flicker of pain. He began to trust this human and left his personal opinions away that day, and gave Anna an adjustment of hope, along with the lending hand of camaraderie and his faithful support. His insight, his aged wisdom, and his leadership skills would touch a tender girl's heart with that of a leader to being Guardian of heaven's realm. This was her time to shine and show her skills.

"Okay, young lady, you are my eyes and ears for what you see is wrong with this plan. I'll take your point of view for what it's worth. Fair enough?" Anna showed a quivering smile, while holding on to a cheerful thought to get plans rolling along. Even though in Anna's point of view, it didn't really matter what he thought of her. She only thought her plan being the best, because it was strategically thought out, not even allowing for him being from heaven. Although he had spent many a day learning extravagant battle tactics to outsmart the enemy, she depended on her own frame of mind. She was in this for the long haul, as they would say, to close every gap in the future struggles that had come along in the perfect sequence of simulation. Anna continued with her overactive imagination as she glared up at this rather concentric immortal. Anna turned to address the others.

"Might and glory is something that needs not to be on display during this battle. For your King has that honor, it's not something for soldiers to do, because they need to keep their heads in the game, focus on only one thing, outsmarting our enemy. We all need to learn to see past those barriers that blind us, beneath the hidden secrets of success, because success is not something that comes without considerable effort but from an open perspective of acknowledging there could be failure. Those of you who spend most of your time examining yourselves in prideful ways, by how you look and feel or your position of glory, have become the most vulnerable, those will be the ones that die first. For basking in glory comes to the deceptive mind, hinders the act of war, cripples the body, enacts the fall, as those Fallen from heaven have done before, setting one foot forward in this field is an act or proclamation. One step worthy of defying a King, for we are all judges and jury of those of a rightful heir without the consideration of a King, for glory is self-proclaimed without remittance of justification or who will be worthy of barring such honors. They are like trophies gathering dust. They are needless to a cause, for we are dust that gathers in the field, of battle which will be carried away by the wind. Let brothers be brothers and men be men, for our end is recompense of a promise each will come to his end. Those who once held position have Fallen into their own entrapments, like quicksand swallowing them up. For glory and personal gain is an illusion for those of a blackened heart and a reprobated mind. They will fail by their conditions, blinded by their lack of insight."

Drew began to understand the representation of their Circle. Anna's way of thinking pushed up a touch of emotion in Drew's throat. He reached for her and took her hand, then slipped his arm around her waist. Gabriel felt Anna's words were worth all their weight in gold. James saw the Circle in his mind's eye, knowing they would serve a purpose in being here. They had an important part of what was to come. James understood she had a redoubtable position to give all her opinion. He was glad that they were here.

"So, what's your plan, little queen" Gabriel proclaimed. Anna sensed a tad of sarcasm in Gabriel's manner, but she also sensed him being a good sport about supporting her along the way.

"Well, for one, you shouldn't let them see a mass of angels waiting for them with these giant Conquerites standing here ready to wipe them out. Have only a few of your soldiers standing about, with most of your warriors hidden within the trees, below the ground and from the sea, that way they'll smell no trap. Never let on that you mean to destroy them. Let them get in and make it look like they are winning the battle, and then when their numbers are the greatest in the center of this meadow, we'll surround them from all sides and overtake them." Anna still looked somewhat unpleased, but released her words slowly after much thought.

She regarded the sky that displayed that azure colors and forest with mounting trees on both sides. There was something missing…

"So, what's going on in your head, my dear Anna? What do you, see?" Drew asked. Anna turned her eyes in a loving manner, smiled but remained uncommitted in her thoughts. Her mind had been running like a locomotive for the last two days.

Gabriel took a seat on the edge of a large rock to take in her words. Drew and the others took a seat. Gabriel considered the young lady's words more than stellar. He then examined Anna's wondering eyes. "Okay, young lady, what troubling you?"

Anna looked up with a touch of emotion crossing her face. "I don't know. Something's not right with this plan. I mean they have wings and can fly up out of this trap like you would. There's got to be another way to overcome them. Something needs to hold them in this place."

Gabriel looked past the trees and discerned a perfect line away from the cabin. Fronting the cabin, and moving toward the lower end, the meadow expanded as moving forward, so the cabin was at the higher end of the meadow where the tree line was much thicker. They were boxed in by the trees at this higher level, causing a cone effect. Maybe a hundred feet lay from east to west, but the north end was narrowed while the south expanded at a distance much wider. From Anna's perspective, the gap looked to be narrowing as it drew closer toward the mountains and wider toward the ocean's door. This was a good point of observation from this pint-sized girl.

"I know what you see, young queen."

Gabriel stood and called his foot soldiers to his side and began to look at the forest and point to several key areas. He also began to make plans for these thought-out conditions. From one end of this boxed in area to the other had Anna hitting on a key element of strategy.

Anna glanced up, trying to find out what was part of the big picture. "So, you understand my point?"

Gabriel shook his head with a hesitant smile as this disruptive gaze flinted across his eyes. He reached down and put a hand on Anna's shoulder. "Well, young queen, it might not be the best plan but definitely inspired by your persistence."

Anna eyes narrowed as she ignored Gabriel's insistent name-calling.

"So, your plan is what?" Anna developed a serious look.

"We should cast these huge nets, which are catapulted from the tops of the trees at these different locations at a set time, when we have them here in these key places, here and here." Gabriel gave an example by pointing toward the tops of the trees to the west and east." And this will trap them in."

"What about your own soldiers that will be trapped also?"

"The nets are only to keep them from flying up out of the area. We'll keep the fight in this valley. That's my main concern. We'll figure the rest out as we go." There was still something missing, something desultory that was left unsaid.

"I see, but how do we overtake them if we're blocked from the top?"

"From the side, young queen, from the trees like first thought." Gabrielle sat on the top of the same rock and looked out. They had a lot of planning to do, and not much time.

Anna looked disappointed. "Well, shouldn't that depend on timing?"

"I believe you're right, young queen. One never knows what will happen when waging war against those of our own kind." Gabriel was taken aback by the young woman's understanding. Anna sensed they would never have complete control, because this was a fight between two like minds that were well trained from an elite class of immortals.

Anna turned back near the Circle, evaluating their gifts. Tommy, Toby and Jim had powers to help keep the Dark Angels at bay, and Drew had his deceptive way of stealing through doors. Anna was thinking the rest of this plan could be left for the Conquerites to contend with.

Gabrielle measured her points of view while looking back at Drew.

"Young man, I hope you can handle this young lady. She's quite the catch." Anna perked from the sound of her name not to take offense to his assumptions.

"I'm not a catch, my Lord. I'm an inspiration."

"That you are, my dear girl, and that you will be."

Gabrielle showed a deep stare that only comes from aged wisdom, bearing in mind Anna's character was not from an ordinary human.

Anna then turned and narrowed her eyes showing a tad of bemusement. "You're not making fun of me, are you?"

Gabriel, with a slight grin, said, "Who me, no, I would never," like he was playing along with her game of intrigue.

The Circle had to loosen up a bit and settled in with James and the Indian princess. They began to talk about their lives on Orbitus and their fellowship with the Aquerian leaders. Anna spoke about how beauty and chaos shared the same space at times, even being a strange place where they have lived as chaos in her many forms at the beginning of life would give back to this thing called life. For life was a subject that would be left for those of a higher purpose to consider, as death and her consorters who steal life away were standing at the brink of destruction.

Then the day followed instructions about how angels and the Fallen all played their part. How they would camp among the trees and covered creases of land. With carefully placed positions for better sight of the mountains, the glaciers of blue ice and their averse elements would frequently take over. They talked about what they were to face in the next few days. They talked about the past and all her conclusive ways as the day wore on and the night would come they'd be ready. The Circle talked about important issues to deal with security and about how communication with each other was one of the greatest concerns, during different stages of battle as it progressed. Anna seemed a little emotional after speaking about issues of the heart, and their inconsistencies as humans. They spoke of love, commitment, and times of sharing. They spoke of purpose and planned-out positions. But most of all, they shared those troubling times that pricked at a tender part of the heart, that reached beneath the lines of commitment and cause. And further, they talked about this place that used to be home. It had its moments of teaching, and reaching, yet the most important thing of all was saving lives, and holding to traditions of giving, and living, and loving others without compromise. For their reasons of giving were the facts that those living was the cause, and dying was a chance to be reckoned with for them all. They talked about new ways of living in the future, with unfathomable doors of hidden wonder, as they were in a place of no rhyme or reason, as the dolorous effect of the dying, had no purpose in Anna's head.

As she walked in mind through the timbering trees, she listened to the gentle sounds of nature, her unwarranted journey. She left a trail of guidance for those who seek her perfections. Anna glanced out the window. She saw wisdom cutting a trail before them, hidden in the panels of experience, the tracks of enlightenment, the footprints of memory. Her beauty was like the unseen ailments of chaos, covered by the soothing touch of comfort that had left this area without a signaled warning of departure. Anna's eyes sparkle as she saw wisdom walk the meadow below and turned her head to smile. She knew this girl behind her would compile worthy info to survive. They had to stay live and strive to move forward, for reasons of wisdom are like reasons of being… a mystery to unfold…

Drew took Anna's hand gently, led her to a secluded part of the cabin and began to talk with the new love of his life. She looked up at him while they sat together, staring out a far corner window, looking for wisdom to show a sparkle of her fleeting light, as distance of space blurred her memories. Her hair fixed like tendrils of healthy vines moving through the cogs of experience with her beautiful eyes reflecting off golden light, pearls of a divine purpose, immeasurable in the eyes of the living, but justifiable in the giving of those pearls. Drew looked into Anna's eyes and saw his reflection.

"So, what do you think?" Anna asked.

"Think about what, my love?" As love goes, he'd already known her love to be there, as they shared not with the words but in deeds done, as the sun rose each day and prepared a pathway for their hearts to find. Both hearts held by her draw.

"You know, this battle…the mood in the air." Drew caught her gaze, outside this place where meadows run through soft bleeding air.

"I think it might get ugly out there. This battle to come is for angels. It's not meant for us."

"Yes, I know, but it's more than that, Drew. We're meant to be here, but I don't understand why? We're not like them. This place called heaven… could it be real… like those demons with wings."

Drew looked suspicious of Anna's thinking. "I don't think their King would allow immortals to be defeated."

"You think so?" Drew saw the look in her eyes as if mysteries were like that of a fortuitous mind, absorbing wisdom through the cracks and creases invented. She was absorbing what she could, by what would follow, as experience lent a hand in the performance of remitting circumstances.

Anna looked up with her big brown eyes. "This is not a game, Drew. These are life-changing events that affect the end of all. Any further success for those of heaven is in someone else's hands, not incurred of our own."

Drew turned to view the serious expression on Anna's face. Dr. Zimmerman walked to the corner of the room and caught the end of the conversation. He smiled slightly as to show his presence between the couple.

Anna turned to meet his glance. "Dr. Zimmerman what do you think about this battle?"

He leaned toward the window and removed his hat, touched her shoulder and wiped his face with a handkerchief. "Well, I don't rightly know, young lady. To be in the midst of all this sounds pretty scary."

Anna looked up in Dr. Zimmerman's eyes. Age had shown under the deep wrinkles in the grooved skin of understanding. Randy and Jim walked in and saw the three in the corner and walked over to be included. Randy's face was perplexed. A sense of worry touched them all.

"So, what's the plan for us?" Anna asked.

Everyone was looking at their professor.

Dr. Zimmerman turned from the window and knew they we're looking at him, like he had all the answers. He saw the worry in their eyes and understood his leadership was expected. "I guess prayer wouldn't hurt."

Anna's eyes widened. "Is that your plan, pray and wait for the end to come? That sound like a cop out, Dr. Zimmerman. We have to do something, and you're a part of this."

Dr. Zimmerman knew she was right, and yes, the statement made was a cop out, so he quickly said, "I don't believe we have a say in the matter, my dear girl. This is not up to us. Never has been."

Anna showed confusion. "Gabriel had an open mind to my suggestions, which seems to tell me more than what's laid out on the table."

Dr. Zimmerman's eyebrow rose. "How so, my dear?"

She looked toward the door. "I'm not sure yet, but it seems Gabriel was shooting from the hip in a way. I saw it in his eyes. He was too open to suggestions. I think that his King is letting the angels settle their differences like he has done for us in the past."

Dr. Zimmerman was a little confused about where Anna was going with her thoughts.

"I think that he's not going to interfere with this battle."

"Why do you think that?"

Anna glanced back at this larger-than-life angel standing outside the door, before looking back at her teacher. "I don't know, but I sensed it in his manner, something hidden. His hands were shaking when he touched my shoulder. And the way he moved, he was nervous."

Dr. Zimmerman was baffled with Anna's sense of intuition.

"Maybe it's more than that, Anna," Randy said. Everyone turned to look at Randy.

"They're brothers. These angels that are getting ready to fight against each other, their common bond between them are that they're brothers," Randy said.

Bella walked over to the small group of Circle members and backed Randy up.

"Randy's right. They're brothers. That's what you see, Anna. In Gabriel's eyes, he doesn't want to kill his own brother. They're bonded by family ties. They played together as children. They are of the same blood."

This made sense. Anna observed Bella, thinking maybe she could read her thoughts.

"So how do you know this?"

Bella smiled as if she had control of the conversation. "Torack was talking to his foot soldiers. And don't you remember when first meeting the Indian princess, she had mentioned something of brothers. They were saying he is not looking forward to going up against his brother. He plans to capture him, not kill him."

"This is getting way out of control. Your team needs to pull out of this. You shouldn't even be here," Dr. Zimmerman said.

"I don't think we should interfere. There's more to this than has been said. This feels like a dispute that's been raging for a long time."

Anna had that worried look about her. What was to become of them? She looked at Dr. Zimmerman with rumination of what was said. "Well, I'm not sure it would come to brothers killing brothers, but think of it. Would you value the people in the house or the house itself? It's a simple equation of blood being more valuable than where they are from. A man can be pulled from his country, but in memory, he never leaves, so his heart still moves as a free spirit, always seeking guidance of brothers, for brothers will always have love for his supporters who remain behind in the woodwork of country. Love of brothers can learn to live anywhere, while left behind is the rubble of war. Destruction is still eminent. They both will have support from opposing sides. The realms might be in trouble if the fallen numbers increase as this battle builds momentum."

Dr. Zimmerman looked over at the Indian princess. "I believe your teacher is in quite the predicament, wouldn't you say?"

The Indian princess's eyes filled with emotion. A tear made its way down her face. "So, you believe the King sees these brothers as sons?"

"Well, wouldn't you my dear?" Dr. Zimmerman whispered.

Anna's body language appeared to change as she folded her arms in front of her and cast her gaze outside the front window. "And the people left behind, what will happen to them?" Anna asked.

Dr. Zimmerman's face took on a serious dictum. "I'm not sure that includes everyone left behind of earth."

Anna wondered what she had missed. "Why should they be left behind?"

"This is the last place you would want to be," Dr. Zimmerman said without answering her question. "There's no hope for the hopeless. There's no cure for a place set for destruction."

The color drained from Anna's face.

Randy turned his head. "So, what do we do now?"

Dr. Zimmerman looked out the window as if expecting company. "I don't know. It's not our job to judge why these predicaments are done as they are but to only considered the alternatives."

Anna's eyes become inset with worry. "And that would be?"

Dr. Zimmerman glanced back at his small group of curious students. "Well, nothing I could explain... but maybe we could ask our friend

Torack. He might have some insight. He sees a future that we haven't fathomed yet."

Jim Carson glanced at Dr. Zimmerman and measured getting Torack with a raised eyebrow. He left to get him, while Anna and the rest of the Circle stood in wonder.

Drew leaned over and gently kissed Anna on the forehead and pulled her close. The others seemed a blur to her at the moment and only believed the young man that had stolen her heart. She was everything they needed right now in this dreadful hour, but she was much more than a justifiable leader. She was keen in thinking they might stand a chance yet only in doing what she concurs them to do. Anna was here to represent her Circle of friends and those who would listen. She had embedded in her heart that true beauty of what her life had involved, not just her physical form, but much more complicated part of beauty that was embedded in her soul that made her more valuable to a King of realms, with her commitment to the eternal structure of this Circle. Her attachment to friends were all she had left. For Anna and those that were a part of her group were chosen from a selected few to represent everyone left. Drew looked down at Anna's hand, delicately made and tender. He reached over and kissed her, soft and sweet, the taste of tears on his mouth. She looked up at him into the starry gaze of love and pressed her lips against his. Drew could see the sunset beyond the window. Anna leaned in and stole another kiss. The clouds opened up, and it began to pour.

13

GREAT-GULF

The rain ceased to give in to the reds of the setting sun as it reflected a torrential downpour that flooded the meadow just in front. The forest went past the level of holding moisture as the darker clouds began to overtake the sky. The air was filled with effervescent colors of the land as it laid waste in the reproductions of iridescence. The wind was blowing at a rate that bent foliage of churning trees near their breaking point. All the young men who had tented the night before were now camped out around the fireplace. They had gathered in the warm comforts of the main room. Bella, Anna and Thaliana had taken to the loft. Dr. Zimmerman had the one-bedroom downstairs, and Torack and his soldiers had used the basement as their resting place. Drew had gotten up first and walk out on the front porch, and noticed Dr. Zimmerman held in memories while sitting on the porch under cover. Looking out past wind and rain, wrapped in a blanket, his face had paled through ages memories. It left a mark on his life chasing after dreams that had never happened. Drew saw him sitting in a rocking chair watching the rain come down.

"Would you care for a cup of coffee, Dr. Zimmerman? The professor looked up out of his reverie to see Drew standing over the top of him with a curious look on his face.

"Yes, that would be good to warm an old man's bones," he said while siding with a chuckle.

Drew left and came back with two cups of hot comfort. He was concerned about their aging teacher, who appeared to be lost in some past memory.

"So, what's the distant look for, professor?"

Dr. Zimmerman turned his stare with a troubling grin. "Ha, young lad, I don't want to trouble you with an old man's past. Its ways are full of projects that have left me many a year to think about. I'm sure it wouldn't interest you." Drew, still standing, was looking out past the puddles of not-too-distant troubles of his own life and placed his hand upon the old man's shoulder.

"Actually, it would be good to hear of your life. I'm sure I can still learn from my teacher." Drew took a seat across from him before saying, "You have my attention."

The professor leaned forward and gave a diminutive chuckle as he took a sip of hot comfort to get a jolt of caffeine. "Well then, my dear boy, relax a while because it does have its connections with you. It may even be of service."

Drew stretched his arms and sat in a chair abreast from his teacher, then pulled a blanket close as he saw the reluctant glare in the professor's eyes. Drew sipped his coffee as he bent an ear to moments of mystery. The professor paused as he took a brief look back to deduct his interest making sure the young leader was ready. Dr. Zimmerman, reflecting a diminutive smile, took another sip of coffee, before slowly unraveling those obscurities.

"I was quite the catch back in the day, as so declared by my peers, with a fair shake of lady friends pulling at my coat-tails, and along with that many troubles that followed. Oh yes, and troubles, my dear boy, can be most revealing of troublesome grief, but you'll find out one day what really sticks with you as the most helpful emissions so critically made. All your years remembered beneath the heaps of self-condemnation. There's no changing the past, my dear boy, but learn from it and pursue only those delicate choices of discretion that become dear to your heart. Love in secret is the cement of survival. You will learn that a woman's love lost will drain a man's soul. Love has it peculiar way of pulling you in all directions. It could ruin a good man's life so quickly, taking away a life of simple pleasures." Dr. Zimmerman bemused briefly by the boy who had stayed on the path first taken. "You look so lost, young man. Soon, this will all make sense to you, in one way or another how to put the pieces together." Dr. Zimmerman looked as if he was gathering his thoughts from distant places, well, hidden in memories as watery eyes of those memories came flooding back, understanding his words to be more personal.

"I was in love once, many years ago. She was from a very prestigious family in England. Her father was a count. She was much younger than me. I had no idea what would become of our connections. My mistake was falling in love with her. She was quite beautiful like Anna. In fact, she reminds me so much of her, my dear Katherine, my precious love. I still remember her like it was yesterday. Her particular ways were so defining of her. She always left me so spellbound by her beauty and grace... such a delicate flower she was. I loved her more than life itself, but she died as your Renee did, shortly after we had made glorious plans of defiant beginnings. Her mother didn't like me. I wasn't good enough for her Katherine, but I did love her so and was willing to sacrifice the dealings with her dreadful mother. Oh, she was the thorn in my backside that made me boil at times, but Katherine was worth it. And most of the time, I avoided the controlling witch as much as possible." Drew looked over surprised by Dr. Zimmerman's assessment of an old woman's anxiety.

"Katherine filled every waking memory of mine with love and commitment bound for a life wanting of most others. I was obsessed with her. She was so passionate about everything. She got pregnant before we married, quite the scandal I do say.

"Her mother refused to let me see her for weeks, so we snuck off and got married on our own. Then my sweet dear Katherine lost the baby months later. Her mother, being the witch that she was, stole her away from me. She destroyed my life as a professor. I was twenty-seven years old and a professor already set to make a name of myself at Oxford University, but that accomplishment was ruined for me, because of her dreadful mother. Shortly after that, I had to leave England to clear my name and start anew. That's how I ended up at Ohio State University. Well, after traveling the world through time, I had to live in a future,

I knew nothing of for time was a pendulum ready to cut the threads I held on to. I couldn't go back to her if I wanted to. She was gone, still in memory, but Katherine had stayed behind, facing her ignominy from the scandal. I felt bad for my mistake, yet there was nothing I could do. I left her behind to go to America because of other inherit goals that were of an eternal nature involving this Circle. She was one of my students, and relations of that order were deeply frowned upon. I lost my position at the University and was banned from ever teaching in England again. A time most enduring when trying to establish a good life. The eighteenth century was a difficult time to build a reputation. My dream had been lost. My heart was broken when I read that she'd died from tuberculosis. I found that out later when searching historical records a few weeks after being of the future. The information was recorded in the library of records. It was a difficult search, yet with diligence it was there. I was amazed, only an infinitesimal article about her death. She was part of a rich family that was well cultured. There was this picture," he said. "I took it and kept it for all these years." Dr. Zimmerman pulled a dilapidated, folded piece of yellowed paper from under his coat, showing this wrinkled article to the boy sitting next to him. A beautiful young lady of that era reflected in eyes of love and intelligence. A tear rolled off the old man's cheek. "I mourned her death for many years. I never married again. I could never find anyone quite like her. Well, until I met your sweet Anna. She is so much like her. Knowing her these last few years has brought us old feelings I once had so many years ago. I mean not toward your Anna, just her character reminding me of a past... I think that's why I took Anna in as a student and brought her to Ohio State University. Yet someone else had other plans." Dr. Zimmerman looked over for a brief moment. "You do love her so, my dear boy, as you did your last?"

Drew expelled a gentle smile as a quiver of eccentricity caused a brief pause in his manner, as if ceded of power. He knew Dr. Zimmerman had pushed a few buttons of his heart.

"She is quite the girl, is she not?" he said as a repeated inflexion.

Drew let out a transparent chuckle at the expense of giving the professor a little comfort in his docility. "Yes, I do love her, even though Renee is still a part of me." Dr. Zimmerman didn't miss the words of what Drew meant. His previous wife's memories would follow him all his life, living in this new world, he already considered home.

"You have to go home before this escalates. I mean all of you. The only reason you needed to be here was because of Anna. I believe she's the key. Her role in this battle between good and evil is not a place for this Circle, but you have to finish what's been started." Dr. Zimmerman looked toward the cabin door.

"Their leader saw what was so special about Anna after spending a few moments with her, and I see it too. She's an aplomb type of woman that only comes around once in a lifetime, too precious to lose like I did my Katherine. Don't stay too long in this mess. We won't have much time once this battle takes place. They'll be after her. Those of the fallen will be on to her."

Drew developed a disconcerting stare. "How much time do we have left?"

Dr. Zimmerman glanced past the meadow as the rain continued. The cabin door quickly opened, and Anna's beautiful face appeared. A hesitant smile graced her face as she saw the professor caught off-guard by her quick arrival. Anna leaned *into* the new love of her life and touched his shoulder.

"Hey, baby, are you hungry?" The words so innocently said caused Drew the raise an eyebrow. A touch of love expelled from crossing glances.

Dr. Zimmerman caught the gesture of love cast by both. He looked up with a quibbling smile. "Are you talking to me or Drew?"

Anna felt heat run to her cheeks. "I was talking to Drew, but you can be my secret admirer professor of an educational mind, if Drew doesn't mind giving away a few moments of time. I mean for educational reasons." Both men laughed, yet Drew still sensed uneasiness about his conversation with Dr. Zimmerman. *Why did he bear his soul so compromisingly, secrets of tenderness, incomplete transitions, and a trip down memory lane?* Drew thought, *what was its purpose?*

He looked over briefly with a troubled expression just before turning to address the beautiful flower hanging on his shoulder.

"Anna, maybe the professor would like something to keep his strength up. We have a few plans to discuss, if you wouldn't mind."

Anna caught the inflection of privacy traced in Drew's eyes. "Oh... yeah... I'll be but a moment," she said, "I'll bring something for the both of you." Anna treated Drew sensibly. The professor could see her commitments to the young man were for an eternal nature, even in the simple light of servitude. They turned to look at each other as she left the porch. Dr. Zimmerman's eyes expelled a flicker of distant light.

Anna returned in just a few minutes with sausage and eggs with two biscuits and honey. The smell of hot food redeemed a reciting hunger, as both men felt the draw of home-cooked food. Drew's mouth was watering as an impenetrable connection was made by the two congenial youths. After remitting both plates, Anna reached down with a warm kiss that left behind a touch of gentle memories of closet claustrophobia, and veritable boys with out of control devices immured of youthful misunderstandings. A chill went through Drew as he sucked in air to get his composure. A light shade of blush washed over the boy's face as passing glances caught love in her mesmeric eyes. Dr. Zimmerman smiled and put his finger on his cheek as if to signal for the young and beautiful to share her moment of affections, and of course, only to the letter of professional courtesy. Anna shook her head with smiling eyes as she walked close to the professor and grazed his cheek with a kiss of comfort, knowing she had his best interests at heart, showing respect for her teacher.

"Okay," she said, "you boys have fun and enjoy the rain." She then left both men in the torrential downpour under cover.

Drew sensed their experiences of that space between the past and present were just a breath away. He turned to look at his professor.

"We have to go to that dreadful place again, do we not?'" Dr. Zimmerman turned to see the expression on the young man's face. He knew Drew's statement deserved an answer.

"Yes, but I'm going with you," he said.

Dr. Zimmerman paused to see Drew's response. "I don't think Anna should go. They're targeting her."

Drew caught the understatement of Dr. Zimmerman's caution.

"I don't want to leave her behind, sir. I think she'd be in more danger staying here."

The professor measured for once that Drew might be right. "You heard Gabriel. We have to go," the professor explained.

"I agree, but James and Thaliana are going with us, along with the wolfdog of theirs." Drew replied.

Dr. Zimmerman already knew that information and prepared mentally for the journey to that indomitable place he wanted to forget. Drew's curiosity perked.

"Why did they take his father?"

"Something to do with the past, I'm guessing," Dr. Zimmerman said.

"We're leaving after everyone's finished with breakfast. We need to talk about the trip before doing so." Drew stood up as he continued to look out past wind and rain. He appeared to look a bit worried from what Dr. Zimmerman could gather.

Drew's eyes met with his professor's gaze. "We're taking Anna with us. I'm not leaving her behind. She's the one with the inspiring intuition. And according to Bella, James's father will be in a place never imagined, a place we haven't seen yet. Bella said that the gulf that lies between worlds has changed, something forbidden of a presence we've not encountered. We'll need every member available. They'll know we're coming."

Dr. Zimmerman regarded Drew's statement as if he spoke a critical aspect of this trip would not be anything they had mentally prepared for. Without saying another word, they both stood and went into the cabin. The morning air hit them of a freshly baked biscuits and coffee that had the homey aroma of warmth and comfort.

The Circle of members was ready to go. James, Thaliana, and Skittles were standing at their side as back up. The *Great-Gulf* gapped between worlds of another place; a nightmare in the worst of forms was about to be breached. Anticipation of the dreary day ahead didn't settle so well at the breakfast table. Torack sat with foot soldiers, examined his friends, along with the family of this strange planet he'd never been. But recourse of priorities he was well aware of. They would be left behind with weapons that they called Element guns, along with swords of that eventful place called home. Where they had lived and survived for the last four centuries. Their intellect and wit were well managed and focused for the day to transpire out of a wilderness like that of Orbitus. He was ready as they said their good-byes and hugs of endearing friendship. Torack didn't want to be left behind but recognized the alternative. Alien to this world and creatures of the air, he felt safer behind the shields of these giant soldiers in front. The Conquerites, held with wings of ineradicable strength to maneuver, to protect, those of heaven in their frenetic world of chaos. They were creatures too easy to disturb.

Noncommittal in his approach, Torack proclaimed. "We should go with you and come back before this battle begins. This is not to be decided in one day for brothers are brothers, and blood is blood. And their internal commitments of their bond will not be broken in a day."

Drew looked at that aged teacher as worry etched in his eyes. "I wish you would stay behind because if you got hurt or any of your fellowship, who'd fly the starship?" Torack understood the meaning and remained disposed for he knew his position was better served on these elucidate matters, preserved for a time much later.

Their professor and the Indian princess were discussing what was to happen between the space of dissimilar worlds. The Guardians and Circle took leave of this place. Bella's dreams began to fill in gaps of fruition. She had this reoccurring dream, invalid of a darker world of portent conditions, as visions of steel castles overwhelmed her. Places unseen by the human eye in earthly terms, a vivid imagination could not place a world more likely.

This vision strung along from a mind-expelling impermanence from time that didn't exist. The eternal reasonings of this place did not make sense. Each time, she would wake in darkness, feeling the cold susurrations of sounds, not recognized of being of the human spirit. Mutterings and moaning of unfulfilled moments lost in unrecognizable faces exacted payment for memories left culpable. For a world disconnected, only imagined from achromatic conditions, a light exposed quiescent as if life ceased to exist. This cold, steel castle reached for disheartening souls. To draw weary tendrils transmogrified in death as to reach for the light of life, to expel strength from those who entered her boundaries, mastered by a heart so black. Convoluted blurring her victims duped. Bella woke up screaming. She shunted the vivid pictures that flashed across her mind. Each room had been a holding cell for souls lost from before.

Each place within heavy dank air, each room was occupied with ghostly imprints of virulent subluxation. A hopeless feeling filled the air. The only person who was able to move independently from room to room was Drew. He was their means to an end, a light at the end of a tunnel. He was a glimmer of hope.

The Circle, along with the Guardians, flew through time and space as corridors remitting dark-dank hallways vitiated incredulity of things crenellated and marked by doom. The Circle slipped through this aperture marked by the dead. Dr. Zimmerman kept them together. Drew waited for Bella to see the right time to enter the correct door as melodramatic colors left behind on a trail of abandonment. The skies all around them were full of sounds of a permeating progeny of the dead. Suddenly, Anna understood this to be a place like her dreams. In her past, she'd tried to find resolve from those detached memories. As the living exist in their world of life and love and purpose, so these things that move in the dark of what used to be took up residence in this castle. This was a place of walls and darker shadows and mysteries. The feelings of apprehension crawled along the nerves and tingled on the back of Annas neck. Life as they knew it was long gone in this elusive edged inhabitation. Those conditions of the night exhibited a lack of necessitations moving toward light. Anna and Bella held on tight to Drew while Jim and Tommy keep the malevolent spirits at a distance. The Indian princess along with James and his protector expelled light in this darkened world. Those of heaven were marked accordingly, brought fright to those entities of the dark. Separated from affable light toward a path drowned in darkness, not procured in any way toward light, for darkness was the domain that pulled them. They were an infestation. Indescribably invested of an entity congestive for the flow of life was not in them. Randy kept close to his best friend as lifelong friends are the best investment. The knowing eyes can see and the ears can hear, but only the soul understands. What crawled and moaned and slithered in the dark were inscrutable. They held no representation of the living. They were an enigma of bad reasoning, disconnected from life, scorned by light. The Circle remained chaste of this place of the damned. Bella was trying to figure out what was inside past these gates that stood at the edge. They were procured forward on this huge lift attached to this monstrosity of a castle. It expanded as each moment pressed. The Circle found each member pulled toward this huge steel plate. They dropped and rolled while catching themselves before flaring off the edge. Each member of the Circle was held suspended, weight without recognition of gravity as no earth existed beneath them. A structure of the beveled gates and walls of trickery held in empty space, cumbersome in size not held to the laws of the living. To them, the living was a forthright visual of the nonphysical, not of reason. Everyone could see what Bella could see. She revealed untruth, for untruths was its intended purpose, and purpose was reciprocal as if mirrored of previous life, sustained as animation in a world turned backward. Anna knew those elicit dreams were coming back full circle. Tears built up in the back of her eyes. Dr. Zimmerman kept Bella focused by placing an arm around her shoulder. He presumed to know what touched her visions. A placid stare reflected in her eyes as she press forward.

She stood at the crossroad of these gates, as if an example of hell lay creeping. This was a lazaretto submerged in confusion. Behind the other side, she saw what looked to be a physical body, lengthy stringy, slithering gray hair, hinged together to the roots of a skull followed by an airy conglomeration of movement. Eerie shadows dance upon the walls gave way to a world more frightening; a deception of fear gripped Bella from moving forward. A creature quite tall took form with hypnotic body and face pocketed by scars. There was perfidy sensed of others that flickered through Bella's mind, separated by a wall of delusions. She saw this apparition lurking in the dark. It was held to the bonds of chains, writhing anklets, as bondage was the epitome of the draw. This entity was held to its room of torment. The creature dragged behind a chain of burden, as memories mirrored a life of wealth, and selfish ways of a deceitful life. Long past the shadow of days unforgotten, young Bella had seen those memories, realizing the pain in those eyes. For this creature impure in appearances, permeating with pong while being tethered by the weight of a past, as if memories were mountains scaled by heavy detrimental crepitation's echoing a harvest causing ruin. This particular creature was hissing and spitting a vile stench through the air. Bella drew back to push down the bile. She was overcome with fright. Young Bella was convinced this demented presence had felt her near for the presence of the living was like blood to a vampire setting a heightened sense of urgencies, as the draw of blood set rage in motion. Bella anticipated long razor-sharp talons finding her and ripping her apart. She turned with a look of fright.

Dr. Zimmerman pulled her back. "Calm down, dear girl. That's their way of drawing you. Don't succumb to this test of wits. We're here for you." Pallor of sweat permeated her face as she felt the heaviness of weight caused her eyes to flutter while Dr. Zimmerman held her up.

Bella looked at her aged teacher with a nod, for the professor had seen past those elusive shadows of familiarity. "There's something on the other side," Bella said, "those of the other side have no fear of living flesh but relish in the moment of sinking their teeth into soft warm bodies."

This caused Dr. Zimmerman to raise an eyebrow but considered his dexterous hindsight, a bit of elderly influence or his mummified self from his many years. He slightly smiled, sensing mothballs and murky memories was a test of ones courage to avoid the bite of those inflicting pain while considering him a mouthful of mush.

This creature lay near, played its card to draw those to discover, for their night and day were the same as time had no bearing on this place, for its intangible ways were unreliable. Bella saw a flicker of light. A small candle sustained a fading breath of life, waned in the balance of this place hither. She knew Robert was here somewhere, but where? She looked back at the Indian princess. Thaliana read Bella's thought by the look in her eyes. She wanted their time to be limited. Anna, from behind, clung to Drew, wrapped in the underside of his shoulder. He could feel her heart slam against her chest. A rhythmic beat vibrated in adrenaline. Drew pulled her close. Her fingernails dug into his arm. Anna gazed at the love of her life waiting for Bella's vision or for Dr. Zimmerman to prod her along. The castle creaked and moaned, sending a message of hesitation through Bella's bones. This structure filled with chains and hooks and blood and stench as if given way to this abattoir. Its existence was an illusion from reprobated minds. It was deluged of depth and meaning. Its message was clearer than a bell that tolls a final cry holding no redemption, for redemption had ceased to reflect a face of comfort. All had drawn nigh to the conclusions of the sufferer. Thaliana didn't like what she felt. Her second sense of reasoning had shed more than a little light on the subject. James and Skittles turned into their heavenly form not waiting for an invitation. Bella screamed a blood curdling high-pitched cry, something off-key, something unfamiliar rose the hair on back of each one's neck. Fear made its own sound that didn't fit in line with the living. It left them feeling empty. Drew saw Bella's twitching with eradicated movements. Her cries echoed a return sound that made no sense.

Drew shouted, "Are you okay?"

Bella blinked twice and then viewed Drew from a few feet to her right. Her heart was almost beating out of her chest, and sweat swanned on her arms and face. Thaliana reached over and touched Bella's arms of a wallowing complexion. She began to feel a source of power run through her, as if the Indian princess had a few gifts attached to her position. She glanced back at her rescuer with a nod of success, willing to understand that Thaliana was not held to the powers of this place. She was two steps ahead of her enemy's one minded thinking.

I'm okay, thanks." Bella informed Thaliana as a quivering emotion crossed her lips.

Suddenly, Thaliana experienced an acute sense of reasoning when noticing a host of Dark Angels moving quickly toward them with agility. She intuited something abysmal was taking form as the space around them began to fill in. Thaliana turned swiftly and took to flight with the two Guardians close on her heels. She released three golden arrows taken to swift flight like gently guided missiles admitting and ineluctable point. All three made contact in a direction of angled flight toward these grayish-black creatures just above the Circle and below. At once, the three turned into an ashy mist and burst into the air. The sky was culled with more frightful creatures as they quickly took up space. Tommy, Jim, and Randy used their own powers at a distance. James above Thaliana, was grabbed from behind by a huge set of hands. His protector sunk feverish teeth into the filthy creature that held James in his bonds. The wolfdog turned Honorite ripped a chunk of flesh from this creature's side. A forfeit of blood poured from him. James quickly acquired his composure for a brief moment but is hit again by another larger force that took him into a spiraling roll of wings and sharp talons. With grunts and groans, they slammed down hard on this steel plated surface. The air pushed from

James's lungs as if being trampled in an unexpected stampede. James's protector was quick to follow. The tumble of feathery wings flapped and scraped as the two creatures twisted and turned in a showmanship of might. James rolled to his left to avoid a knife that scrapped against metal, creating a shower of sparks. Jolted to respond, the Circle backed up. Jim Carson split two a part with the swish of his hand. Light and smoke and ash were released in thin air. Another arrow released sank into the back of another creature's head. This enemy brought their very best.

Without hesitation, James pulled his golden whip from his side, as he tried to make stride with this creature. He slashed and struck out with anger. James slashed at confusing shadows. His anger pushed him toward an end. His golden whip snapped off a right hand.

"You want a piece of me...come on!" Jim yelled. Yet Jim Carson used his gift and threw four unannounced enemy against a far wall. They hit the gate with a sizable crunch, slamming body and bone leaving stains of three kinds. Jim rammed a three-foot stake through another one's back. He turned his head quickly, leaving no room for reprise. From behind, another creature knocked Tommy to the ground. As air left his lungs, he gasped for breath focused to his left on the Indian princess. James flew back to the steel plate and tackled another predator. Anna glanced up and saw two more making tracks.

"Look behind you!" she yelled.

James did a Bruce Lee move. His slid at an angle whipping his wings in an outward motion. He sliced through the air to make contact. Bella and Anna pushed to the corner to make room. Their moment of denial was drawing near to a test, which caused Bella to lean against the wall to find a moment of peace. Yet Bella stepped backward, not her best step forward, a trap door in the floor, for this corner held an obvious anomaly. Bella's honor and feet, along with Anna were taken out from under them. Both young ladies toppled into a nest of an unnatural kind, hurled below into darkness. A rancid smell permeated the air. Bella's visions of previous began to crawl beneath her skin. Her dreams had been a forewarning of dreams to come. Both girls lay in a bed of sweat, injuries, and unconscious dilemmas.

Bella had hit her head. Anna fell at an angle of this trap door in the floor. They were more than surprised after Anna felt something broke below the knee. She screamed. When Bella woke, she could not see. The darkness had overtaken them. She could hear a faint cry a few feet away. Bella reached for Anna, a whisper's touch from her grasp. She sensed Anna's pain.

Drew turned and saw the girls were missing. His heart sank, knowing they had slipped from their grasp. Something hidden had taken them. He moved his eyes toward Randy, who was fighting off one of those creatures on his own. Tommy jammed the end of his knife into another's creature's ribs. The Dark Angel roared in pain as a black mist hit the wall just in front.

Drew yelled out, "The girls, they're gone!"

Tommy's eyes glared with indignation. "We can't stay here. They're endless."

"Where'd they go?" Drew insisted.

Randy and Tommy turned to see the girls were nowhere. Drew moved in Randy's direction. Toby came around the corner and had speared a Dark Angel right through the chest.

"I have to find them!" Drew said. Toby reached up and pulled free his spear before turning.

I'm going with you," Tommy said. "Besides, none of you know Bella like I do. She's unpredictable." Toby heard the words yet keep silent.

Dr. Zimmerman nodded. "Go before they're moved," Dr. Zimmerman replied. A chill went through the air.

"She shouldn't have come with us," Tommy said. "She doesn't have a way to protect herself."

Drew knew Tommy was talking about Anna. "I know, but leaving her behind wasn't an option either. No one knew what to do."

Dr. Zimmerman stepped forward. "Keep your heads, boys. They can't be far."

The Indian princess shot two more arrows that burst into the light of bliss. A hole of light had parted a host of Dark Angels as they fell left and right.

Randy acknowledged the worried look in his best friend's eyes. Jim Carson finished off another Dark Angel and stood to leap toward another member of their Circle. Dr. Zimmerman held his cane like a weapon stretching further toward off these creatures. His calmness set an example, as the Circle started losing confidence. Randy considered the heart of his closest friend. He remembered when they were just boys of youthful beginnings. How they used to stand together in everything. A remembering tear welled in Randy's eyes. Loss a difficult thing to endure, as life reveals imprinted souls so delicately made. He remembered his life of struggles of a broken family, punishments unrelenting, a mother gone of his youth, and a father, showing a lack of concern, yet Drew would always show up when he needed assistance. He had sacrificed much of his time to help a family member who did not know what real love was until experienced from a best friend who lived across the street. Randy jolted back to this reality." We're going with you." Randy stared at Tommy. "Besides, you need our powers to fight your way through them." Jim, Dr. Zimmerman, Toby, and the Guardians stayed behind. Thaliana and James were still battling in a good dozen Dark Angels. James cast his whip toward another one of the Fallen and splits him in half.

Drew took off in a dead run toward the corner where he had last seen both girls. Randy, catching up, began to feel around for a hidden panel.

Drew brought a flashlight out to expose a step hidden below. entrapped diminutive colors not perceived as normal, as all things of this castle were here for perfidy.

The girls were cold and afraid. Anna had broken her leg from the fall. She lay twisted in a heap of sweat and heated tension. Bella could hear small whimpers of agony come from her right. The darkness of this place was absolute. Tears rolled off Anna's cheeks down onto the cold steel floor, as comforts of the Circle had been left behind.

Thaliana could feel their despair from another area of this condemned place. Bella felt around in the dark. She reached for Anna in her miseries. She felt Anna trembling. She knew that Anna was starting to go into shock.

From a distance, Bella felt something looming inside the room, she sensed a presence. Whatever it was, it began to make a noise as it moved closer to them by each second that went by.

She pulled a small penlight from her pocket and clicked it once. The room was about twenty-five feet wide and sixty feet deep, but she couldn't make out what was making this insidious noise. She could hear a hissing plosive of air coming from twenty feet away. She stood up and reached for Anna's shoulders and began to slide her toward a corner away from the sound that had taken her adrenaline to an all-time high. She stood sheltering Anna, understanding this thing of the dark lay lurking forward, for this creature sensed purpose as before. Once Bella had Anna moved into a comfortable position, she flicked her penlight directly across the room. A building shadow had crossed the path of the flashlight. Her light flickered off. Bella shook the small penlight to get it to come back on. She turned to look up. And eerie shadow stood over her with protruding teeth dripping fluid from its mouth, like an alien creature seen in a horror movie with an acidic breath spraying across her face-except this was real. She knew this because the spray hit her burning her skin. Bella screamed. She could feel hot breath coursing across her face. She held back from vomiting. She screamed again and drop the penlight...

Randy turned his eyes toward Drew with raised eyebrows. "Can you take us with you?" Drew didn't answer because he felt Bella calling to him and knew he only had seconds to save the girls. He glanced over his shoulder at Tommy and Randy. "I have to leave now!"

He grabbed hold of Randy and Tommy as they held on, and then they were gone.

Jim looked around and saw that Dr. Zimmerman had backed up against him. Toby was slamming a malignant creature between him and another wall with the flick of his hand. Jim saw a bright light expel from the end of Dr. Zimmerman's cane. A diamond-shaped ball shot light from the end of what Jim understood to be a little strange. Dr. Zimmerman had a few tricks up his sleeve, puzzling his rival as he raised an eyebrow and shook his head. His quick stroke of genius turned the Fallen into a darkened mist. The professor grabbed Jim by the arm and backed up slowly against the wall of the castle's gate as Toby followed after them. They were faced head-on with over a dozen of these dark malignant creatures of the dammed. Dr. Zimmerman stayed between Jim and the steel plate in front. The professor had a few tricks still to pass on. The main gate of this monstrosity behind them began to open. Jim turned and saw a mass of Dark Angels standing stoically on the other side of the gate. The three of them became surrounded. Jim Carson turned to look at the professor. "Look, boss, the little angels went to play, and they brought their toys with them." Jim pulled a pipe bomb from the backpack, lift it, and slid it, which rolled across the floor into a hazy mist and *boom*! The pipe bomb took out seven more Dark Angels. Jim picked up a large framed steel door that had been torn from its frame, made a mental connection before starting to swing it back and forth at a high speed, mind over matter as blood would splatter all over the walls and floor. He was making a mess while knocking Dark Angels off their feet and smashing them up against the wall, three insidious creatures turned into puce of smoke. Jim began swinging the door like a helicopter blade at an even higher speed as a pendulum with purpose. The air filled with a putrid stench. The gate had opened up, leaving them vulnerable on all sides. The more that had come closer, the harder Jim swung this door like a sharp impediment leading to the flow of blood for the day of the dying was here. Yet fear held no part of the living, as the dying moved forward like automatons marching to the beat of dread. More accursed creatures splashed against the back of this steel plated wall into liquefied abrasions to fit the occasions. Thaliana and James had freed themselves from the twenty or so Dark Angels and made their way back to the steel plate. More of malignant creatures landed on the steel plate facing their dread.

Drew, Randy, and Tommy appeared in the long-beveled room where the girls lay thrown to one corner of the floor. Just in front of them, the carrion creature that Bella had envisioned was standing over the top of her as if to suck the very life from her. They saw Bella shaking as she tried to recover from her state of shock. Tommy grabbed the creature with his gift of telekinesis and slammed it against the far wall, as he sensed it to be neither male nor female but something else. The creatures shrieked in a high-pitched frenzy, as if pointing out painful mysteries. It quickly stood and ran toward them again. Tommy flipped around to notice it was bent on killing them. He pulled a serrated knife from under his belt that looked like it was used to skin alligators. Tommy gripped it in his left hand, a perfect fit for a five fingered hold. The steel blade sparkled off silvery light that came from someone's flashlight. The entity leapt where others dared not follow. Forward into unmannered bliss, it jumped toward Tommy. Timing and preparation were two separate conditions coming together to meet this foe. The creature looked like no living beast that they'd ever seen before. It raked a craggily claw across Tommy's face, as blood spilled and splattered down Drew's chest standing just behind him. The misery of Tommy's twofold condition woke Drew up. He looked down at the depleted cowboy with bewilderment. Bella scream when she made a connection of what was in front of her. Drew picked up the knife that Tommy had dropped and lunged at the beast. A look of hatred set in the young leader's face as he sunk his blade into the creature's throat. He gutted his enemy to keep it from forward progress. Blood had covered the front of this beast as its muscly flesh dropped to the floor. The creature slithered side to side in a mass of liquefied filth and heavy breathing. The foul order reminded Drew of an image of a hellhound he once had recognized from childhood comic books. Drew looked back at the girls and noticed their condition. They were sprawled out on the ground in the worst of positions. He recognized Anna's apparently fast-depleting condition while looking back at Bella. A surge of emotions got stuck in his throat. Anna's pale color painted a drab picture as blood from the break soaked through her jeans. Her body trembled in eradicated moments, and tiny whimpers of being exuded from her lips. Drew could see a bone protruding out of Anna's lower right leg just below her knee, as reflected from Bella's penlight. Emotions weighed heavy on Drew's mind, causing his stomach to churn in knots. He looked back at Tommy who lay unconscious. Blood was oozing from the cut across his face. *This is chaos,* Drew thought.

Bella saw bite marks in Drew's shoulder. He dropped down on both knees to reach for Anna's face. He could feel her body heat leaving her, as she emanated a diminished heartbeat. He turned toward Randy with a look of concern.

"She's in shock. Randy, lend me your jacket." Randy took his jacket off and put it around Anna's shoulder. Bella got up and went over to where Tommy was laying out in the hollow of the floor. She felt for a pulse. "He still alive," she said, as she ripped off a portion of her shirt to dab the blood off Tommy's face. Bella turned to look at Drew.

"Are you okay?" Drew blinked to clear his vision, not answering right away. He tried to take notice of any doors that might be available, but none could be seen. Drew looked back at Bella in the dim light left in this room while acknowledging the torpor view of Anna's face.

"Yes, I'm okay, just a little shaken up, that's all." He was worried. Randy took a few steps toward Drew and knelt down by Anna's side.

He looked in his best friend's eyes. "She's going to need some medical attention, or she won't make it." Randy and Drew both understood she landed in a way that a piece of bone speared through an artery. A serious expression crossed his best friend's face. Randy saw the look and knew something had to be done.

"The Indian princess, she's the only one that can help." Randy acknowledged by a shake of his head. He knew something like this was going to happen. Drew looked up into Randy's eyes.

"You know we're not meant to be here." Drew paused for a minute before finishing. "And you wonder why this is going south."

"This place will change soon," Bella said, "and then it will become something else."

Randy had a puzzled look on his face. "Why change…what do you mean change?"

Bella stared at the two Circle members kneeling beside Anna with worry flashing across her eyes. She wondered if there condition would worsen as time progressed.

"I'm sorry we had to come to this place all over again," Drew spoke. There was a long pause before anyone spoke again. Drew reached down and stroked Anna's paling face. He wasn't concerned about himself; only the others crossed his mind. Seeing her eyes move back and forth made him worry. He knew she had dreams of this place. He should have known better. Drew ripped a long piece of cloth off his shirt and tied it tight around Anna's knee to slow the bleeding. A tear leaked from Anna's eye. Drew started rambling.

"She has this strong personality. You know, she's never accepted life for what it seems to be. She's like a fragile flower. She would never give in to others without knowing the true path to take," Drew broke out a nervous twitch. He blinked when Randy interrupted.

"We need to find Robert before those creatures find us." Nodding, Drew bent to hold on to Anna. Everyone touched Drew and Bella connecting them with Tommy. Drew slipped through the next door and appeared where they had originally started. The Guardians ran over. All the Dark Angels were gone for the moment. Thaliana reached for Anna, knowing she was injured the worst. Her healing power flowed through her. Anna's current condition was effaced. The color began to slowly come back in Anna's complexion. They could hear the bone snap as it in conjecturally moved back into place. Their leader turned his head for the briefest of moments. Thaliana then reached for Tommy. She held onto Tommy longer than Anna. He opened his eyes. Anna moved slightly, and then she saw Drew holding her in his arms when looking up. She smiled and touched his face with cold fingers. The tickle caused his lips to quiver, an early enlightenment of young love. A smile of understanding flashed in their eyes. He grazed her lips with a kiss. Thaliana warmed Drew's shoulder with a healing touch. She stood and looked at them with serious intent. Dr. Zimmerman stood a far.

"We need to find James's father and leave this place. We can't stay here much longer."

Randy looked over at Drew and understood. They stood together and joined hands. Drew took them to another place, another room on the other side of this obscurity, a room that lay beneath this castle. Bella pointed the way. The room was full of chains and hooks and streaks of blood. A dank smell of rotting flesh pulled at them. They could hear soft whimpers of mourning in the distance. A shadow hung with knees bent, feet behind him, suffering with a suffused light flickering above him, clothes torn and badly beaten. He was hardly recognizable. A tear rolled from James's cheek. He saw him first. The corner was obscured by shadows elongated against the walls. James felt his father at his limits. An infinitesimal twinkle of light broke through shadows, casting moments of pain procured by a lack of desire. This was the end. James saw the Dark Angels sitting quietly with their backs turned as a surge of rage welled up in him. Thaliana reached up to hold James back. Two Dark Angels were guarding Robert's bloody body obtained to the wall. He was hanging in thin lines of life; sweat and blood ran down his face and neck. His arms looked bent in a manner that showed they were pushed beyond limits. A whimpered moan leaked from James's lips. Thaliana carefully stood angled in shadows and shot two arrows before they could signal any others to come. Both shadows of that darker world vanished in thin air. They were alone now. Robert's body seemed lifeless, lonely gentle whispers of breath expelled from a fading heartbeat. James reached up and ripped the chains away from the wall and floor in a matter of seconds. His rage had been building since entering the room. His father was pale while both eyes were almost completely shut from being beaten. Yet his recognition of James caused a grin to grace his face.

Thaliana reached for him and placed her hands on his shoulders. His wounds began to heal right away, and his normal color began to return. Robert leaned his head upward and blinked. James bent the shackles off his father's wrist and legs. They fell to the floor with a clink. Father and son reunited with tears. A cry of forgiveness encased between the father and son, there was hope again. He saw the look in Thaliana's eyes." We can't stay. There's not much time." The Circle and the Guardians held hands and slipped through time and space as colors of two worlds apart began to mix as they were thrown forward. Memories and dreams were the same as time and space. For the briefest of moments, it didn't make any sense.

They were pulled forward by this current time spot, passing the hot blue stellar spectral of stars, Puppis, supergiant's a mass strung throughout the universe. The smaller red dwarf suns graced the heavens flashed by at immense speed, quicker than the eye, quicker than dreams that pass leaving to a different part of the universe. They could see colors of brilliant proportions, like the Orion Nebula with its extensive swirls of ghostly glows of gases floating in the cosmos. The darkness of night gave way to the blending of newness all around as dark empty space gave way to light from the sky above and below remixing colors together as it brought them closer to life. An explosion of light circled all around them as the brilliance of this universe was only showing a flicker of the heavens. Sounds of wind and billowing clouds began to gather around them as they kept falling toward earth, as light and darkness coexist. Dr. Zimmerman reached out and directed the Circle through a gate. Drew closed the door as they advanced to a world of the living. Anna turned and wrapped her arms around Drew as they appeared inside the cabin. They left behind that place between worlds.

Thunderous sounds surrounded the cabin. It was engulfed in the throes of battle. No one was in the cabin but them. They were shocked to leave one world of chaos to only enter another. Thaliana, James, and his protector head out the front door into battle. Thaliana's eyes peered toward the heavens, blackened by night and dashed by wind and rain. The sky filled with thousands of the Fallen, her heart started to race...

14

THE FIRST BATTLE

The Conquerites held an angelical splendor, when they slew Dark Angels with each stoke of their swords, without their enemy seeing what was coming. They held to their bargain of keeping their enemy away from the borders of this valued cabin, way out beyond the borders of a normal way of living, beyond any typical way of thinking. There was no just cause in the dying except to meet this night that was before them with a conclusive end. For dying held no purpose. It was only a place to find body and soul emptied out, to ruse in the range of emotions, to set each member free. Life at the moment held no value except to show each member of this battlefield that certain decisions made emotionally had a no return policy on those it was enforced upon. Thaliana could feel a heavenly strength come to her as did James and his protector. They were wrapped in a bed of emotions. They jumped into the fight that lay before them. In the short distance of raze, Thaliana could see the swarming of swords and other weapons clanging and slashing to the sounds of death. Blood flowed this day of all days and chaos filled this meadow that clung close to the edge of timbering blackness. Strength and finesse was closely guarded as this day of the dying was quick to follow a place of the dead. Thaliana realized a better tomorrow was by the unyielding of her sword. They were drawn to a bitter day by the edge of her blade. In death there was the end of rage, the end of an enemy fighting to choose to walk along side of the grim reaper of overshadowing darkness, as death held the scythe to remove heads from bodies on a better road to dread. For light did not dwell in the hearts of the dead. They were of a darker world confused by the light, confused by the fulfillment of glory.

The Guardians, along with their alien friends were already fighting, using their instruments of destruction to slay the enemy. Torack had a force field around his small circle of Aquerian soldiers. The Dark Angel's, swords and arrows would not penetrate their shield, thankful for advance weapons from a more advanced race. The Aquerian soldiers had weapons replicating a laser, cutting through the ranks of darker shadows, known as an Element gun. Gabriel looked behind glad to have them as backup. Torack and his Aquerian soldiers were having better luck at reducing their numbers, because they didn't have to go hand-to-hand combat with those of the Fallen. All they had to do was point and shoot from a distance. Watching from a distance, a hundred yards from the cabin, Cornelius face appeared frustrated by his numbers being reduced so quickly. He knew something was strangely guarding the cabin's borders. Cornelius backed up to get a better perspective of the total battle scene, then he moved to the front left of the cabin, close to the edge of the forest, and signaled a half a dozen Dark Angels to free themselves up.

From inside the cabin, Bella could visualize Cornelius's plan to dig a tunnel to reach down under, she knew then Anna's prediction was right on. This was their plan all along. Something Anna had seen from her intuitional mind. Anna was truly gifted. Cornelius took flight at the front side of the battle scene, were dirt had been piled high off the side, hidden in behind the first rows of trees, which was blocked the vision of others. This deceptive group of Dark Angels dug in deep, under the close scrutiny of three sets of eyes. Those creatures of a deceptive leader were up to something. Bella sensed their deviations hidden away from the battle scene.

Not too far from little brother, Gabriel began to swing the modified Morning Star above his head. The spike steel ball with the rod and chain were the perfect diversion of necessity. It caught most everyone off guard, both the Fallen and those of heaven. A few stopped to look back at the edge of the forest. The Morning Star stole the moment as it divested space with a high-pitched whistling. Gabriel's muscles flexed through broken light. He brought this galvanic weapon up to speed while quickly pushing back the crowds. The trilled sound produced caused a quelling pressure to strafe the ears of those who witnessed the draw this high-pitched sound, along the building of speed created a wind tunnel. Its combative form weighted heavy on the few that were close by. Its distressing pressure began to form a black hole with a buildup of illusive clouds surrounding the mouth of its imposing force. A hand full of Dark Angels were sucked in and slammed against the spinning ball of terror, and anything else that was closed at hand. The indiscriminate weapon sprayed the meadow with blood and unrelenting ferocity. Those of the Fallen had sensed a habitual fate toward a dismal end. Cornelius saw the Morning Star in the background and knew what it was yet only shed of glancing acknowledgment and pulled a lightning bolt from behind his back. He ran with intemperance and slung the bolt of lightning in the direction of Gabriel. It left his hands with such speed it knocked the Morning Star from Gabriel's hands with the crack of thunder. Gabriel was knocked off his feet and flew a good hundred yards landing hard on muddied soil slamming against half a dozen angels from both sides. Cornelius flew to where his brother lay and picked up the Morning Star and snapped the ball and chain off the end. He reached for his brother and grabbed his hand to help him up. Gabriel laid a piercing stare, as little brother only smiled being aware of their predicament.

"Hey, next time no cheating. By the way, where did your friends come from?" Cornelius cast a shadowing expression, wondering about these bizarre alien friends.

"They're not my friends. They belong to someone else." Gabriel eyes looked back, untrusting. He had once deeply loved his little brother, yet so many inimitable happenings since their youth had come between them. They had spent thousands of years together, playing in the courts beyond their mansion. The fields were graced with orange blossoms of effervescent colors. They had learned as young warriors about a past quickly lost from innocence. Their days were spent on golden walkways cobbled many pathways toward freedom. They played were adolescents could learn about their world so angelically created, staying in the protection of a guiding force of a kingdom's love. Gabriel remembered taking a smaller brother's punishment when getting in trouble with a father seeking only perfection from his two sons. Something buried deep in the younger boy's heart that led to facing their present-day situation. Their realities had finally come back full circle. Cornelius wanted nothing better than to best a brother giving of his total commitment. He smiled as he pulled him to his feet. They had spent countless years training together in youthful days of yesteryear. Gabriel has been a tutor to little brother. He was a much-needed mentor, one who could be looked up too for guidance and encouragement throughout his whole life as two young lives began to grow and form. A King's honor and glory had been their main focus as youthful lads. They were geared to become leaders of further creations of realms. Yet something went wrong between two brothers that led to a King's broken heart. There had become a gap of separation, a gap of love and jealousy, and a gap of differences that festered in a young warrior's heart. Gabriel learned more about love that day. The love of a brother pushed to the edge of existence. Where would this end? When would it stop? Brothers turned immortals, set out on the edge of eternity, as a visual of life flickering by. Even in battle, Gabriel knew he could not put his sword through his brother's heart. The memories of youth and love shared caused a lump of emotion to rise in his throat, emotions he hadn't felt since the last time seeing him. Gabriel held back the sentiments that pressed on the back of his eyes.

"Thanks for the info," Cornelius said, "I'll see you soon…"

Gabriel saw Cornelius leave the ground and threw his same thunderbolt toward the Aquerian protective barrier. The bolt slammed against the force field, breaking through, spilling the guts of an Aquerian soldier. Torack whipped around to see his comrade with body torn in pieces. He became enraged yet held his composure to save the others. The Dark Angels yelled a victorious victory. Infiltration into the Aquerian stronghold had been a major breakthrough. Half a dozen hellhounds came out of the forest on both sides of the tree line. They took down several archangels at the edge of the battlefield. Thaliana, James and his protector turned their focus toward the hellhounds, a creature thought to only exist in mythological legends, or from comic books for young minds of myths foretold of places thought not to exist. But to James, they looked real enough to blow back your hair with their foul stench. The hellhound was a fierce competitor with protruding teeth and wings shimmering of a darker world. Each beast contained a stinger beneath their tail catching most off-guard before they knew what hit them. The hellhound exhibited as frenzied emotion of rage. Each beast left a trail of drool and blood remitting from mouth of venom. The hellhound held to only one purpose, sensed only one pleasure, and was driven by malevolent intentions. Their skin was layered thick, tougher than the hide of an alligator with jaw-tight razor-sharp snapping teeth. Their wings were fitted on edge with improved hooks at best knocking their victims off their feet. The hellhound had spikes ridging on top of their backs and claws ready to tear into soft flesh. The stinger whipped back-and-forth like a scorpion set to vouchsafe a quick end. Their poisoned barb gave no mercy, left no victim living, only giving of an assured instant death.

Thaliana shot three arrows quickly and took out the first beast. It turned into ashes and splashed against her next victim. Gabriel pulled his sword from behind his back and cut a trail to the front side of this battle scene. He took out another beast by removing his head, which bounced several times before rolling face up-the left eye blinked open under James's feet then winked. James looked down and kicked it a good fifty feet hitting the back of another beast. Thaliana noticed James taking down another of a larger shadow by a foot sweep and ran a spear through his chest. Each blade used set aglow in an amber-blue color of light before sucking the life from each victim. He was given this present by Toby who'd looked over and only showed a grin of southern hospitality, just inside the barrier. Another beast headed his way. James leapt to the side and came in at an angle against another hellhound as he mimicked a famous Bruce Lee move to the tee. His protector snapped off one of his back legs, leaving it handicapped. The beast flew through the air bleeding, soon to be finished off by another angel in flight. Thaliana shot two more of the Fallen out of the sky. The land below looked like an invasion of impersonal bees protecting their queen. They were headed directly towards James who had been cut down in mid-flight. Thaliana's only concern was guarding James at a distance. She. kept a watchful eye as she fought her way toward him. Suddenly taking up space behind him, she flew to his side, sensing he had become the main target.

"You need to go back into the cabin. Stay with your father!" she insistent. James didn't want to leave, but at the same time, he didn't argue. He turned back toward the cabin with Skittles knitted to his side. The Conquerites pressed heavy to keep this enemy from advancing. These stoic warriors of heaven recognized James and his protector and let them pass through a small opening and then quickly closed up the gap behind. The Dark Angels still hadn't figured out what was keeping them from passing across the threshold of the cabin. Their consistencies through futility were a constant barrage of violence that keep them focused for a prize they could not keep. These creatures of a darker world tried to take this impenetrable barrier by the pure force of the rage of clashing of swords. Yet something quite large with invisibility had blocked their way from getting through. The Conquerites, battle shifters, planet enders were a force to be reckoned with. There was so much confusion with everything set aflame that Gabriel couldn't follow through with his original battle plans; too many of his soldiers of leadership had been defeated. Then Anna's words came back to him in full force. When the chaos begins, you won't have time to integrate your plans. The battle will take from them all manner of logic. Their numbers were down as the slain in the field left a flow of blood and a sense of emptiness. Gabriel was concerned. Cornelius, from the other side of the meadow, had focused on reducing the numbers of the leaders-not giving value to the foot soldiers that were slowly depleted. Gabriel began to notice rules of engagement he had taught younger brother so well. The catapult nets were a no go. Too many of his captains were already gone. Gabriel began to see the cracks in his defense. Little brother had learned quite well from older brother that had taught him so much. Deception was the key to this distraction. Gabriel had noted Cornelius setting the stage for an unexpected surprise. James and his protector had shot passed the door. Jim Carson, in the protection of the cabin, was equipped with more pipe bombs. He filled the table with half a dozen other weapons. James looked down and considered their chances.

"What are those for?"

Jim, showing a rusty grin, looked up. "Robert had an idea about drawing those creatures into the mine. Maybe we can take back the lead. There a part of a better idea, to cause a little bit of disorientation." Jimmy said while filling a duffel bag quickly. James looked over with a hint of confusion.

"Who is going on this little adventure?"

Drew stood and looked over. "You, I, and your protector, and maybe your father... if he's feeling up to it." Drew looked back at Robert who seemed infused mentally to the battle raging outside the cabin's door. Then he looked back at James." I heard your dad has the tunnels almost memorized?" James wasn't too thrilled about Robert making the trip down into the mines again, but Drew tried to reassure him. "I can get us to the end without having any trouble, as long as I have someone who knows the way. We're here for a reason," Drew said. James looked up, somewhat disconnected. "We'll go back after they've been pulled through..." Drew hesitated, "just before boom ...they won't know what hit them."

James had a peculiar look about him that said yeah right. "What makes you so sure we'll have time to get through without being seen?"

Drew had a distant stare in his eyes, and then blinked. "I'm not one hundred percent sure about anything, but we have to help them somehow. Their numbers need to be reduced, unless you have a better way."

Anna looked down from the loft a bit surprised. She wasn't too thrilled about the love of her life cutting through the backcountry being chased by those creatures, bad enough contending with the wolf packs and now, these winged creatures with inhuman strengths.

She yelled down from the top of the loft, "Drew, you shouldn't do this, unless Thaliana goes with you. She's the only true Guardian with training." Robert looked at Anna with a deep impeding stare.

"Drew, please," she said, "it wouldn't be right to go without her. And getting trapped..." she hesitated, "if you ran into a snag, you'll need her assistance."

Robert handed James a walkie-talkie. "Here, you and the protector will go first and cut a trail behind. They'll be led right into our trap." He looked back at the young leader. "Drew and I will go through one of the portals. We'll be okay," he said with hesitation in his voice. "They won't know we're there until it's too late."

Anna didn't like the fact that Robert was using her new boyfriend in a way to take revenge.

"Maybe you might think this'll work, but that's assuming everything goes the right way." That appeared to be an assumption rather than fact. "Don't be fooled. Those creatures won't be so easily led astray. You have to remember Drew. Cornelius was trained by their best. I'm assuming you haven't missed that?" she said.

Robert looked up shaking his head." So, young lady, how can I convince you otherwise?"

Anna's eyes flared toward Robert. "You can't, unless you can get one of those massive Conquerites to follow them up the mountain. And I'm sure it's going to be hard not to be noticed."

Robert stood and placed his hand on his head, wondering about this girl. "Well, young lady, who put you in charge anyhow. This isn't your fight. How would you like to be tortured as I had been? What you're considering will leave this cabin open for those creatures getting into our little place of safety... not quiet conceivable from my point of view. That's just madness."

"And your way of thinking is better served, for what?" Anna said. She felt a building of frustration. She saw the pain in the old man's eyes. The scars of his many years had left him a bit shaky. His face was full of unanswered questions left to the wind.

"Gabriel will bring his troops in closer." Robert said.

"And your point is?" Anna asked.

Robert couldn't believe this girl with the quick interventions of an already chaotic plan. "My point is stay out of this," he said.

"Look, I'm not trying to jeopardize anyone's life. To help Gabriel, and to find success, we have to take one of the Conquerites up that mountain. They still outnumber us two to one, and without doing anything to the extreme, we don't stand a chance."

Suddenly, Torack and two of his Aquerian soldiers burst through the front door. All three were wounded. One had been pulled toward the sky, almost torn apart, before Gabriel intervened. Torack had an arrow sticking out of his back. Drew looked over and saw their condition and got up quickly to retrieve the healing stones. Thaliana was still out on the battlefield, soaked in adrenaline with blood splattered on her golden shield and hands, with mud knee high on her boots as the rain washed down in the torrents of the night. Her powers were stronger than the healing stones, yet she was indisposed of for the moment, fighting alongside her teacher. Her fellow kinsmen had kept all projects to an even keel, although being outnumbered. It was like the dead were rising from the muddied soil beneath their feet, in a steady stream of unmatched heat. Death in battle wasn't held to disparaging conditions of one's heart but held to the conditions of wit and strength. It was fought between thin lines of the quick and fearless. Drew didn't even consider Thaliana. He placed the blue healing stone on the first soldier with fleeting conditions. He looked over and pushed down a lump of emotion that started to rise in his throat. From the other side of the room, Bella, Tommy, and Anna came over to lend a hand. The healing stones brightened the room to a peaceful glow. Within five minutes, the stone went back to its normal state. The first Aquerian soldier sat up with a burst of breath as he reached for his chest. He was disoriented from the violent repercussions left in memory. Their time in this place was fleeting for hope and dignity and whatever was left had flown out the window. The second soldier, once clearing the door, had collapsed. Drew moved to the second soldier and placed the blue healing stone to the next. The stare in his eyes told a story of those creatures outside were of a different breed. Drew looked to his left and noticed Torack's paling face and felt his cold hands. He was quickly losing him. Anna got up and went for a blanket. Then Drew noticed Dr. Zimmerman, standing, looking outside the window with a distant stare in his eyes. Dr. Zimmerman turned and noticed the look. The professor had never been in a battle scene so gruesome, until today, first dealing with the Great-Gulf and now seeing a battle between immortals. There was too much blood, too much rage, too much dying. Nothing had gone right since they'd started on this trip. Drew could tell by his paling condition he'd been overwhelmed. He whipped his head to look at Anna, who stood next to him. He got her attention. She saw the look in Drew's eyes and knew what he was thinking. Her gaze crossed the room toward the professor. Anna quickly went to his aid. Anna reached up and took his hand as she was leading a child in the right direction. She shouldered him to the back bedroom and helped him get in bed. She took his coat and hat while draping them over a chair. He looked up at her like viewing an angel, a quiver of a smile, a blink of elderly eyes. She brought a small hand towel and soaked it in water. She reached down and wiped his face and neck, while brushing the graying hair out of his eyes. Anna thought, *He needs a vacation.* He only smiled while looking up.

Back in the main room, Drew looked at Torack's face. "I have to remove the arrow before we can use the healing stone," he said yet expressed hesitancy. He could see the arrow was close to his heart. Drew didn't want to cause any further trauma to his superior alien friend. He tried to reassure him with a pat on the shoulder and a cautious grin yet hesitated.

Thaliana came barreling through the front door at the perfect time. She was concerned about their Aquerian leader also. She had seen them burst through the door just minutes previous. Thaliana veins burned with adrenaline. She saw the daunting few. They were sprawled out on the floor in a puddle of blood and mud and fading conditions. She looked at Drew and wondered what was going on. She came over to lend her assistance, steady and ready and focused. She reached down while getting on her knees. Her face was set aglow. The Circle of members hovered around the wounded like school children waiting for their teacher. Thaliana sensed Torack was close to death, losing body heat with a sallow color reflected in his eyes. His hands were shaking when he reached out to touch him. Torack floated in and out of consciousness. Thaliana remarked while kneeling beside him.

"I've got this one." she said. She gently took over as she put her hands on this well-respected teacher. Thaliana hesitated when seeing where the arrow was.

"I'm not sure how to do this," she said. Torack's eyes suddenly sprung open. She gently turned him on his side, trying to figure out how to remove this blackened arrow. She knew these arrows were made like fish hooks, scaled with barbs that force the flesh to lock down on each arrow. Thaliana looked up. "It needs to come forward. Backward might cause further damage."

Jim Carson came over to lend a hand. "I've seen this type of wound before."

Torack reopened his eyes. "Young man, my body is… not like that of humans. My heart is on this side of my chest, encased in bone." He said while placing his left hand over his heart. Jim nods in his approval. Quickly, Jim Carson snapped the tail end of the arrow and pushed it through. Torack flinched while taking a deep breath, almost passing out.

"Sorry, I'm not familiar with your species," Jim said.

Torack showed a quivering acceptance. "Okay, so I'm my own species?"

Jim acknowledged the Aquerian leader with a cooperative grin and pat on the hand.

Thaliana reached over and touched his chest. Her healing power surged through him. They were running out of time. When finished, Thaliana got up and looked for Drew and then showed a raised eyebrow toward James.

"What's going on?" she asked. "What scheme or plan have you been devising, without my approval?"

"We were making plans to draw the Dark Angels into the mine shaft," James said.

Thaliana's memory went back to when she first met Robert and James. She recalled the many times she had sacrificed herself for the better of her people. She understood these chosen few were trying to help. Gabriel and his archangels' time were set on short notice.

"So, what's the plan?" Thaliana asked.

Drew went through the process all over again, explaining what he planned with James and the others. But he looked up at Anna, seeing she didn't agree with the strategizing of putting them back in harm's way. Thaliana turned suddenly and looked toward Robert and then changed their plans.

"You're staying here," she told Robert. "I'm taking your son and his protector with me. Torack and his Aquerian soldiers will stay to protect the Circle. The Aquerian soldiers and Jim Carson will stay behind. I want to separate you and your father for a brief time. We'll be back in only a moment. I know away. Drew and Tommy will set the bait. They'll start with the front of the mine, setting the explosives before heading to the bottom and seal them at both ends like you've agreed."

Drew slapped his hands together, surprising the rest of his members. "Okay, let's do this."

Anna leaned in toward Drew and quickly touched his arm. He took her hint and pulled her close. Her eyes flashed his way showing a hint of worry." Don't take any chances that would put you in danger," she said.

It ended with the kiss and tender touch of hands.

James glanced back at the couple. "We're going first and then Drew can do that disappearing thing he does so well. I'll cover crowd control. You guys go for entrapment." He looked at the Indian princess. "Thaliana will cut a trail across the sky to draw them in. Once they're in the trap, close the door and seal them off. Have any questions?"

Skittles barked twice as if in anticipation.

Drew's face was set in a serious tone. "Yeah, lead them through the mountains, but don't give away our position."

Tommy got up off the floor as his face lit up. "Okay, let's go."

Randy looked across the room.

Thaliana nodded. "Okay, Tommy will go with Drew, but you need to be smart and fast. Don't stop to smell the flowers."

Drew sensed that Thaliana thought Tommy sometimes didn't use common sense.

Tommy shook his head. "Oh brother. Come on, guys, this isn't a game. I know what's at stake here. Let's just do this thing…all right."

Randy stood and slowly walked over. His eyes showed he wanted to help. "Drew, I'm going too." He turned and stared at James.

"Load up the shotgun. It's my best weapon of choice, up close and personal. Besides, I wouldn't mind giving a few of those putrid looking predators a rib-ticklin' surprise."

Drew's face showed bewilderment, knowing Randy had a country sense of humor, and kicking butt was on his mind. The trip was set, and the three young men were quickly to follow. They would spend their last few moments together ironing out bits of details, plans among friends and Guardians. And then James looked over, wanting to know where they were to ride. Thaliana looked up at one of the Conquerites just past the door. James looked at her and shook his head. "You're kidding me?"

Cornelius was waiting for a signal from one foot soldier to another. On the east side of the forest, straight across paralleling the cabin, was their mark of digging. Their leader kept a watchful eye for any stragglers coming his way. They began to show success digging underneath the forest floor, forty feet in, then sixty, then eighty. Not much more before they were hitting their mark. Six Dark Angels had been working at it nonstop, dripping with sweat and dirt and mud and small puddles of rain splashed all around. Their mark was to dig twelve feet deep and one hundred and forty feet across. Cornelius made sure, the work in progress was covered sufficiently, for their view of treachery was left undercover as their enemy would quickly discover they'd been duped. Within minutes, they would be right where they wanted to be, smack in the middle of a Circle of friends. Cornelius stood at the edge of the forest, looking in the distance of a slow burning light, soon to be diffused of existence. He knew something was different, some type of force field or something blocking the way, causing havoc, because he could see his soldiers running into a wall of confusion, and then falling back. He could see the invisible pendulum swinging back and forth, remitting the Conquerites' merciless form of death. They tore through the ranks of Dark Angels left and right, leaving bodies and blood strewn all over the ground. Cornelius took his bolt and heaved it toward the cabin. The bolt hit one of the Conquerites hard, given way to their position for just the briefest of moments, only a flicker of light shown through gothic like transmutations in perfect form. Cornelius reached down and picked up his bolt, smiled and wondered what he had missed from a King so astoundingly secretive. *Warriors of a different kind.* Cornelius thought. He found his deception so revealing and signaled his soldiers to back off. Thousands of the Fallen had lost their lives that day. The damned had called their soldiers to back away from this field flowing with the blood of brothers. They kept their distance from the cabins edge and waited for their master to give them direction, whose emotions had set the stage for what was to come.

Gabriel looked across this field of battle to see his little brother toward the edge of a blacker world of timbering trees. He'd sensed foul play and trouble around the next corner. He took flight with a half dozen archangels at his side, taking the fight in another direction. Quickly noticing a mass of mud, dirt, and rocks piled to the side, Cornelius stood guard against intruders looking to the side below while missing big brother coming down at an angle. He had a half a dozen of his biggest soldiers displaying weapons he hadn't seen before.

Gabriel was on him before little brother could see him. Several Dark Angels were knocked off their feet and flew past the hole. His archangels backed him up as they stood waiting for the leader to come forward. Cornelius looked up, suddenly surprised by Gabriel coming near. For a minute, he just looked at him not knowing what to do, but then he saw a softer look in big brother's eyes and knew he didn't have the heart to kill him or have another take his life. They were family, as far as he was concerned. There had to be another way to solve their issues.

Gabriel moved forward and grabbed younger brother quickly and through him to the ground while standing over the top of him. "You can't win this battle. Why even try?" Gabriel said.

Cornelius's face was flushed with anger and spite. "Futility is not what I see. There's always a way to overcome, brother. Don't you remember his teachings as a boy? There's always a way, big brother."

Gabriel looked past his little brother's insinuation of the bleak hole that sparkled from his eyes. "He had always favored you, little brother. So much potential and natural ability."

Cornelius was not impressed. "Your words have empty meaning to me, big brother. Too much has happened between us that shows the end of us. We're running out of time. Your king is only allowing this battle for his old amusement. He's just passing the time away until the end."

Gabriel considered his brother's insinuation of what a King would do. "This is much more than that, little brother. He wants us to settle our differences in a civil way."

Cornelius shot a piercing stare back. "This is not exactly civil, big brother. This is war. Don't you get it? He wants us to kill each other out on this no man's land, a place where dreams and hope will die out among this cold, wasteland where the bodies of the dead are forgotten so he can forget he ever created us. We have no future or past that he wants to remember or realizations of a better tomorrow. Our lives are only what we can salvage from this rubble of a cause."

Gabriel walked back and forth, considering his little brother's speculations, which seemed to be heated from being emotionally traumatized by his many experiences left by the roadside. Gabriel grabbed Cornelius by the shoulders and hauled him to his feet. "What went wrong inside you, little brother? I never stopped caring for our lives together. You gave up on your dreams. You're tied to this eternal commitment that eats at you day and night, but why?"

Cornelius's eyes reflected fierce impediments full of remorse and bitterness. "I lost my dreams of any faith when your King began to pick and choose between us, the better of the two. You were his choice, not I."

Gabriel began to sense that what his little brother was feeling seemed not to be birthed against their King but from a spark of jealousy between two brothers. He stood for a while looking into his little brothers' eyes sensing pain beneath the surface of the rough disposition.

"If we had to do it all over again, I would have given you the keys to the kingdom and would have given up my rightful position. It means nothing to me without my true brothers at my side. The love of brothers is much more fun consuming of me than the right to a throne. I wish none of this but that of a brothers love in return. Your own soul means more to me than all that's been birthed throughout history. How can I convince you otherwise?" A tear shot down Gabriel's face.

Cornelius shook his head in disbelief as a look of pain was etched in his eyes. "That's the thing he sees in you, big brother, that he so inherently clings to that draws him. You're so blinded by your emotions that you live in denial. It's too late big brother. He's already chosen the outcome of this battle. He knows my heart, and I cast no doubts about my attentions. We know of a place not of this world that shows a glimmer of hope for me and my Dark Angels. Who knows? Maybe this might give me a chance to look at circumstances from a distance, maybe seeing the effects of a better future, a better tomorrow, because there is to be no tomorrow for this place." Cornelius spoke as if there was a way out of this dilemma.

Gabriel knew not his brother's heart, yet his eyes watered over with a brother's sentiment as he tried to reach for some distant draw of his youth that had been separated by years of hateful sentiment that had dug itself deep in the heart of the younger. Cornelius's face was filled with embittered thoughts of impalements to cause raze. Gabriel responds as a last rebuttal.

"He won't allow this. You have to let this personal vendetta go, little brother!"

Cornelius pulled away from Gabriel's loving grief while drawing his sword. "Prepare to die, big brother! It's the only way that I'll give into this madness!" Gabriel, surprised by his brother's quick assumption, pushed back away from the distance of his sword.

Drew, Randy and Tommy had the shotgun loaded with two extra boxes of shells and the backpack full of pipe bombs loaded and ready to go. Drew looked at his two Circle members who were to accompany him. He turned to look at Anna one last time and then again at his friends. Robert showed Drew on several maps the location of the mine and gave him a copy after studying it. Drew pictured mentally a physical position of the passageway in front of the mine.

"Are you two ready?" He asked. Both Randy and Tommy nod in their approval. Drew put his arms around his two friends and took them where no other man could follow.

Once at the entrance of the mine, Drew pulled both his endeared friends quickly off to the side from the frontal face of its opening. He was sensing intuitively they were not alone, out of the view of others. Drew leaned in to Randy and whispered in a low tone, to draw him in, as their time had been measured. They had a small window of opportunity to make this work.

"We have company," Drew said, as Randy whipped his head around suddenly, bewildered by the statement. "Inside the front entrance, I saw two Dark Angels sitting off to the left." Drew put his hand on Tommy's shoulder.

"The shotgun will draw attention. We need to get past them somehow."

Tommy looked confused. Randy glanced into Drew's eyes, "How do we get past them without drawing attention to ourselves? We don't know if there are others."

Tommy quickly pulled away from his two confused friends and faced the opening of the mine without hesitation. He chuckled, looked relaxed, while putting on a show. Then he slowly pulled his hands out of his pockets. Too confused to know what was going on, the two Dark Angels stood up suddenly. Tommy tried to make conversation like the local boys would be chummy.

Tommy said, as if tipping an imaginary hat in a red neck fashion, "How's it hangin, big boys? Sure, is great weather were having." Tommy then looked at his wrist like wearing a watch. "Well, it's about time you guys give up?" This confused them even more. The cowboy kickin' farm boy thought they were two horseshoes shy of a good gallop. Drew wondered what was going on, and why all of the sudden did Tommy become so brave? He and Randy were shocked, fit to be tied, standing out a way in the distance and leaning toward the lower end of the road. He was a bolstering idiot, according to Drew. The two Dark Angels walked out toward their uninvited visitor. They drew their swords as they walk toward Tommy. Tommy reacted by raising his hands and said, "Now, now, there's no need to get hostile. I'll be a good boy."

Both Dark Angels looked at each other briefly nonplussed by Tommy's words. Yet Tommy had something else on his mind. He quickly used his telekinesis against both Dark Angels. An inflection of power pushed forward by turning their swords against each other. Though surprised, both Dark Angels stabbed each other without being able to do anything about it. A heap of ash covered the ground. Tommy put his hands together like cleaning off leftover dust and calmly viewed his two friends, who were mystified by his quick recital. "Come on, times a wasting, you two. We got pipe bombs to plant."

Drew, still in shock, shook his head while pushing past the entrance. With the loss of words, they went to work. Then he looked over. "I forgot you can do things like that. I guess it was good to bring you after all. "A southern grin broke out on Tommy's face, and then he chuckled while twisting his face to one side as far as a country boy would allow.

"That's just one of my many talents. I'll hook you up sometime when you're not so busy."

Randy looked over and couldn't believe what he was hearing yet stayed silent.

Tommy's ego was floating higher than usual. "I'm not the Hick boy from the back fields of Ohio as you've all assumed."

Drew showed a bit of troubling uneasiness. Ignoring Tommy's last comment, he grabbed the backpack and slung it over his shoulder and handed out several pipe bombs to his closest of friends while Drew looked back at Tommy. "Well, are you going to help me or just tell us how great are you?"

Tommy raised an eyebrow then leaned in to take two pipe bombs, showing a dumbfounded look on his face, like cowboy heaven was just around the next bend.

"Where do you want them?" Drew's eyes rolled toward Tommy's position.

"Somewhere that will cause the most damage but hidden from view, get me?"

Tommy tipped an imaginary hat and spit on the ground. Randy backed up like a stork standing among alligators.

"Dude, are you serious?" Randy muttered.

Tommy pulled a walkie-talkie from his jacket.

"I'll call the Indian princess and let her know we're almost ready." Drew looked over and nodded in Tommy's general directions as Randy started connecting fuses to their little surprises.

He turned the static box on and tuned it to channel three, and then pushed down on the call button. After he heard the static through the speakers, he did a test run with a spark of pleasure glinting in his eyes. "Big bad wolf calling little red riding hood, do you read over..." Drew turned his head around in a gaze of wonder.

Tommy repeated the call. "This is the big bad wolf calling little red riding hood, do you read? Over!"

Drew shook his head. "Who thought of that call sign?"

Tommy turned to answer. "I did. You like it?"

There was a voice on the other end that came in over the speaker. "Little red riding hood, go ahead, what's your twenty?"

This time, Randy turned around, curious, wondering why Tommy and Thaliana, we're playing children's games with the walkie-talkies.

Tommy pushed the call button again. "We're almost done on top, headed for the bottom in a few minutes." Tommy released the call button again and waited for an answer.

"Roger that, big bad wolf. Little red riding hood on her way with a basket full of goodies."

Tommy smiled while looking at the two stunned friends.

"Ten four, little red. Got your back and making tracks."

Tommy returned an answer. He turned off the walkie-talkie and stuffed it back into his jacket pocket.

Randy and Drew looked at Tommy for a moment. "Are you having fun with your new toy?

Tommy smiled. "It's no big deal. She said it sounded all right when we talked about it briefly."

Drew wondered where all the creativity had come from. "It's fine. You just surprised us. That's all. Are you ready to go?" Drew looked back over his shoulder one last time, looking around, making sure they weren't discovered.

"Ready as a rodeo clown. Let's do this thing."

The three closely knitted Circle members huddled together for a brief moment, and Drew took them through an elusive door. When the three members appear in the bottom tunnel, Drew looked up and saw two shadowy, silhouettes reflecting off the wall.

Thaliana looked across the cabin, and whistled to get James's attention. "We need to go. We're taking one of the Conquerites with us."

James had a puzzle expression in his eyes. "How will we accomplish that?"

Thaliana glanced back. "I'm in charge. Do you doubt my position? You don't think I have game, just short of fame?" He looked back curious.

"Well come to think of it, I wasn't quite sure what your boundaries of power were?"

Thaliana's eyes lit up. "The Conquerites are commissioned to follow my lead. If I need their assistance, I only have to touch one, and they read my thoughts and then react to my will."

James looked outside past the door. "You think the other two Conquerites will be able to hold them off?"

Thaliana considered the statement. "They'll be fine. Let's go."

James walked toward the porch as Skittles came from behind to catch them. "Yeah boy, you're going with us, wouldn't want to leave you behind." Skittles looked up and barked at his sidekick to consider his words of approval. James, with a concerned stare, held out his arm to the princess. With a wavering smile and curious stare, she looked down at him while taking flight.

"It doesn't quite work like that. I have my own way of doing things. Besides, I'm not an old woman needing to cross the street in heavy traffic."

James gave a flash of confusion. "I guess I had that coming. It looks a bit drafty up there. You sure we'll be okay riding up that high? I could easily get a nosebleed. Maybe I can take a horse," James said while trying her patience.

Thaliana looked past the odd hesitation in his eyes. She made a trivial response by raising an eyebrow. He grabbed his whip and tucked it on the side of his Kilt.

"Speaking of drafty," he said this is cooler than normal. Shouldn't I be wearing pants?"

Thaliana cupped her hand over her mouth and covered a smile. *How could I teach him?* she thought. "Stop talking. You're a major distraction. You know that?"

James grinned and looked down at Skittles. "Come on, boy. We have a mission to get done." Skittles followed James out on the porch and flapped his wings reaching for the sky.

They looked down toward Torack and his Aquerian soldiers one last time. "Guard this place and keep them safe," she said. Torack only acknowledged with a nod of his head. He wouldn't argue with the Indian princess, knowing only minutes ago she had saved his life. James was fluttering slightly over the top of the first Conquerite, still somewhat hesitant. "So, where do I sit? And where does he sit?" Skittles looked at him and whined.

Thaliana shot a heated stare.

"On the top of his shoulder. Where do you think?"

"I think winging it would be safer than riding on his shoulders."

Thaliana shrugged her shoulders while losing patience. "Suit yourself, but if you see arrows flying your way, he can't protect you, unless you have a direct connection with one of them."

James wondered if the ride would be safe. "Do you have insurance? I mean at least liability. I'd hate to get hurt and have to sue you. Who's your insurance agent up there?"

Thaliana had no idea what he was talking about.

"You need to touch him. Make contact," she said.

"Who wants to touch him? I Just need to ride. I'm not looking for a relationship." James said. Now Thaliana was totally confused, yet after getting his joke, she expelled a translucent smile.

"Are you going to act this way on the whole trip? You're becoming a major distraction, and we've got work to do."

"I only talk when I'm nervous princess." He was still a little unsure about his ride.

Thaliana looked at her new trainee with a touch of disappointment shown by her awkward stares.

"Don't worry about staying on him. He'll know of your presence and help keep you close."

"This doesn't mean we're a thing. You know, I have other commitments."

Thaliana rolled her eyes. "Whatever. Just be quiet and get on. Thaliana's expression turned serious. "Don't be a big baby." She started to say as her impeding glare took them to new heights.

James closed his eyes when looking down. "I'm ready," he said while leaving only partial eyes open.

The three Guardians left the ground on the shoulders of a heavenly beast created by a King of realms. The flight of them leaving the ground caught the attention of Cornelius. He pointed to a legion of Dark Angels to follow after. Momentarily, streams of the enemy followed this beast of the sky in a myriad of numbers. The sky filled with these blackened winged creatures. The Conquerites held a greater esteem than these lowly creatures following him. Arrows flew by unwavering, making no penetration. He did his job by drawing this enemy in a long position to follow. The Conquerites made no effort to fight, for he was on a mission to meet up at their appointed destination, as so directed by the Indian princess. Within a shorter period of time, they saw the opening of the mine about a quarter mile, the last flap of a wing before settling down on a rocky edge. The Conquerite landed in front, facing out as his three riders dropped down behind him. Thaliana looked up before quickly taking cover. This colossal beast was the epitome of the draw. An unbridled giant drew the attention of these swarming bees confused about the host. He scattered them with the whip of his sword, swinging fervently, cutting them down like withered trees ready with a steady hand for an open fire. He slew Dark Angels that were close to his physical mass. James, like bait, became the draw, consisting of a fox being chased by wolves. He stepped forward, out of the mouth of the cave's opening. From building emotions from a father badly treated, he found his voice. His bottom lip moved with a quivering emotion, yelling at the top of his voice with a heated face. James thought to draw them in.

"Hey you, black winged vipers. I'm here!" James yelled as if thinking about the gold left behind. "I'm here, you devils of the night! Come take your treasure." Then it made sense why he and his father had been pulled by the draw of the mountains hidden secrets. It was here to teach them about life, about love, about convictions. This moment caused James's heart to soar.

The Dark Angels turned from the sky and took the bait, like bats to a hornet's nest, disturbing their sanctioned place. They saw this defiant single-winged creature egging them on for a fight, a draw of encouragement, hastily beelining their numbers toward the opening.

James abruptly comprehended that he had become the main target of intense trials of flight, resembling a dam breaking as a flood of water was sinking fast toward the collapsing of this mine.

James and skittles shot down the first tunnel to quickly to follow their leader as she led the disturbed angel-size hornets back into the hive. The pied piper illusion carried them into the depths of this abyss, beneath thousands of feet of rock and earthen soil. Hundreds upon hundreds of Dark Angels poured into the mouth of the opening into an endless stream of reprisal. Drew, Randy, and Tommy suddenly appeared outside of the mine's entrance, as soon as the last stream of the enemy passed by. The massive Conquerite blocked their retrieval with his mighty frames. With Drew's ability to slip through doors, his timing was perfect. Randy lit three pipe bombs quickly. Drew thought, *Those of the Fallen would never know what mystical plan was devised against them.* Then the first line of explosions went off. Hurriedly, Drew took them through another door.

Drew, Tommy, and Randy were back inside the cabin, just when a massive force powers its way up through the cabin's basement floor. Bella and Anna screamed. Tommy, Jim and the Aquerian soldiers began to light up the Dark Angels beneath the basement boards. Randy took the first Dark Angel out with both barrels taking off his head. The gothic angels turned to ash and dropped to implore. Drew took Robert straightaway to the far corner of the room and steered him in the direction of the lost. Jim was in charge of guarding Robert yet kept a watchful eye on the skirmish from below. Jim moved physical objects with his mind and heaved them toward the enemy. Bella and Anna made their way quickly to the top of the upper floor. They got away from the direct fire of the guns and arrows. Torack sent a continued barrage of laser firing from his Element gun. They lit the basement up with a constant barrage of firing. They killed at least a dozen Dark Angels, who were forcing their way up past the opening, without first considering death, precariously meeting them with open arms, knowing their leader would not accept failure as an option.

Torack flashed a look toward the upper floor. "Keep them from getting up there." Jim smiled an unarmored salute with two fingers loosely thrown toward his head. Torack caught the gesture of sarcasm and hoped his success, considering him like his best armed corporal hanging on to his bootstraps. The barrage of fire continued toward the opening in the basement's floor. Echoes of screams, groans and grunts filled the air with uneasiness. Drew's mind began to churn thoughts of reprisal as butter churning in a mixing bowl. He jumped down from the upper floor. His shadow cast against the door. An idea came to him from before, so he clutched his backpack filled with explosives, with pipe bombs ready strategically to plant, sighed heavily, and walked through another door...

From the bottom of the mine shaft, Thaliana and James, with Skittles could feel the first pipe bombs go off about them. The ground and the mountains shook above with violent quakes of fury. Thaliana could see the shadows of a great force flying fiercely toward them. An elusive rumbling of shadows darkened a swirling motion of impact. She and James had just lit the last of the pipe bombs, trapped whomever remained between them from the top, resembling a sealed glass bottle being cork at both ends. The mine was sealed off both ways once the pipe bombs had drawn their deductions, a simple case of leaving hundreds of Dark Angels buried alive inside the mountain. The Indian princess and her companions dove into the hidden room that was next to the water basin, into calling shadows deeper running channels of clean dark waters accompanied from memories past. The natural aqueduct led them straightway into the underground canals of marine life, twisting and turning through the liquefied movements of unnatural churning, in currents of underground corridors of water, reflecting back a world from peaceful suggestions, of traveling voices coalesced to this world below, tuned and pitched with the creatures of the sea.

They glided from end to end, underneath the hidden canals, before the last set of pipe bombs could go off. The mountain began to shake more at her refusal of giving in, guiding to undisturbed explorations, through the glistening aqua-blue pleasures of the deep. Two Dark Angels made it past the last line of explosions and were on their trail but not without injuries to amend. James's protector turned in the opposite direction in an imposing corner to draw the enemy on a different course.

The first Dark Angel fell in line to be led away in another direction. Skittles whipped his barb-tail at just the right moment to pierce the heart of the one so near. A flow of liquefied puce dispersed in the Black Death. The Dark Angels disappeared. The protector took off in pursuit of the others.

The Conquerite had blocked the mouth of the mine, changed his body to be invisible. He sent crashing winged creatures slamming into his immense body and sword. He finished the last of those blasphemous witches, who sluggishly rose from the holes of brown-covered ditches. Staggering bodies from mindless conditions, with incomplete solvents of battered renditions, with dust and dirt and clouds of reprisal and heaps of cuts and bruises in the making, with quivers aloft and hands still shaking, covered in mud and liquefied abrasions, left in the call of unsolved equations, covered in blood under revenged evasions. Robert's plan seemed to work, as so eloquently thought of while tormented between worlds. His trapping's success left them buried in the depth of the old mineshaft. Their work here for the moment was done.

The Conquerite smashed what remained of the Dark Angels with his sword's invisibility. They knew not what was coming, a rampant of disparity leaving nothing to chance.

Thaliana, James, and Skittles made it through the water with no further trouble and came out above a glacier of a bluish tint. They pulled themselves up on a large piece of ice to catch their breath before finding their way back home. The sky was clear of Dark Angels for the moment, but darker clouds of the violent kind would soon roll in, showing their enemy wasn't far behind. Thaliana reached over and touched James on the chest with her hand, showing merit for his considerations. "Are you okay to go on?"

James turned his view away from the sky and looked into her eyes. She showed a touch of consideration. She sensed his heart yearning for an explanation yet none was to come.

"I'm okay." James tried to draw her attention away from what he was thinking. "How long will this battle go on? And my father…?" James lost his train of thought when lightning struck just above them.

Thaliana felt commissioned to flee the immediate area, sensing a furthering storm was closing in. "We've destroyed half his forces that were with him, but they'll regroup and make their way back with a different plan."

James eyes gave a timorous stare of unanswered questions. The Indian princess knew she couldn't answer those deep-seeded questions that lay so near. There was but a bleak hope that they would get out of this unscathed. Each intervened motion of a greater force was not seen or perceived to be made known. Their sudden ride hovered them as they looked up.

"Our ride's here," James said, as they stood, flapped their wings, and made the connection.

"You think we'll make it out of this mess?"

Thaliana eyes revealed a hint of worry. She seemed unable to cope and kept silent about future bouts with those creatures left behind, entrapped by their own snares. It all still seemed blurry, even though she had a heart full of faith and a mind well trained by those Guardians commissioned by her King. She held in reserve a King's motive of the end.

"You and your father will be all right. You need to go with the Circle so better protect them. Make sure they're safe, and get them on that starship. They're going back home." Thaliana's eyes flashed with a bit of concern. Her companion saw the flinch of uncertainty, the drop in her eyes, and the movement of her hands without purpose. She looked at him unguarded in her expressions. She was being tested, being pushed back to learn of her purpose, as all had their journey. Where would she go? What would be next?

Suddenly, James asked, "What will happen to my family?"

Thaliana's expression changed. "They're not to go with you. It's too dangerous. They must stay behind." Yet Thaliana couldn't finish saying what she'd learned by the passing of time.

"Why am I to leave them behind?"

Thaliana felt heat rush through her skin and touched her face." I don't know the purpose of my King for your family. Your journey is somewhat different." Moments went by before further words were said. They sat on the top of this heavenly beast looking up into the heavens. James noticed a shooting star go the full length of the night sky and turn a purple color at its end.

James began to wonder about what would come next. He was shaking after seeing so much blood that day and death covering this field of battle so rapidly. This humbled him completely just thinking of it. Worry set in his face. He thought each individual had their own journey to travel, and this was his, for each road was different. Each filled with bends and curves or unannounced pit falls along the way. No sure-footed journey to take on this road he called his own. Only misery and death had followed him this day toward an end. He did not have all the answers to life's questions. Sometimes a troubled mind accompanied him. Death had walked by his side this day, as a good friend who taught him well. Even though he had never viewed death as a friend, he had always stayed by his side, always giving his advice, pointing the way ahead. He would move on and pick up the slack where others had lacked. He would fight this good fight and never look back.

Drew appeared at the end of the tunnel. The Dark Angels were still fighting below to break through. He lay hidden beneath the feet of the enemy and placed several pipe bombs in strategic areas into the walls of hidden secrets. When the mouth appeared clear, he lit the last remaining two and was quickly gone. The pipe bombs went off and seal the outside world from the Dark Angels, leaving them trapped beneath the surface. There was only one way to exit now, through the basement floor where rapid gunfire and a barrage of arrows were blasting the enemy unrelentingly. Drew appeared inside the loft, as his gift had given him passage. The other Circle members were gathered with Robert, Bella, and Anna. Jim was below with Tommy and Toby, helping push back the last of the resistance.

Anna reached over and touched Drew by placing her arms around him. "Are you alright?" Drew focused on her eyes.

"Yes, I'm fine. Just sealed the other end of the tunnel so no more can get through." Drew noticed Jim in the distance for just a brief moment. He pulled another pipe bomb from under cover. It was the last hope to seal the deal.

"This one should finish this," Jim said as he rolled the pipe bomb back through the basement and heaved it into the tunnel. Cornelius envisioned the bleak remission of their fate. He called his reduced army from the fields of battle and took to the skies.

To be continued...

www.ingramcontent.com/pod-product-compliance
Lightning Source LLC
Chambersburg PA
CBHW020439130626
46549CB00001B/212